‘BREAD AND CIRCUSES’

‘BREAD AND CIRCUSES’

Euergetism and municipal patronage in Roman Italy

edited by
Kathryn Lomas
and Tim Cornell

LONDON AND NEW YORK

First published 2003
by Routledge
11 New Fetter Lane, London EC4P 4EE

Simultaneously published in the USA and Canada
by Routledge
29 West 35th Street, New York, NY 10001

Routledge is an imprint of the Taylor & Francis Group

Typeset in Garamond by
HWA Text and Data Management, Tunbridge Wells
Printed and bound in Great Britain by
MPG Books Ltd, Bodmin

British Library Cataloguing in Publication Data
A catalogue record for this book is available from the British Library

Library of Congress Cataloging in Publication Data
Bread and circuses: euergetism and municipal patronage in Roman Italy /
edited by Kathryn Lomas and Tim Cornell
p. cm. – (Routledge classical monographs)
Includes bibliographical references and index.
1. Rome – Politics and government – 284-476. 2. Benefactors – Rome.
3.Patron and client – Rome. 4. City-states – Italy – History.
I. Title: Bread and circuses. II. Lomas, Kathryn, 1960–
III. Tim, Cornell. IV. Series
JC89.B69 2002
306.2′0937–dc21 2002068020

ISBN 0–415–14689–5

CONTENTS

CONTRIBUTORS

Kathleen M. Coleman, Professor of Latin, Department of Classics, Harvard University.

Tim Cornell, Professor of Ancient History, Department of Classics and Ancient History, University of Manchester.

Jill Harries, Professor of Ancient History, Department of Classics and Ancient History, University of St Andrews.

Claire Holleran, Department of History, University of Manchester.

E.D. Hunt, Senior Lecturer in Ancient History, Department of Classics and Ancient History, University of Durham.

Kathryn Lomas, Lecturer in Ancient History, Department of Classics, University of Newcastle.

John R. Patterson, Tutorial Fellow and University Lecturer, Magdalene College, Cambridge.

Rowland B.E. Smith, Lecturer in Ancient History, Department of Classics, University of Newcastle.

Thomas Wiedemann, Professor of Latin, Department of Classics and Ancient History, University of Nottingham.

PREFACE

This volume has been a very long time in the making, having started out life as a collection of papers given at a conference, organised by the editors and held at the Institute of Classical Studies, University of London in 1994. It was held as part of the 'Ancient Cities' research project, funded by the Leverhulme Trust and based at University College London, the purpose of which was to document and examine the processes of urbanisation and the nature of urban development in pre-Roman and Roman Italy. The topic of euergetism, benefaction and public patronage is one which is central to our understanding of urban society in the ancient world. These activities had a major influence in shaping civic life, from determining the physical form of the city to influencing many levels of social interaction and behaviour within the city, and mediating relations between communities. The aim of the conference, and of this volume, is to explore these themes in relation to the cities of Roman Italy and to the relationship between these cities and Rome itself. The majority of the chapters reproduced here were offered at the conference, but a significant number of others have been added in order to extend the scope of the volume, and in particular to cover the history of Italy in late Antiquity.

The editors would like to thank the Director and Secretary of the Institute of Classical Studies for their assistance in hosting the conference, the Leverhulme Trust for its generous financial support for the project of which it formed part, and Mr Richard Stoneman and Ms Catherine Bousfield of Routledge for their patience and forbearance during the preparation of the manuscript.

ABBREVIATIONS

AE	*Année Epigraphique*
AJA	*American Journal of Archaeology*
AJP	*American Journal of Philology*
Annales ESC	*Annales: économies, sociétés, civilisations*
ANRW	*Aufstieg und Niedergang der Römische Welt*
BCH	*Bulletin de Correspondance Héllenique*
BICS	*Bulletin of the Institute of Classical Studies*
BullCom	*Bulletino della Commissione archeologica communale in Roma*
Byz. Zeit.	*Byzantinische Zeitschrift*
CAH	*Cambridge Ancient History*
CEFR	*Collection de l'École Française de Rome*
CIL	*Corpus Inscriptionum Latinarum*
CQ	*Classical Quarterly*
CSEL	*Corpus Scriptorum Ecclesiasticorum Latinorum*
CJ	*Codex Justinianus*
CTh	*Codex Theodosianus*
Diz. Epigr.	E. de Ruggiero, *Dizionario epigrafico di antichità romana*
DOP	*Dumbarton Oaks Papers*
Eph. Ep.	*Ephemera Epigraphica*
FIRA	C.G. Bruns, (1919) *Fontes Iuris Romani Antiqui*
IG	*Inscriptiones Graecae*
IGRR	*Inscriptiones Graecae ad Res Romanae Pertinentes*
Inscr. It.	*Inscriptiones Italicae*
ILS	*Inscriptiones Latinae Selectae*
JDAI	*Jahrbuch des Deutschen Archäologischen Instituts*
JHS	*Journal of Hellenic Studies*
JRA	*Journal of Roman Archaeology*
JRS	*Journal of Roman Studies*
JTS	*Journal of Theological Studies*
LCM	*London Classical Monthly*
LTUR	*Lexicon Topographicum Urbis Romae*

MDAI(R)	*Mitteilungen des Deutschen Archäologischen Instituts, Römische Abteilung*
MEFRA	*Mélanges d'Archéologie et d'Histoire de l'École Française de Rome, Antiquité*
PBSR	*Papers of the British School at Rome*
REL	*Revue des Études Latines*
RG	*Res Gestae Divi Augusti*
RIC	*Roman Imperial Coinage*
SEG	*Supplementum Epigraphicum Graecum*
TAPhA	*Transactions of the American Philological Association*
ZPE	*Zeitschrift für Papyrologie und Epigraphik*

INTRODUCTION

Patronage and benefaction in ancient Italy

Kathryn Lomas and Tim Cornell

Paul Veyne, in his ground-breaking work *Bread and Circuses*, famously defined the phenomenon of euergetism as 'private munificence for public benefit', a means of harnessing the wealth of the elites of the Roman empire to provide the public amenities needed by cities and to provide entertainment for their citizens. Veyne's magisterial analysis explored the motivations of these elites, the types of activities undertaken, and the impact of their benefactions extensively and in detail. However, there is one major gap in his analysis: his work covers Hellenistic kings and kingdoms, the cities of the Roman provinces, and the role of the emperor as *euergetes*. He does not, however, include any detailed discussion of the role of euergetism, benefaction and public patronage in the cities of Roman Italy, restricting his comments to observations that the benefactions and privileges to Italy were part of a more general development of the emperor as *euergetes* on a global scale (Veyne 1990: 362, discussed further by Patterson in Chapter 5).

This constitutes a major gap in the literature on ancient patronage and benefaction. The cities of Italy occupied a unique – even anomalous – position in the Roman empire. Until 90BC, they had been allied to Rome and were for the most part autonomous and self-governing city-states, rather than administered by a provincial governor. After that date, they were communities of Roman citizens – part of the Roman state in a way that most provincial cities never could be, but in practice continuing to govern themselves and occupying an ill-defined relationship with the central power of Rome. Italy did not constitute a province, and therefore did not have an army or any administrative structures controlled from the centre, and ultimate responsibility for Italian communities was sometimes a matter of debate between senate and emperor (Tac. *Ann.* 14.17). Italian cities were thus in a highly anomalous position. In many respects similar in their social structure to the cities of the provinces, they were nevertheless subject to a range of different conditions and constraints. The physical proximity of Rome gives an added twist to the history of benefaction and public patronage in Italy which it does not possess elsewhere in the empire. The nobility of Italy began to be absorbed into the Roman senatorial order in larger numbers and at an earlier date than was the case in the provinces, thus creating different motivations for benefaction and different arenas for it to take place. From the Augustan era onwards the presence of the emperor in Rome adds a further complicating factor. Euergetism in Italy does not, therefore, necessarily manifest itself in the same way as it does in the cities of the provinces – although it has strong similarities – but at the same time it does not fit Veyne's Roman model of euergetism, which focuses on the benefactions of the Republican senatorial elite and on the emperor as benefactor.

The purpose of this volume, and of the conference on which it is based, is to explore aspects of public patronage and euergetism in the communities of Roman Italy, and to examine the effects of the close relationship between Italy and Rome on these phenomena. There is a vast – and steadily increasing – wealth of information on this subject. Excavations in Italy have produced much new evidence in the form of inscriptions, and archaeological traces of public buildings and other benefactions. In addition, a number of important studies of particular sites and aspects of this topic (Zanker 1988, Jouffroy 1986), and several monographs and volumes of conference proceedings (Cébeillac-Gervasioni 1996, 1998, 2000) have illuminated specific aspects of the social and cultural behaviour of the Italian elites and their relations with Rome, but none of these have focused specifically on the mechanisms of benefaction and municipal patronage.

Chronologically, the main focus of this volume is the Principate. Networks of patronage and benefaction were undeniably important in Republican Italy, but are less well documented and therefore much more difficult to identify and analyse. Epigraphic evidence exists in significant quantity only from the Augustan period onwards, reflecting the general trend for a much higher output of all types of inscriptions in the first two and a half centuries AD than in earlier or later periods (MacMullen 1982). For the Republic, we have a much smaller body of epigraphic evidence (but *cf.* Panciera 1997, and Pobjoy 2000 for examinations of the evidence for euergetism in Republican Italy) and are consequently more reliant on literary sources which give a predominantly Romanocentric slant on the topic. The chances of finding factual information either about benefactions within Italian cities, or about the motivation for euergetism amongst the Italian elite, are much smaller. For the Principate, on the other hand, the quantity and range of evidence – especially the epigraphic evidence – is vast, but at the same time, is often still relatively limited in what it can tell us about the motivation for specific acts of euergetism. Euergetic inscriptions are frequently brief and factual to the point of terseness, leaving the motivation of the *euergetes* and the extent of his (or sometimes, her – *cf.* Forbis 1990 on female euergetism) connection to the recipient community vague. Nevertheless, it is clear from the evidence we do have that civic benefactions were an important part of municipal life in both republican and imperial Italy. The problem, from the historian's point of view, is that it is much more difficult to disentangle euergetic behaviour and patronage towards a community from the more general and all-pervasive phenomenon of personal patronage (Saller 1982, Wallace-Hadrill 1988). This, however, may be inherent in the patron–client relationship as it operated at communal level. Some studies of public and civic patronage in more recent periods of Italian history (Silverman 1977: 12–14) have suggested that the benefits accruing to a community from a civic patron might actually be rather small, and the real value of such a patron may lie in the prestige and aura of protection conferred by his connection with the city rather than in services rendered. Equally, the partial nature of our evidence means that less tangible benefits – e.g. preferment for individuals – from the patron–client relationship are less likely to be documented.

Cicero, for instance, was a high profile patron of a number of communities, as well as being a source of some useful insights into the morality of benefaction as he saw it. He deeply disapproved of what he regarded as frivolous and needlessly extravagant acts of euergetism (Cic. *Offic.* 2.60–1), which he defined as the traditional 'bread and circuses' – public meals, games and other public spectacles and entertainments, and construction of buildings. Instead, he advocated acts of financial assistance or practical help to individuals, such as loans for dowries, and money to ransom prisoners of war or victims of piracy, rather than the more obvious forms of euergetism (*cf.* also Seneca, *Ben.* 1.2.4 which also identifies financial assistance as the prime duty of patron and client). Both of these examples relate more closely to personal patronage than to the relationship between civic benefactor and community, but in other contexts we find Cicero in the role of high-profile civic patron. In these instances, the emphasis still seems to be on the patron as a legal and political fixer rather than a source of material benefactions. In the abstract (*Offic.* 2.61), donations of money for the construction of public buildings are grudgingly admitted to be more-or-less acceptable, although less worthy than other forms of benefaction, provided that they were utilitarian structures. In the particular, there is no direct evidence that Cicero was ever a *euergetes* in this sense of the word, but devoted his energies to interceding on behalf of his client communities to sort out specific legal problems such as expediting the collection of rents owed to Atella and Arpinum (Cic. *Fam.* 13.7, 13.11), and deflecting plans to settle a veteran colony at Volaterrae (Cic. *Fam.* 13.4). In this context, benefactions appear to have taken the form of services rendered rather than the later euergetic activities of provision of buildings and amenities, and public entertainment (on patronage in the late republic, *cf.* also Wallace-Hadrill 1988: 63–88).

The complexities of the links between personal patronage, euergetism, and wider social and economic behaviour are examined in a wide-ranging opening chapter by Wiedemann, who explores the role of patronage as an interface between economic and social activity. Personal patronage in the Roman world had a close connection to financial support and obligation, and Wiedemann's paper argues that the Roman systems of banking, trade, and financial management – traditionally studied as purely economic activities – should more properly be examined in the context of the household and of the patron–client relationship. The need to protect one's financial assets by depositing them with a stronger and more influential individual could effectively turn a patron into a form of deposit banker. On the other side of the equation, patrons and clients had a mutual financial obligation, and either could be called on by the other for loans when required. This could, as indicated above, be a primarily private transaction, to fund a private purchase, a ransom, a dowry, or even social promotion (Pliny, *Epist.* 1.19), but in other contexts, this form of patronage spills over into public life and public benefaction. Rites of passage such as funerals were just as much public events as private ones if families of significant status were involved, and frequently involved public benefactions such as games and distributions of food and money. Such activities involved a significant outlay, and Wiedemann argues it was commonplace for families to call in loans or request help from relatives, patrons, or even clients to fund this type of benefaction. Similarly, there is evidence that the euergetic displays demanded by elections and by holding public office required financial assistance from similar sources. Assistance could also go beyond the purely financial sphere. Perhaps one of the most famous examples of a request of this sort is Caelius's persistent pestering of Cicero, his friend and mentor, to supply him with panthers to enhance his aedilician games (Cic. *Fam.* 8.6, 8.8–9, 11.11). The connections between euergetism, patronage and finance are perhaps less clear in the context of municipal Italy than they are in the case of Rome, but it is entirely possible that the personalisation of banking and finance was even more pronounced in smaller communities. Pliny seems to have fulfilled the role of private banker as well as public patron and *euergetes* at Comum and a number of other communities of which he was patron (e.g. Pliny *Epist.* 1.14, 1.19, 3.6, 4.1, 6.18, *CIL* V.5262) and there is no particular reason to assume he was an exception. Inevitably, given the prominence of Ciceronian evidence, this emphasis on the interplay between personal patronage and public benefaction appears most striking in the later years of the Republic, but as Wiedemann makes clear, it was no less important in later periods of Roman history. In order to maintain a clear focus for the present volume, many wider aspects of patronage and patron–client relationships have been deliberately excluded, but Chapter 1 is an important reminder that there are few real divisions between public and private behaviour and between economic and socially-driven interactions in the Roman world.

From the Augustan period onwards, evidence for euergetic activity proliferates markedly and is much more varied. Inscriptions record a wide variety of different types of benefaction, and there are perceptible shifts in the identity of benefactors, their social, cultural and political motivations, and the impact of their benefactions. There is also a distinctive chronology of euergetism, with some forms of benefaction more popular than others in specific periods of history. In the first century of the Principate, for instance, there was a public building boom which resulted in the physical transformation of many cities in Roman Italy (Jouffroy 1986). In the second century AD, there was still a substantial amount of building undertaken, but there was also a much greater emphasis on marking public and private occasions with public dinners and distributions of food and money at private expense (Mrozek 1972, Andreau 1977). Games and spectacles were a frequent form of benefaction throughout, partly because they were a legally required duty of certain magistrates as part of the annual cycle of religious festivals, and partly because there were social expectations of games on certain other occasions such as funerals of prominent citizens. The importance of euergetism and civic patronage in the life of the Italian city can also be seen in the growth of an extensive body of law which governed the procedures for appointing civic patrons, recording of patron–client relationships, and regulating the permitted forms of euergetic activity (Nicols 1980, Johnson 1985, Duthoy 1986).

One of the most direct results of this changing pattern of benefaction in Roman Italy was the transformation of the urban environment in many cities. As Lomas argues in Chapter 2, the development of cities and consequent changes in uses of urban space in Italy were closely linked to programmes of public building and to the benefactions which funded them. The same process can also be seen to be linked to the Romanisation of the urban landscape, thus producing a complex set of connections between buildings, benefactions, and changes in cultural identity. Public buildings can be approached as reflections of both communal identity and self-image, and of the preoccupations and priorities of the individuals and groups who paid for them. The marked chronological variations in types of buildings – fortifications in the late Republic, theatres in the Julio-Claudian period, baths and amphitheatres in the second century AD – indicate that cultural choices were being made about what to construct and how the urban landscape should develop (Gabba 1994, Jouffroy 1986). Inevitably, this means in most cases that they reflect the agenda of the urban elite or of individual members of it, but other factors can come into play. Some structures were paid for by municipal patrons from outside the city, for instance, or even by the emperor himself (Millar 1986; Patterson, Chapter 5 of this volume), while others were funded by less elevated groups such as *collegia* or Augustales (Duthoy 1977, Patterson 1994), which became a significant source of finance for urban development in the second century AD. The motivation of the *euergetes*, the cultural signals sent out by particular types of building, and the impetus for adopting particular types and styles of building are complex and not always easy to decode. The notion that Italian cities adopted a particular style, with monumentalisation of fora, construction of theatres and introduction of temples of the imperial cult, as a result of direct imperial or senatorial prompting during the reign of Augustus (Zanker 1988), or of displacement of competitive euergetism from Rome to the municipalities (Eck 1986), places the emphasis firmly on a top-down approach driven by an imperial and Roman agenda. However, it is possible that choices about what to build, and how to shape the appearance and amenities of the city were driven just as much by local concerns as by the wishes of the emperor, the cultural agenda set by Rome, or the decisions of a senatorial patron. Competition for prominence between local nobles, or rivalry between cities in a locality could be just as powerful a motivation for a *euergetes* to invest in a particular type of building as his benefaction to the community. In particular, the emergence of non-elite groups – principally the upwardly-mobile freedmen who formed the bulk of the *ordo Augustalis* and the membership of various *collegia* – as major public benefactors and civic patrons suggests that public building programmes were driven as much, if not more, by local rivalries and interests as by a centralised Romanising agenda.

The interplay between Rome and the municipalities of Italy is a particularly problematic area when considering the questions raised by public building programmes, who funded them and why. One of the great paradoxes of urban development in Roman Italy is that although Italian cities came to acquire a fairly standard set of Roman amenities such as baths, theatres, amphitheatres, basilicas, monumentalised fora, and temples of particular Roman cults – often as a result of the generosity of private benefactors – they remained significantly different from Rome itself. Many of the Roman colonies founded from the third century BC onwards were laid out with a significant degree of regularity and endowed with similar sets of buildings laid out in a similar manner. For obvious reasons, municipia were less clearly regimented and many developed in a much more piecemeal manner, but by the end of the first century AD most of them had acquired the buildings listed above either at the expense of the community or by the generosity of benefactors. Where public buildings already existed, it was not unknown for them to be rebuilt in a markedly more Romanised style. Rome, on the other hand, lagged behind Italy significantly in the construction of public buildings and regularisation of layout. This discrepancy between patterns of public building in Rome and in the rest of Italy has been the subject of much debate over the years, and is revisited here by Holleran in Chapter 3, who provides a critique of previous attempts to explain this discrepancy. She sees the relative paucity of buildings for public entertainment in Republican Rome as a result of the political culture of the city, which gave kudos for the presentation of games and funding of temporary structures to house them, but which inhibited the creation of permanent theatres or amphitheatres. The breakdown of the social and political pressures which limited individual displays of euergetism can be seen as part of a more general shift to a political culture dominated by the quasi-monarchical behaviour of a small number of dominant individuals. Thus, in Holleran's analysis, the construction of buildings for public entertainment is intimately linked with the shifts of political behaviour which characterised the end of the Republic, and with the emergence of the power of the emperor.

This difference between patterns of elite euergetism at Rome and in the rest of Italy in the context of public entertainments is also addressed by Coleman in Chapter 4. She also examines the general significance of the construction of buildings dedicated to public entertainment, but in the more specific context of the role of Augustus in construction of euergetic buildings at Rome. It has long been recognised that the establishment of the Principate fundamentally changed the climate of euergetism in Rome. During the Republic, the giving of games and the construction of major public monuments were part of the duties of the Roman nobility and were particularly associated with the celebration of a triumph. During the reign of Augustus, however, the right to celebrate a triumph was severely restricted and the urban regeneration of Rome became so closely associated with Augustus himself that it became much more difficult – if not impossible – for anyone outside the emperor's immediate circle to initiate major public buildings. The effect of this was to displace elite munificence into other spheres and other arenas, possibly even to the direct advantage of some Italian cities (Eck 1986), but also to contribute to the disjunction between the urban development of Rome and that of the rest of Italy. The most noticeable difference is the absence of an amphitheatre from the Augustan building programme, despite the strong evidence for his sponsorship of imperial spectacles and entertainments. The various possible reasons for this, as explored by Coleman, cast light both on the motivations for – and restrictions on – imperial benefactions in Rome, and on the variations in euergetic behaviour between Rome and the rest of Italy. Coleman's chapter underlines strongly the differences between the colonies and municipia of Italy, on the one hand, and Rome itself, on the other. Italian communities – already well ahead of Rome in some regions – acquire or enhance a characteristically 'Roman' set of structures for public entertainment, while Rome lags behind this respect.

Imperial benefaction in Italy is a significantly different process from imperial benefaction in Rome. This is one area of euergetic activity in which we have some insights into the possible motivations of the *euergetes*, but even so, there are some frustratingly grey areas. As Patterson notes in Chapter 5, the political and military centre of gravity shifted away from Italy after the end of the Republic (see also Dyson 1992, 89–121; Millar 1986), yet it remained the focus of significant imperial attention. This attention was not consistent, however, and appears to be focused on specific types of communities and specific types of benefaction. It was also more important to some emperors than others, with Augustus, and later the Antonines, featuring largely in the record of imperial benefactions, but other emperors being much less generous. At one level, this looks distinctly odd. Veyne defines the figure of both the Hellenistic king and the Roman emperor as the supreme benefactor, whose gifts were intended as a display of regal splendour and generosity, and also as a 'super-patron' whose subjects lived under his protection and looked to him for benefactions (Veyne 1990: 102–3, 377–8). In relation to Rome, and to some regions of the empire, this model of the emperor as universal patron and benefactor appears to work well, but Italy fits into it rather less convincingly. Far from being a universal benefactor acting as *euergetes* by virtue of his office, the emperor in Italy appeared to direct his patronage to specific communities and for specific – often personal – reasons.

Patronage and benefaction remained important in Italy throughout Antiquity, but the changed conditions of the Later Empire bring about some interesting and significant changes in the ways they operated and the impact they had on communities and individuals. As the imperial court became increasingly detached from Rome and Italy, the form, the symbolism, and the impact of imperial patronage changed. Christianity prompted further changes in the rhetoric and practice of euergetism as the elite ethos of patronage and benefaction was modified by Christian ideas of charity and social obligations towards the poor. This led to some interesting changes in expectations and a certain amount of philosophising about what was the appropriate expression of euergetism for a Christian senator. It is clear that it was not just a case of grafting a new religious framework on to established forms of social conduct, but that there were serious moral and philosophical issues at stake. The extent to which this new Christian world-view could be responsible for significantly changing interpretations of well-established euergetic behaviour is demonstrated by the debate over the nature of alimentary schemes in Roman Italy. The long-standing view that *alimenta* were primarily imperial poor-relief schemes designed to boost the population of Italy has been effectively challenged (Patterson 1987, Woolf 1990: 197–202) on the grounds that the only evidence which attributes these schemes to a wish to provide charity and relief to the poor (*Epit. de Caes.* 12.4) is from a fourth-century source which approached the problem from a distinctively Christian viewpoint which may have had a very different understanding of the motivation behind the schemes. Even without the cultural shift which resulted from the Christianisation of the empire, the intensely competitive public life of the late Empire ensured that the discourse of patronage and benefaction remained both a central and a problematic aspect of elite activity.

The politics of building programmes could be particularly complex in late Antiquity, with the contrasting programmes and iconography employed by pagans and Christians to represent their identity and stake their claim to power and influence. This is particularly graphically demonstrated in Rome, where, as Hunt demonstrates in Chapter 6, Maxentius' ambitious but incomplete pagan building programme was taken over and subverted by Constantine as a means of symbolising his own regime and its Christian ethos. Structures begun by Maxentius were completed by Constantine and dedicated in his own name, and new monuments, such as the arch of Constantine, which depicts his victory over Maxentius, were constructed. At one level, this represents a traditional use of benefaction and building activity to represent power and denigrate a defeated opponent, but in another context it was an important representation of the new order, with an ambitious programme of church-building and endowment of shrines. This gave prominence to monuments, not just to Constantine's victory and political power, but also to the new belief-system of Rome both in the centre of Rome, and at key points – such as the Via Appia – on the approaches to the city. The implications of some of these locations are still debated, but the extent to which Constantine utilised public building to establish the identity and authority of his regime is not in doubt.

The contrasting, and potentially conflicting, views of the pagan and Christian dignitaries of the late Empire are explored by Harries in Chapter 7 from a variety of standpoints. At one level, the dynamics of euergetism appear to be similar to those of earlier eras. Patrons, local notables and visiting dignitaries were important sources of benefactions. Voluntary gift-giving was practised as a way of enhancing personal status and prestige, and communities had a variety of strategies for actively 'encouraging' potential or reluctant patrons and benefactors to fund euergetic projects, and also for acknowledging gifts given (on the status and prestige accruing to the patron more generally *cf.* Duthoy 1986, Forbis 1996). On the other hand, there were significant differences. The benefactions and euergetic activities of the pagan senator Symmachus appear in many ways to be similar to those of his earlier counterparts. He organises games and wild beast shows for popular entertainment, in conjunction with his son's quaestorship, and displays a preoccupation with the acquisition of impressive and rare animals for these events which is very similar to Caelius' hankering after panthers for his aedilician games (e.g. Symm. *Epist.* 2.77, 5.59, Cic. *Fam* 2.11, 8.2, 4, 6, 8–9). He recognises – and to some extent deplores – the pressures on notables to provide lavish and expensive entertainments, while continuing to do so as a means of maintaining his own and his family's status. At the same time, the emergence of prominent Christians introduced new attitudes to euergetism. Christian senators were subject to the same pressures as their pagan counterparts when it came to providing games and entertainments, but religious opinion was at best ambivalent and often downright hostile to traditional 'bread and circuses' and some religious leaders began to elaborate an alternative. Shrines, cults of saints, and the festivities associated with the feasts of local saints were promoted as alternative sources of public entertainment or targets of euergetism by divines such as Paulinus of Nola. It is notable, however, that even these promoters of Christian rather than pagan forms of euergetism did not escape their more traditional duties and that many of them were induced to pay for buildings and amenities in the communities they visited.

The wider patterns of euergetism, however, are less certain in Italy than they are in late imperial Rome. As Smith points out in Chapter 8, there is some evidence that patronage and euergetism became significantly more centralised in the fourth century AD, with a distinct absence of local benefactors in the cities of Italy, and a much stronger emphasis on the role of the external patron and Roman notable as a source of benefaction. Many of the inscriptions in honour of Roman patrons may be an attempt to gain favour and extract benefactions from an otherwise distant *patronus*. In Rome, by contrast, the volume of patronage and its relation to the status of the patron expanded significantly. The development of the new imperial capital at Constantinople meant that the Roman elite could act as benefactors without the danger of seeming to trespass on the preserve of the emperor and the wealth of many members of the elite ensured that they had the means to generate euergetism on a grand scale. The intense competitiveness, and the need to generate status through display, which Symmachus so deplored by created an upsurge of benefactions and elite activity within the city of Rome.

The patterns of euergetism can be seen to have changed dramatically over the course of the centuries, from the late Republic to the end of the Empire but there are, nevertheless some underlying continuities which can be discerned. The focus of activity may have shifted in emphasis, from the local communities of Italy to Rome, and socially from the local elites to the senatorial nobility and the emperor, but this was not a linear development. The increasing dominance of Rome brought about changes in the patterns of benefaction but did not wipe out euergetism in the Italian communities. Similarly the establishment of the Principate initially made some forms of euergetism unavailable to the senatorial elite while leaving them still open for local notables, but the developments of the late Empire and the removal of the imperial court from Rome allowed senators to undertake ever more flamboyant forms of euergetism. There was also a wide variety of forms of benefaction and ways in which euergetic activity could be conducted. What continues throughout, however, is the fact that the process of benefaction was never entirely top-down. As both Smith and Harries point out, the behaviour of the people within a community, whether in Rome or elsewhere in Italy was an important factor in instigating and shaping euergetic behaviour in the late empire. In an earlier era, a powerful driving force seems to have been local pride and rivalry between communities and, sometimes between sections within a community. Even at the height of the empire, when the emperor was a dominant patron in many areas of activity, euergetism in Italy remained as much about local competition and the establishment of local identities and hierarchies – whether of individuals or groups within a community, or of communities within a region – as about a response to central power.

References

Andreau, J. (1977) 'Fondations privées et rapports sociaux en Italie romaine (Ier–IIIe s. ap. J.C.)' *Ktema* 2: 157–209.

Cébeillac-Gervasioni, M. (ed.) (1996) *Les Élites municipales de l'Italie péninsulaire des Gracques à Néron*, Naples and Rome: Centre Jean Bérard and École Française de Rome.

Cébeillac-Gervasioni, M. (1998) *Les magistrats des cités italiennes de la seconde guerre punique à Auguste*, Rome: École Française de Rome.

Cébeillac-Gervasioni, M. (ed.) (2000) *Les Élites municipales de l'Italie péninsulaire de la mort de César à la mort de Domitien: Classes socials diregeantes et pouvoir central*, Rome: École Française de Rome.

Duthoy, R. (1977) 'La fonction sociale de l'Augustalité', *Epigraphica* 36: 134–54.

Duthoy, R. (1986) 'Le profil social des patrons municipaux en Italie sous le Haut-empire', *Ancient Society* 15–17: 121–54.

Dyson, S. (1992) *Community and Society in Roman Italy*, Baltimore and London: Johns Hopkins University Press.

Eck, W. (1986) 'Senatorial self-representation: developments in the Augustan Period', in F. Millar and E. Segal (eds), *Caesar Augustus: Seven Aspects*, Oxford: Clarendon Press.

Forbis, E.P. (1990) 'Women's public image in Italian honorary inscriptions', *AJP* 111: 493–512.

Forbis, E.P. (1996) *Municipal Virtues in the Roman Empire. The Evidence of Italian Honorary Inscriptions*, Stuttgart: Teubner.

Gabba, E. (1994) 'Urbanizzazione e rinnovamenti urbanistici nell'Italia centro-meridionale del I sec. A.C.'. In *Italia Romana*: 63–104 (= *Studi Classici e Orientali* 21 (1972): 73–112).

Johnson, D. (1985) 'Munificence and *Muncipia*: bequests to towns in classical Roman law', *JRS* 75: 105–25.

Jouffroy, H. (1986) *La Construction Publique en Italie et dans l'Afrique Romaine*, Strasbourg: AECR.

MacMullen, R. (1982) 'The epigraphic habit in the Roman Empire', *AJP* 103: 233–46.

Millar, F.G.B. (1986) 'Italy and the Roman Empire. Augustus to Constantine', *Phoenix* 40: 295–318.

Mrozek, S. (1972) 'Crustulum et mulsum dans les villes Italiennes', *Athenaeum* 50: 294–300.

Nicols, J. (1980) 'Tabulae patronatus: a study of agreement between patron and client-Community' *ANRW* ii(13), 535–61.

Panciera, S. (1997) 'L'evergetismo civico nelle iscrizioni latine d'età repubblicana'. In M. Christol and O. Masson (eds), *Actes du Xe Congrès International d'Épigraphie Grecque et Latine*: 249–90, Paris: Publications de la Sorbonne.

Patterson, J.R. (1987) 'Crisis: what crisis? Rural change and urban development in imperial Appennine Italy' *PBSR* 55, 115–46.

Patterson, J.R. (1994) 'The *collegia* and the transformation of the towns of Italy in the second century AD', in *L'Italie d'Auguste à Dioclétien. Actes du colloque international de l'école Française de Rome*, Rome: École Française de Rome.

Pobjoy, M. (2000) 'Building inscriptions in Republican Italy: euergetism, responsibility and civic virtue'. In A. Cooley (ed.), *The Epigraphic Landscape of Roman Italy*: 77–92, London: Institute of Classical Studies.

Saller, R. (1982) *Personal Patronage under the Early Empire*, Cambridge: Cambridge University Press.

Silverman, S. (1977) 'Patronage as myth'. In E. Gellner and J. Waterbury (eds), *Patrons and Clients in Mediterranean Societies*, 7– 19, London: Duckworth.

Veyne, P. (1990) (O. Murray, trans. and ed.) *Bread and Circuses* (abridged translation of *Le pain et le cirque* (1976) Paris: Seuil), London: Penguin.

Wallace-Hadrill, A. (1988) 'Patronage in Roman society: from Republic to Empire'. In A. Wallace-Hadrill (ed.), *Patronage in Ancient Society*, London: Routledge.

Woolf, G. (1990) 'Food, poverty and patronage: the significance of the Roman alimentary inscriptions in the epigraphy of early imperial Italy', *PBSR* 58: 197–228.

Zanker, P. (1988) *The Power of Images in the Age of Augustus*. Ann Arbor: University of Michigan Press.

1

THE PATRON AS BANKER

Thomas Wiedemann

A generation ago, analysis of the economic structure of the ancient world, where it did not concentrate on the effects of slavery, tended to be in terms of the polarity between a 'primitivist' and a 'modernist' interpretation. Early twentieth-century 'modernists' such as Meyer and Hasebroek emphasised those elements which seemed to have analogues in nineteenth-century economics such as the search for colonies in response to the need for raw materials, long-distance trade and increased population; the 'primitivists', influenced by Marx, Weber and Polanyi, saw the ancient economy as embedded in social structures and therefore quite different to a modern industrial world in which capitalism had made the economy autonomous and supreme. In his discussion in the 1970s of the origins of the Peloponnesian War, de Ste Croix minimised the role of the commercial interests which Cornford in the heyday of European imperialism had posited as controlling Athenian policy. Finley in particular preferred to see the ancient economy as based on small-scale units of production centred on the individual *oikos* or *domus*, and aiming at self-sufficiency rather than producing for the market-place.[1]

Finley (and other scholars who followed Marx and Weber) appeared to have won the argument in favour of the 'primitivist' approach, and the view that antiquity was fundamentally unlike our own world continues to be important to the way in which it is represented by many social historians. But there is now a large corpus of detailed work on different aspects of the economy of the ancient world which shows that the two views do not need to be as mutually exclusive as Finley's polemics made them seem. Finley's lasting contribution to English-speaking scholarship was to draw attention to the importance of slavery and the primacy of agriculture. By the 1980s scholars – some of them Finley's own students and collaborators – had moved on to look at the ways in which other kinds of labour were being exploited, and at the complexities of agriculture and manufacturing in specific contexts; amongst the new influences have been feminism and environmentalism.[2] It became clear that the model of the economically self-sufficient household, while a useful starting-point for an analysis of the ancient economy, was indeed only a starting point. Antiquity may have had institutions which, whether 'primitive' or not, were quite unlike those of the modern world, but they did not inhibit economic and commercial activity of great complexity – or at any rate, if they prevented some activities, they enabled other things to be done, in ways that might be quite different to those of the modern world. But it is perverse to be apologetic about the economic impact of (for example) a project such as the construction of Hadrian's Wall because it employed a state-funded workforce with no formal negotiating rights and directed by state officials rather than venture capital freely provided by private individuals with a view to maximising their profits.[3]

A further element in recent years has been the interest in quantification and the recognition that accounting is not merely a fashion of modern business administration, but something that had been of major significance in Roman culture in particular.[4] The Roman need to quantify will have had several roots. Apart from the unusual interest in census figures required by a state in which military requirements were given unusual emphasis, we may identify one such root in the competitiveness of political life: a simple way of proving one's superiority over a rival to the electorate was by quantifying one's deeds. Hence the sometimes nauseous precision with the number of enemies destroyed in battle is specified. Pliny the Elder tells us that the temple which Pompey dedicated to Minerva boasted of the 12,183,000 persons routed or scattered in battle or killed or surrendered, 846 ships sunk, and 1,538 towns and cities capitulated. Caesar's account of the defeat of the Helvetii and their allies in 58BC gives figures for before and after. Statistics were broadcast of wounds received in battle and of decorations awarded (Pliny *NH* 7.97f.; Caes. *BG* 1.29.2f.; Pliny *NH* 7.101–6). We might also associate the Roman interest in statistics psychologically with the practice of successful imperial domination over long distances, and socially with the integration of Italy following the Social War and the development of a single market in land of a kind not seen again until the nineteenth century (Rawson 1976: 85–102). The landowner who had inherited or acquired estates all over Italy but spent most of the year in Rome needed statistical reports on a scale which had previously only been seen in the redistributive palace economies of the Near East.

The cultural effect is striking: we just have to think of the way Catullus notoriously quantifies erotic acts. Lesbia's kisses are counted in hundreds and thousands. The poet's 'puella' embraces 300 lovers; he hopes that intercourse will take place nine times in succession; the departing Caecilius is called back 'milies' by his girl; Ameana is described as mad for asking him for 10,000 sesterces for sex; Catullus wishes to kiss Iuventius' eyes 300,000 times. But quantification occurs in a wide range of Catullan contexts: a friend (Furius) is worth more than 300,000 sesterces, and elsewhere told not to beg for 100; his villa is said to be mortgaged for 15,200. An enemy is threatened with 300 lines of hendecasyllables, one of Caesar's officers lampooned for consuming 200,000 or 300,000 sesterces (Catullus 5.10f.; 11.18; 32.8; 35.8; 41.2; 48.3; 9.2; 23.26; 26.4; 12.10; 29.14.).

Quantification, accounting, financial management, were crucial in Roman culture. We have seen that they were used to make moral claims in the contexts of political competition and of erotic literature. But those who have assumed that they could be found in the context of anything like modern systems for supplying credit and investing savings have been disappointed. It may help to explain that absence of evidence if we distinguish between different functions to which the modern concept of banking is applied, and the different kinds of 'bankers' associated with them. Analyses of Roman bankers show that the range of services they provided did not correspond to that provided by modern bankers. Jean Andreau (1987), in his *La Vie financière dans le monde romain*, mentioned two main approaches to the topic, the legal and the philological. Kirschenbaum's *Sons, Slaves and Freedmen in Roman Commerce* (1987) is very much in the first tradition, and Andreau's own approach seems to be very much tied to the philological method which he criticises for restricting itself to literary texts. He carefully examines epigraphic as well as literary evidence for a range of Latin words, and then assigns some of them to the category of 'bankers': *argentarius* (provider of currency), *coactor* (debt collector, often on behalf of the state), *stipulator* (moneylender in the sense of creditor), *nummularius* (currency exchanger), *mensarius* (paymaster, including one who paid out coin on behalf of the state), and the Greek word *trapezites*; while the words *saccularii* (swindlers) and *mutatores* (dealers in goods), he decides, cannot be held to refer to financial activity. These groups of professional Roman money-handlers (those for whom, as for other traders and craftsmen, their skills provided their livelihood) typically were involved in dealings which were not just relatively small-scale, as short-term.

The distinction between a moneylender or pawnbroker and a banker may be a fluid one.[5] But the professions identified by Andreau clearly did not provide Romans with the range of financial services of modern bankers. For leading, high-status figures such as the Rothschilds, Barings and Warburgs, we clearly have to look elsewhere, and Atticus is the obvious example of such a figure (Perlwitz 1992). He has nothing in common with the *argentarii* who changed money in the forum except that, two millenia later, both could be classified in modern European languages as 'bankers'. Rather than analysing all possible Latin words for 'banker' (and incurring disappointment at the results), what is required is to look for the contexts of different financial activities within Roman society, as Edward Cohen and Paul Millett did so successfully for Athens (Cohen 1992; Millett 1991). This is not to suggest that the small-scale, short-term and low-status context in which *argentarii* etc. worked was not unimportant – Vitruvius pointed out how essential it was for someone laying out a new forum to provide for their booths (Vitruv. *Arch.* 5, 1.2) – but the sophisticated provision of credit and of investment opportunities occurred within a quite different context, not the familiar 'market' but the apparently 'primitive' context of the *domus*.

Recent studies have shown that it was the requirements of supervising the management of estates, especially over long distances, that lay behind the development of the competence of the procurator in Roman practice and law; his role should be seen as an extension of that of sons within the household, not a response to the needs of long-distance trade or shipping (Aubert 1994). The 'modernists''

mistake was not to assert that the legal powers and economic potential of the Roman procuratorship were sophisticated, but that they developed for reasons more familiar to nineteenth century economic practice but anachronistic in ancient terms. And it is within that same apparently 'primitive' context of the Roman household and its wider connections that the provision of financial services, no matter how sophisticated, should be located: in particular, the relationship which the Romans called *amicitia*, though in many cases the 'friendship' was so asymmetrical that it is properly translated as 'patronage' in English. As ancient texts discussing friendship make clear, friends are supposed to help each other not just with advice, but with money. Indeed, Seneca puts money first in the list he gives at *De Beneficiis* 1.2.4: 'Help one man with your money, another by standing surety for him, another by applying your influence, another by giving him advice, another with helpful maxims'. *Res*, money, heads the list.[6]

If we want to see in which respects the management of money in the Roman world was a function of patronage, and how that affected the provision of banking services, it might help to consider the basic if banal distinction between accepting money, and providing money: deposits and loans. Economic historians sometimes seem to have been more interested in examining the provision of loans, large or small-scale, e.g. to governments or long-distance traders; assumptions about the superiority of medieval banking provision over that of the ancient world appear to be based on the ability to fund long-distance trade or travel (including crusading) and to provide for the financial needs of rulers and particularly of the papacy at one end of the spectrum, and to lend money in return for security on a small scale (i.e., pawnbroking) at the other.[7] But it is obvious that no banking operation can survive unless it attracts more money than it provides, in the form of deposits from investors as well as interest from debtors.

It has been held to be one of the characteristics of pre-capitalist cultures that producers do not produce so as to maximise income, but only to cover expected needs. But good harvests cannot be avoided any more than poor harvests. What could a Roman do with his surplus? A surplus of agricultural produce can of course be stored against time of need (though the storerooms and granaries of Roman villas are more likely to have been intended as protection against the annual shortages of the months before the next harvest than for long-term insurance). Alternatively, they can be marketed and converted into cash; agricultural textbooks note how important it is that estates should have access to road- or water-ways in order to minimise the cost of marketing surplus produce (Varro *RR* 1.16.2 and 6. On markets, Frayn 1993). But cash, too, needs to be securely stored. Providing such security has been one of the functions of modern banking systems; but at Rome that was not a service provided by any of the professions listed by Andreau. Treasure was kept in the house, in the strong-box (*arca*). If additional security was required – for instance, if someone would be absent from home for some time – it could only be provided by persons who both were more powerful, and could be trusted. One could assume that both conditions were fulfilled by the gods: their temples were structurally more resistant to damage than ordinary buildings, and also protected from robbery by laws against sacrilege. Temples or churches have always been normal places for depositing valuables securely.[8] Alternatively, one could turn to a human 'friend'. What was needed here was a guarantee that that person would return the deposit when it was needed; and that required, not the anonymity of a business arrangement with a professional banker, but a strong inter-personal bond the breaking of which would have dire consequences for any partner who felt powerful enough to do so. That bond was expressed by the Latin concept of *fides*, the responsibility which the stronger partner in an asymmetrical relationship had not to exploit the weaker. The emphasis of ancient sources on *fides* as a component in the unequal relationships between Rome and her allies, or of formal patrons to their clients, shows how the Romans found the psychological security that we have traditionally look for in our bank manager in their *amici*. *Amicitia* implies *fides*.[9]

The other aspect of financial provision is the need to borrow. Surpluses deposited in the *arca* or with *amici* regularly need to be drawn upon for family or household expenditure. There are predictable surges in expenditure associated with annual ceremonies of feasting and gift-giving, as well as unforeseen expenditure as a result of accidental damage or loss, perhaps through lightning or flooding. The life-cycle brings its own predictable expensive ceremonies. Provision for one's own funeral was one of the motors for life-insurance in nineteenth century Britain; the costs of a Roman funeral could be substantial, especially if the *munus* included a gladiatorial display. The provision of a dowry for daughters has been an even greater expense in many European societies: it is interesting that one of the first early modern state banks, the 'Monte delle Doti', was set up at Florence in 1424/25 (Molho 1971: 138–41) precisely to provide dowries for the daughters of investors who deposited money when their daughters were born (if the daughter died before marriage, the investment was forfeit). On such occasions, reserves of cash kept in the *arca* might not suffice. Where there are bankers or pawnbrokers, people will be prepared to incur interest rates in the range of 24 per cent per annum; those are typical rates for modern credit-card companies, and correspond to the maximum rate of 25 per cent which Florence imposed on its (Jewish) moneylenders in the fifteenth century. Rates as high as the 48 per cent notoriously charged the Salaminians by Brutus are known,[10] but these were for very short-term periods indeed (i.e., 4 per cent per month or part of a month). Most frequently, they were raised by Florentines of high status in order to cover expenditure over religious festivals such as Easter and Christmas; they would be paid off as soon as other funding became available, and were incurred only because other sources of funding could not immediately be mobilised.

Some of the occasions for extraordinary domestic expenditure in the Roman world were analogous to those in fifteenth-century Florence or in our own society. What appears to have been quite different was that it was exceptional for a Roman of standing to approach the *argentarii* operating in the public forum for a loan. If this was done, then only as a short-term measure, and possibly in order to avoid publicising the transaction for which the money was needed. The property market in the city of Rome was notoriously elastic, and anyone who wished to buy tried to maintain secrecy to prevent prospective vendors from raising their prices: this may have been the reason why Cicero borrowed from *faeneratores* to finance the purchase of a town house.[11] Far more typical was the Younger Pliny's plan to raise the 3,000,000 sesterces needed to buy an estate in Umbria by calling in loans he has made to others, and calling on the resources of his mother-in-law's *arca*. The persons one turned to, even for short-term financial support, were relatives and friends, patrons and clients.[12] As in Renaissance Florence, dowries head the list of concerns: 'qui aes alienum suscipiunt amicorum, aut in filiarum collatione adiuvant aut opitulantur in re vel quaerenda vel augenda' (Cic. *Offic.* 2.56). In the case of freed slaves, the patron had the moral right to call on the financial support of his former slave when (for example) he needed to raise money to provide a dowry for a daughter.[13] A poem of Martial's makes the point that if you had the misfortune of losing your house in a fire, your friends might provide you with more than it had been worth.[14] There were of course other, distinctively Roman, occasions when funds were required quickly – perhaps to pay a court fine.[15] Loans were required to cover the costs to members of the elite of electoral campaigns and of the vastly expensive spectacles which many magistrates were obliged to present, not always with the support of public funding.

One important implication of the way Pliny proposes to raise his 3,000,000 sesterces is that he does not perceive the money he has lent to others as less accessible than any other element of his savings. To lend money to others is not perceived so much as a productive business activity, as a way of depositing surplus cash as securely as if it remained in the *arca*. Of course this is not meant to imply that Pliny (or Brutus) were not interested in making money, but I would suggest that that element was secondary to their wish to spread the risk of losing their cash as a result of theft or accident.

Apart from being kept back against a possible particular crisis, or celebration, savings may also be built up with a view to financial protection over the longer term: against illness or old age. There is no need to document the extent to which in the Roman world, as in most other agrarian societies which are not controlled by the market, it was assumed that the normal source of material and emotional support in illness or old age would be the family. Columella said that that was the reason for taking a wife, and there is a wealth of literary and epigraphic evidence explicitly stating that that was the primary reason for having children. Those who had no children, or whose children had predeceased them, might adopt a child (invariably a son) from another family, or raise a slave-child as a substitute child, *alumnus*.[16] But there will have been couples, and individuals, who faced infirmity without such support; that situation will have been compounded in Italy during the first centuries BC and AD by the frequency with which soldier-sons did not return to their place of origin because of death or because after completing their service they chose to settle, or were settled, in the province where they had served. Who supported their parents in their old age? As the absence of a Latin word for 'spinster' shows, there were no unmarried daughters;

the obligations of married daughters were to another household. Failing sons, there were friends and neighbours. Latin epistolography abounds with references to the obligation to visit sick *amici*; such obligations are likely to have extended to material as well as moral support (e.g. Pliny *Epist.* 1.22; Aul. Gell. *NA* 7.9.5f., 18.8.1f.; 19.10.1; Fronto Loeb vol.I p.74; 80). But to encourage such friends, it would be wise to keep a nest-egg, a *peculium* in the sense referred to by the jurist Proculus (Celsus (quoting Proculus): *Dig.* 32, 79.1). Such coin-hoards would be assembled by those worried about their future health, and without close kin on whose support they could rely. It is not surprising that after their owners' death, many such coin-hoards should have remained undetected for centuries – and sometimes detected: stories such as those of Plautus' *Aulularia* or that of the Corfidius brothers told by Pliny the Elder suggest that the idea of finding hidden treasure had a place in the popular imagination (Pliny, *NH* 7.52.177). It has been customary for archaeologists and numismatists to assume that coin-hoards are invariably connected with political instability, especially civil war or 'barbarian' invasion. That may certainly in some cases be the explanation why someone hid a great deal of treasure and failed to return to recover it, but it need not apply to all cases: those who needed to amass savings because they had no dependents whom they trusted were precisely those most likely to die without telling anyone else where they had hidden it. A hoard, like recourse to an *argentarius*, was a last resort.[17]

The last resort that was not available to the physically or socially weak in antiquity – symbolically, 'widows and orphans' – was to be provided for out of the income from savings deposited in a bank. That was of course one of the major sources of income for British provincial banks in the eighteenth and nineteenth centuries, without which it would have been impossible for them to transfer the financial resources of some parts of the country (mainly southern and rural) to other areas to finance industrial development. Up to 90 per cent of the individual depositors (not the money deposited) with English county banks in the early nineteenth century were widows who needed to keep their nest-eggs secure, and were more interested in a high immediate yield than in long-term capital growth.[18] If that framework was not available, there was another, not open to today's widows: to buy additional household members in the form of slaves. Records of slave sales in the eighteenth century West Indies show that up to 10 per cent of vendors were women, and studies of American slavery show how marginal groups such as widows, the old, the infirm and indeed free blacks were enabled to keep alive by having access to the surpluses produced by slave craftsmen at a time when they had no access to a reliable banking system (Goldin 1976; Koger 1985; on the position of widows and orphans at Rome, Saller 1994, ch.8.).

In the first instance the source of support for a Roman widow or orphan was the *tutor* normally appointed in his will by the deceased husband or father (or by the praetor if such an arrangement had not been made). To refuse to act as *tutor* was deemed a gross violation of one's obligations as an *amicus* of the family. Among the other obligations of *amici* was to look after one's property if one was away for any length of time: Roman law made special provision for who was responsible for losses incurred under such circumstances. Pliny acted to find a suitable *amicus* – i.e., a lower-status client – to look after a friend's estate; and it is interesting that the Heroninus archive from third century AD Egypt suggests that the estate administration included unsalaried persons of a similar social status to that of the owners (Pliny *Epist.* 6, 30.3f.; Rathbone 1991: 70f.). It was to *amici* that one would turn for financial assistance in the face of all sorts of immediate needs. Thus Pliny gave Romatius Firmus 300,000 sesterces to make his census-rating up to that of an equestrian: 'The length of our friendship is a guarantee that you will remember this gift'.[19] In terms of quantity, most evidence naturally relates to the financial support given by the greatest patron of all, the emperor. Augustus' provision of money to buy land for army veterans, although after AD6 financed by taxes paid to the *aerarium militare*, was perceived as support for faithful *amici*. An extreme example of such a gift to be used as support in retirement is the 100,000,000 sesterces Augustus gave the ex-centurion, and later consul, Lucius Tarius Rufus to buy an estate in Picenum. Tiberius' support for impoverished patricians is part of that same social support system. So is the distribution of largesse to citizens of any age in the wills of Caesars from Julius on (Pliny *NH* 18.7.37; Tac. *Ann.* 2, 37f.; Suet. *Aug.* 42).

It was one of the functions of wills to signal *amicitiae*: by making solemn and formal public statements about degrees of friendship, they reminded survivors of the social obligations they had to the deceased and his descendents – i.e., to offer them protection and if necessary financial support. Hellenistic kings who had been formally declared 'rex et socius et amicus populi Romani' such as Attalus III, Ptolemy Apion of Cyrene, and Ptolemy X had nominated the Roman people as their heirs; the emperors had more incentive to enter upon the inheritance. In this as in other respects the paradigm for imperial behaviour was Augustus. 'It was his custom to return all legacies and portions of an estate left to him by anyone who was a parent to their children immediately, or else (if they were still minors) to have them returned together with the interest on the day the boy took the adult toga or the girl got married' (Champlin 1991, ch.7; Suet. *Aug.* 66.4).

Powerful patrons were supposed to provide protection, advice,[20] and money. The relationship of trust, *fides*, represented by the institution of friendship performed the function which in later societies was to be performed by savings banks: and one effect of this was of course that no autonomous financial institution could develop which had a specialist interest in financing economic growth. What we call 'loans' were perceived in Roman law as an exchange of gifts between persons whom Roman law realistically recognised as having unequal social power. Borkowski's recent (1995) *Textbook of Roman Law* has a fourfold categorisation of loans.[21] The first is *mutuum*, the mutual exchange of fungibles, such as grain or money. In this case, the exchange did not have to be of sums of equal value: there could be an agreement, *stipulatio*, that the borrower's counter-gift would make provision for interest at a certain rate. Hence *mutuum* can be considered as a commercial loan, which is presumably why modern commentators award it primacy. There are also two further categories of loans both of which have to be gratuitous: *commodatum* (the loan of non-perishable goods) and *depositum* (the lending – or entrusting – of movables, which may not however be used by the person with whom they are deposited). Neither of these can be of much interest to commerce; and they make it clear that *mutuum*, too, should not be seen primarily as a commercial institution, but as an aspect of the support expected from friends, particularly in the face of sudden need (Aul. Gell. *NA* 20.1.41: n.22). One citizen gives another perishable goods which he cannot use himself, and in return he later expects to receive not the same objects (which will have been consumed or perished), but other objects of equivalent value. If interest was stipulated, then that was not essential to the arrangment. This makes the distinction between loans and gifts unsustainable in terms of Roman law: a loan is a gift made subject to the understanding that there will be a counter-gift. Literary texts suggest that it might not always be clear to the parties concerned when something was a permanent gift, and when it had been intended as a temporary loan.[22]

The Roman law of lending makes it clear that the provision of loans to those who need them has to be seen as part of the institution of *amicitia*, not of a system of banking. There was no such system: the absence at Rome of bottomry loans for maritime trade, of the kind that had been developed in fourth-century BC Athens, has often been remarked on. At Rome, maritime trade was financed by those at the top of the social hierarchy within a wider system of social obligations binding patrons (with capital) to clients (ships' captains, owners, or part-owners), in some cases with added incentives provided by the state, e.g. for those shipping grain to Rome; but this was done without recourse to a banking system (Sirks 1991).

What about the provision of finance for enterprises on an even greater scale, such as the construction of roads and aqueducts? In terms of scale, it is warfare that represents the most large-scale of activities, requiring liquid funding at levels that are erratic and frequently unforeseeable.[23] From the Middle Ages on, such funding has been provided by bankers: the Rothschilds' provisioning of the Napoleonic wars is a prime example. In the Roman world the costs of warfare had to be met primarily, but not exclusively, by the central government out of taxation (after 167BC, almost entirely at the cost of the provinces). Rome's perceived power was so unchallengeable, and therefore her ability to exact the taxes demanded so effective, that there were few occasions on which the bullion could not be found with which to pay soldiers and those who supplied them. One exception was during the occupation of parts of Italy by Hannibal, when the state had to borrow coin and precious metals: but we may note that these loans were made by directly private citizens (in large numbers), not brokered by 'bankers'. As with any government that lacks institutional means to raise money by borrowing, the Roman state occasionally faced serious shortfalls as a result of unexpected increases in military expenditure either from unforeseen wars, or changes in the 'tax base', a decline in the number of those who were paying. I suspect that the frequent references to the problems that the Roman state had in providing its troops with pay during the period from Sulla to *c.* 63BC was the direct result of an increase in the cost of the army by a factor of 250 per cent as responsibility was transferred from Italian communities to the *aerarium* when the Italian allies became Roman citizens after the Social War. The substantial public building activity in Italian municipalities which followed the Social War is well-attested archaeologically; it was financed by income which had previously gone to pay the allied contingents in the Roman army.[24] It may have been Lucullus who first identified the problem, and saw that the answer was to widen the tax base by conquering more of Asia. That was done by Pompey, and thereafter there were no longer regular deficits: the cost of the 60 per cent of the Roman army previously born by Italian allies had been shifted onto the shoulders of the population of Asia Minor and Syria. Under the Principate too emperors could win popularity by shifting the costs of government from taxes on citizens to provincials: hence Tiberius' integration of Cappadocia in AD18, and Caligula's of Mauretania in 38. In contrast, extending the tax-base on Italians was so unpopular that the literary sources generally describe such attempts as gross injustices: e.g., the proscriptions and imposition of *tributum* by the Second Triumvirate. Augustus only managed to introduce the *vicesima hereditatis* for his *aerarium militare* against strong opposition (Wiedemann 1975: 264–71).

Apart from raising revenue, the other way in which a central government can deal with a deficit is by cutting expenditure. Parallels with other periods show that this has a largely symbolic function. If those in control show that they are tightening their belts, then they feel more justified to impose sacrifices on others. What emperors could do (especially in times of military need) was to cut down on the costs of public ceremonies, or auction off surplus furnishings belonging to the *domus Caesaris*; such acts would take place in the full glare of publicity, thus drawing the attention of property-owners to the seriousness of the situation and the legitimate need for raising revenues.[25]

Although the Roman state was able to raise loans from individuals during the Second Punic War, it did not take the opportunity to create a national debt of the kind which the British state was able to institute following the 1688 revolution. It is interesting that Mommsen, in his lectures on Rome under the emperors, pointed to the absence of a national debt as a major difference between the contemporary fiscal system and the Roman one (Mommsen (trans. Wiedemann) 1996: II.89 = p.250). He had two explanations. The first was that no-one would lend to the Roman state because it was in a monopoly position (unlike modern or Hellenistic regimes); it would therefore have offered only the lowest possible returns. The second factor is less implausible: there was no legal recourse against the government should it renounce its debts (and that, Mommsen argued, was effectively what Roman governments did whenever they depreciated the currency). Rome might last for ever, but there was no guarantee that particular present or future emperors would see that it was against the long-term interests of the political system to renege on the state's debts. If a loan was perceived as a gift deposited into the *fides* of someone who could be trusted to reciprocate, then the absence of loans to the state is an indication of lack of trust. This may be borne out by one very interesting exception. Tacitus records a proposal in the Senate in AD70 to lend money to Vespasian to assist in the restoration of the state's finances after the civil wars, an offer which was soon forgotten. This was not a missed opportunity to create a national debt. It should rather be seen as an attempt by a group of senators to re-define the emperor's position as in some sense that of a responsible Roman – to limit the new regime's freedom to act without the Senate (Vespasian himself had not yet arrived in Rome) and to diminish an emperor who was being reported as exercising divine powers in Alexandria.[26]

If borrowing by the central government was impossible because there was only one state, there was a plurality of municipalities, and loans by Italian and provincial municipalities were not unknown. Why did these communities not institutionalise a system for raising loans to avoid the financial embarrassment of building costs that had spiralled out of control (like Pliny's Bithynia), or of tax demands that could not be met out of current income (like Cicero's Salamis)? These cities might have competed for liquid cash by offering rich provincials (or Romans) with cash surpluses competitive interest rates: if security was needed, then apart from income from future revenue, there was municipal land which could be pledged as security (and repayment would be guaranteed under the *Pax Romana*). The *alimenta* sounds like a system of loans of precisely this kind. But the alimentary schemes of different municipalities did not compete with each other within one empire-wide funding system, and lenders could not pull out: the *alimenta* were more like the forced loans, the *prestanze*, imposed on their wealthy citizens by late medieval Italian cities. The *alimenta* had to be created artificially because there was no structure for lending surplus wealth to a local community. Those who had such surplus wealth did not lend it as bankers, they gave it as patrons or *euergetai* – e.g., Pliny and Comum, or Tifernum Tiberinum (Duncan-Jones 1974, ch.1; Pliny *Epist.* 4.1.5) – much as Atticus provided his contemporaries with the cash they needed not *qua* banker, but *qua* patron or *amicus*. Because that was the structure for directing surplus cash to communal projects, there was no system for raising loans when the cash ran out because the project was underfunded.

That did not only apply to building, but also to irregular public ceremonies like celebrating the *adventus* of an emperor; in the Roman world, these had to be paid for through euergetism – grants, not loans. On similar occasions, other societies have had recourse to different systems. On 13 June 1429, Florence had the pleasure of putting on a pageant to celebrate a visit by two nephews of Pope Martin V. In an ancient city, one or more patrons would have had the honour to fund such an occasion; Florence raised a forced loan of 1/12th of a cataster, i.e. 1/24th of one percent, out of the property of its wealthy citizens (it is not clear what proportion were liable to forced loans at this time: in 1390/92 there had been 83 contributors). A pageant was considerably cheaper than warfare, of course: during a military crisis in February 1431/3, a loan of 36 catasti, 18 per cent of property values, was imposed.

If we wish to explain why the Romans did not develop a centralised banking system, then instead of seeing this as a 'failure' in contrast to the development of institutions for the lending and transfer of money by Lombards in the eleventh, Jews and Templars in the twelfth, and Tuscans like the Medici in the fifteenth century, it might be more helpful to consider how institutions which the Romans did have managed to fulfil effectively so many of the functions for which other societies needed banks. It was precisely because institutions associated with the family and the household – *patriapotestas*, slavery, the *fides* of friends and patrons – were able to fulfil requirements such as those of education, healthcare, care of the elderly and emergency fire insurance cover that the Roman elite had no need for the kinds of institutions which in the modern world have enabled the development of commercial and industrial investment and government activities in peace and (especially) war. There was a (lowly) place for small-scale professional moneylenders and changers; in contrast, there was little need for a separate category of financiers providing long-term credit and – just as crucially – safekeeping for the deposited savings of those served by a network of friends and patrons.

Acknowledgement

My particular thanks are due to John Rich, Jim Roy and Richard Saller for their comments on this paper. This does not imply that any of them was convinced by every argument.

Notes

1 De Ste Croix 1972; Cornford 1907; the late 1960s saw considerable interest in the Peloponnesian War in response to the issues raised by the Vietnam conflict. Finley advocated the 'primitivist' approach particularly in *The Ancient Economy* (1985); see the review by Frederiksen (1975).

2 Garnsey 1980; Wood 1988; Osborne 1985: esp. 142ff.; Foxhall 1990: 97ff. The argument about the relative importance of slaves in agriculture continues, with Jameson 1992: 135–46 maximising the importance of slavery. For female workers, Kampen 1981; Günther 1987; Grassl 1990: 13–17; Scheidel 1995a: 202–17 and 1995b: 1–10. Production in a wider context: Garnsey 1988; Gallant 1991; Sallares 1991.

3 The economic effects of Roman state activity on frontier regions in particular were examined by Hopkins 1980: 101–25. A systematic study of the economic effects of the requirements of Roman army provisioning over the centuries (rather than of particular aspects such as the wine trade) seems to me an urgent *desideratum.*

4 An approach which for many years has been associated with the work of Duncan-Jones: see *inter alia* Duncan-Jones 1974, 1990, 1994. It is interesting that one of the first to draw attention to the importance of ancient accounting practices was Ste. Croix 1956: 14–74: he emphasised the shortcomings of Roman book-keeping.

5 But on occasion the point at which a moneylender becomes a banker can be pinpointed: in 1863, the Warburgs stopped referring to themselves as 'Geldwechsler' and called themselves 'Bankier'. Chernow 1993: 13.

6 Sen. *Ben.* 1.2.4: 'Alium re, alium fide, alium gratia, alium consilio, alium praeceptis salubribus adiuva'. Material help does not of course only include providing money: but we might compare the way in which a powerful Roman's network of *amici* throughout

Italy enabled him to stay in their homes while travelling to a modern network of cash machines. Cf. Shatzman 1975; on the different functions of private patronage, cf. Saller 1982.

7 Such financial support was typically given by Lombard or Jewish moneylenders. Cf. Poliakov 1977.

8 We may note the major impetus which the temporary absence of a considerable proportion of male property-owners in north-west Europe (perhaps 25 per cent) in the Crusades gave to banking: property was entrusted to religious orders (who would be able to resist pressure to seize it), particularly the Templars (who also had the means to communicate between the eastern Mediterranean and home, thus obviating the need physically to transport cash). Cf. Barber 1992. In the medieval *Drama of St. Nicolas*, a Jewish money-lender leaves his property in the care of the saint's church when he goes away on a journey.

9 Cic., *Lael.* 18.65. The vast literature on *fides* is surveyed by Becker 1969: 801–36; cf. Fraenkel 1916: 187–99. We may also note the strong feelings expressed against *novae tabulae* (eg. Vell. Pat. 2.23.2): reducing debts struck at the heart of Roman social relationships.

10 Cic. *Att.* 5.21.10–13; 6.1.3-8; 6.2.7–9; 6.3.5–6. We may note that Brutus did not act himself, but through the 'mandators' (M. Scaptius and P. Matinius) to whom he had entrusted his savings.

11 Volatile prices: Cic. *Cael.* 17. Secrecy is emphasised in Aulus Gellius' account of Cicero being lent 2,000,000 sesterces by P. Sulla to buy a house: 'mutua sestertium viciens tacito', *NA* 12.12.4. *Faeneratores*: Cic. *Fam.* 5.6.2; *Att.* 2.1.11. Rauh 1986: 3–30.

12 Pliny, *Epist.* 3.19.8: 'aliquid tamen fenero, nec molestus erit mutuari: accipiam a socru, cuius arca non secus ac mea utor'. At 3.11.2 Pliny boasts of giving his client Artemidorus a loan 'while other, richer friends delay'. Aulus Gellius (*NA* 20.1.41) underlines the function of borrowing to cover the short-term needs which are faced by everybody: 'in pecuniae mutuaticae usu atque commercio … subsidium hoc inopiae temporariae, quo communis omnium vita indiget'.

13 Waldstein, 1986: 68f., 365, shows that *obsequium* entailed moral obliations that were not legally enforceable: *Dig.* 37.15.

14 Martial 3.52:

Empta domus fuerat tibi, Tongiliane, ducentis:
abstulit hanc nimium casus in urbe frequens.
Conlatum est deciens. Rogo, non potes ipse videri
incendisse tuam, Tongiliane, domum?

15 Following the condemnation of Lucius Scipio in 187BC: 'collata ea pecunia ab cognatis amicisque et clientibus', Livy 38.60.9.

16 Columella 12.pr.1 (citing Cicero's translation of Xenophon's *Oeconomicus* 7.19ff): 'adiutoria senectutis, nec minus propugnacula'; the assumption is that a younger woman will look after an older man. Children: Wiedemann 1989: 39–43. *Alumnus* as support in old age: Stat. *Silv.* 2.1.69: 'Tu domino requies portusque senectae'. Saller 1994: 48, estimates that at age 55, 20 per cent of women and 12 per cent of men would have had no surviving children.

17 One example of the assumptions that coin-hoards point to destruction by 'barbarians': James 1988: 37. Political instability does not rule out an increasing need for *peculium*-reserves, as individuals become deracinated. Note how the increasing number of coin hoards in late republican Italy may reflect periods of civil war, the personal dislocation caused by those civil wars, and the increasing monetarisation of Italy as Italian communities became more interdependant (see n.4 above). The closeness of the correlation between coin-hoards and war in late republican Italy is illustrated by table 10 of Crawford 1992: 162.

18 With effects on the investment strategies of British banks which remain with us today. See Ollerenshaw 1988: 55–82.

19 'Te memorem huius muneris amicitiae nostrae diurnitas spondet' (note the quasi-legal term): Pliny *Epist.* 1.19.3. We may also note that giving someone a present also served as a public statement that a friendship had not terminated: Sen. *Ben.* 3.27.3.

20 I hope to examine the ways in which advice was given and received in a forthcoming study of the Roman domestic *consilium*.

21 Borkowski 1995: 283–90. I leave aside his fourth category, *pignus*, which seems to have had more to do with indebtedness.

22 The resulting unwillingness to lend is the theme of some of Martial's epigrams: Saller 1982, ch.4.

23 Duncan-Jones 1994, ch.3, suggests that the proportion of the imperial budget that was directed to supporting the army was in the region of 70–75 per cent: some of his detailed arguments may be questioned, but the order of magnitude is surely right.

24 That allied Italian communities had to finance the contingents they contributed to the Roman army before 90BC is hypothetical; but note the sudden growth in the role of *Praefecti Castrorum* (such as Theophanes of Mytilene for Pompey, and Cornelius Balbus for Caesar, during this period). Building: Crawford 1981: 153–60.

25 Nerva: Dio 68.2.3; Marcus Aurelius: Zonaras 12.1 = Loeb Dio vol. IX, p.70. Martial speculates on the scale of the auction that would have to take place in heaven if Domitian were to call in all his gifts to the gods: 9.3.1–4.

26 Tac. *Hist.* 4.47: 'Ceterum verane pauperie an uti videretur, actum in senatu ut sescentiens sestertium a privatis mutuum acciperetur ... nec multo post necessitas abiit sive omissa simulatio.'

References

Andreau, J. (1987) *La Vie financière dans le monde romain*, Rome: École Française de Rome.

Aubert, J.-J. (1994) *Business Managers in Ancient Rome*, Leiden: Brill.

Barber, M. (1992) 'The Templars and the supply of the Holy Land'. In B.Z. Kedar (ed.), *The Horns of Hattin*, Jerusalem: Yad Izhak Ben-Zvi.

Becker, C. (1969) *Realencyclopaedie für Antike und Christentum* 7: 801–36.

Borkowski, A. (1995) *Textbook of Roman Law*, London: Blackstone.

Champlin, E. (1991) *Final Judgements: Duty and Emotion in Roman Wills*, Berkeley: University of California Press.

Chernow, R. (1993) *The Warburgs*, London: Chatto and Windus.

Cohen, E.E. (1992) *Athenian Economy and Society: A Banking Perspective*, Princeton: Princeton University Press.

Cornford, F. (1907) *Thucydides Mythistoricus*, London: Arnold.

Crawford, M.H. (1981) 'Italy and Rome', *JRS* 71: 153–60.

Crawford, M.H. (1992) *The Roman Republic*, 2nd edn, London: Fontana.

de Ste Croix, G.E.M. (1956) 'Greek and Roman Accounting'. In A.C. Littleton and B.S.Yamey (eds), *Studies in the History of Accounting*: 14–74, London: Sweet & Maxwell.

de Ste Croix, G.E.M. (1972) *The Origins of the Peloponnesian War*, London: Duckworth.

Duncan-Jones, R. (1974) *The Economy of the Roman Empire: Quantitative Studies*, Cambridge: Cambridge University Press.

Duncan-Jones, R. (1990) *Structure and Scale in the Roman Economy*, Cambridge: Cambridge University Press.

Duncan-Jones, R. (1994) *Money and Government in the Roman Empire*, Cambridge: Cambridge University Press.

Finley, M.I. (1985) *The Ancient Economy*, 2nd edn, London: Penguin.

Foxhall, L. (1990) 'The dependant tenant: land leasing and labour in Italy and Greece', *JRS* 80: 97–114.

Fraenkel, E. (1916) 'Zur Geschichte des Wortes *Fides*', *Rheinisches Museum* 71: 187–99.

Frederiksen, M.W. (1975) 'Theory, Evidence and the Ancient Economy', *JRS* 65: 164–71.

Frayn, J.M. (1993) *Markets and Fairs in Roman Italy*, Oxford: Clarendon Press.

Gallant, T.W. (1991) *Risk and Survival in Ancient Greece*, Cambridge: Cambridge University Press.

Garnsey, P.D.A. (ed.), (1980) *Non-slave Labour in the Greco-Roman World*, Cambridge: Cambridge University Press.

Garnsey, P.D.A. (1988) *Famine and Food Supply in the Greco-Roman World*, Cambridge: Cambridge University Press.

Goldin, C.D. (1976) *Urban Slavery in the American South 1820–1860*, Chicago: University of Chicago Press.

Grassl, H. (1990) 'Zur Rolle der Frau in antiken Hirtenkulturen', *Laverna* 1: 13–17.

Günther, R. (1987) *Frauenarbeit – Frauenbindung*, Munich: Fink.

Hopkins, K. (1980) 'Taxes and trade in the Roman Empire (200BC–AD400)', *JRS* 70: 101–25.

James, E. (1988) *The Franks*, Oxford: Blackwell.

Jameson, M.H. (1992) 'Agricultural Labor in Ancient Greece'. In B. Wells (ed.), *Agriculture in Ancient Greece*: 135–46, Stockholm: Svenska Institut i Athen.

Kampen, N. (1981) *Image and Status: Roman Working Women in Ostia*, Berlin: Gebr. Mann.

Kirschenbaum, A. (1987) *Sons, Slaves and Freedmen in Roman Commerce*, Jerusalem: Magnes Press, Hebrew University.

Koger, L. (1985) *Black Slaveowners: Free Black Slave Masters in South Carolina, 1790–1860*, Jefferson: McFarland.

Millett, P. (1991) *Lending and Borrowing in Ancient Athens*, Cambridge: Cambridge University Press.

Molho, A. (1971) *Florentine Public Finances in the Early Renaissance 1400–1433*, Cambridge, MA: Harvard University Press.

Mommsen, T. (trans. Wiedemann) (1996) *History of Rome under the Emperors*, London: Routledge.

Ollerenshaw, P. (1988) 'The Development of Banking in the Bristol region, 1750–1914'. In C.E. Harvey and J. Press (eds), *Studies in the Business History of Bristol*: 55–82. Bristol: Bristol Academic Press.

Osborne, R. (1985) *Demos: the Discovery of Classical Attica*, Cambridge: Cambridge University Press.

Perlwitz, O. (1992) *Titus Pomponius Atticus* (Hermes Einzelschrift 58) Stuttgart: Steiner.

Poliakov, L. (1977) *Jewish Bankers and the Holy See* (Engl. trans.), London: Routledge and Kegan Paul.

Rauh, N. (1986) 'Cicero's business friendships', *Aevum* 60(1): 3–30.

Rathbone, D. (1991) *Economic Rationalism and Rural Society in Third Century AD Egypt*, Cambridge: Cambridge University Press.

Rawson, E. (1976) 'The Ciceronian aristocracy and its properties'. In M.I. Finley (ed.), *Studies in Roman Property*, 85–102. Cambridge: Cambridge University Press.

Sallares, R., (1991) *The Ecology of the Ancient Greek World*, London: Duckworth.

Saller, R. (1982) *Personal Patronage under the Early Empire*, Cambridge: Cambridge University Press.

Saller, R. (1994) *Patriarchy, Property and Death in the Roman Family*, Cambridge: Cambridge University Press.
Scheidel, W. (1995a) 'The most silent women of Greece and Rome: rural labour and women's life in the Ancient World I', *Greece and Rome* 42(2): 202–17.
Scheidel, W. (1995b) 'The most silent women of Greece and Rome: rural labour and women's life in the Ancient World II', *Greece and Rome* 43(1): 1–10.
Shatzman, L. (1975) *Senatorial Wealth and Roman Politics*, Brussels: Latomus.
Sirks, B. (1991) *Food for Rome*, Amsterdam: Gieben.
Waldstein, W. (1986) *Operae Libertorum*, Stuttgart: Steiner.
Wiedemann, T.E.J. (1975) 'The political background to Ovid's *Tristia* 2', *Classical Quarterly* 25(2): 264–71.
Wiedemann, T.E.J. (1989) *Adults and Children in the Roman Empire*, London: Routledge.
Wood, E.M. (1988) *Peasant Citizen and Slave*, London: Verso.

2

PUBLIC BUILDING, URBAN RENEWAL AND EUERGETISM IN EARLY IMPERIAL ITALY

Kathryn Lomas

One of the most high-profile, but possibly one of the most problematic, forms of euergetism undertaken by the elites of Roman Italy was the construction of public buildings. This a vast range of activity in both scope and cost, ranging from dedications of small structures or repairs and refurbishment of existing buildings to the construction of vast new complexes and remodelling of whole areas of a city.[1] It was, therefore, a form of benefaction which had a unique impact on the physical development of the urban environment, and also provides a powerful reflection of the cultural identity of a city and the way in which it was shaped by civic patrons and benefactors. Paradoxically, it is also one of the areas in which patterns of benefaction, and in particular the motivations for it, are least clear. There is a wealth of evidence – mostly archaeological and epigraphic – for the construction and reconstruction of public buildings in Roman Italy, but the reasons for preferring certain types of building at particular times, and for undertaking the cost of a construction programme at all, are frequently ambiguous. One of the reasons for this ambiguity is that it falls into a grey area between euergetism in the strictest sense, undertaken at private cost and by private initiative, and activities which formed part of the responsibilities of the civic magistrates (Pobjoy 2000: 89–92). Given the importance and high profile of much of the rebuilding programmes and their impact on the development of the urban environment, an examination of who was choosing to build what, and the motivations involved, may give some useful insights into definition and redefinition of cultural identity in the Italy of the late Republic and early Empire. Study of the patterns of public building can provide us with a way of studying the world-view of the municipal elites of Roman Italy, their relationship with the central power of Rome and the emperor, and their role in shaping the identity of their communities.

The construction of large-scale public buildings, and the patterns of euergetism and benefaction associated with this, were vital elements in the changes taking place in urban structure and urban culture in the late Republic and early Empire. A notable feature of the development of urbanisation and urban culture in Italy is the extent to which cities underwent a physical transformation during the period between the Social War and the end of the first century AD. The impact of this, and the precise form it took, varied considerably from region to region depending on a number of factors such as the extent of pre-Roman urbanisation and the level of Roman colonisation during this period, but nevertheless it is a phenomenon which can be traced in most parts of Italy. In most regions, there are three principal phases of construction and urban renewal. These broadly correspond to period immediately following the Social War and the dictatorship of Sulla, the Augustan renewal in the aftermath of the civil wars, and the era of Trajan and the Antonine emperors. In Campania and some parts of southern Latium, there was also an earlier phase of intensive building and urban development in during the second century BC, but the reasons which lie behind this may be very regionally and historically specific (Gabba 1971; Frederiksen 1976; Cébeillac-Gervasioni 1990: 715–22), and it is not replicated in all regions of Italy. The implications of these changes in the period between the Social War and the reign of Trajan are far-reaching – both in terms of what they indicate about Romanisation, and in terms of what they can tell us about benefaction and the motivations for it – but it is still not clear where the impetus for them was coming from, and whether they are attributable to the central power of Rome or to local communities and the activities of local benefactors.

There has been an increasing degree of recognition in recent years of the extent to which changes in urban space reflect changes in social behaviour.[2] Research on urban space has emphasised just how far the evolution of the city is determined by the world-view of its inhabitants, particularly those in a position of power, and also the extent to which the physical form of the city shapes social behaviour and interactions. It has also highlighted how urban space can impose changes on patterns of social interaction, and the extent to which public imagery in its various forms can be tailored to provoke specific responses or highlight specific agendas. Examination of urban development can give some important clues as to how elite perceptions of a city changed. This may, in turn, suggest something about changing social and political conditions within cities, and about relations between Italian municipalities and Rome. For instance, Zanker's exposition of Augustan iconography as something which was manifested in both monumental architecture and public art and monuments (Zanker 1988) points to a strong connection between the physical structures and the culture and power structures of the society which generated them. One of the weaknesses of this approach, however, is that it is essentially a top-down view of the process. It places a heavy emphasis on Rome and the emperor as the motivating forces and the definers of the agenda but it does not define the role of the municipalities. Given that the role of the emperor in municipal benefaction is at best ambiguous (Millar 1986; Patterson, Chapter 5 of this volume) a more holistic approach which locates the local elites of Italy at the centre of the debate is required. The aim of this paper is to review the structure and form of the Italian city as it evolved in the first century BC and first century AD – what public buildings were being constructed, who was undertaking the construction, and why – but also to suggest some ways in which this can throw light on about the social dynamics of the city in this period, on the role and motivation of benefactors in shaping these changes, and on the role of the city as a vehicle for acculturation and Roman unification of the peninsula.

There is no doubt that public buildings were regarded in Antiquity as a significant part of the urban landscape and vital to the city's status and identity. Careful consideration was given to regulating who was allowed to build structures, on what basis, and where (Cébeillac-Gervasioni 1990: 99–101). Conversely, the demolition of buildings was a serious activity and was carefully regulated and covered by statutes to ensure that this was not carried out lightly. Municipal and colonial laws and edictsd contained clauses to regulate both of these activities. The surviving portion of the Lex Tarentina, contains provisions to regulate public building (*CIL* I^2. 590.25–38 = *FIRA* 27.32–9 = Crawford 1996: 307–8) and the Lex Genetiva Julia from Urso in Spain contains restrictions on demolition of buildings (*CIL* I^2.594.73–81 = *FIRA* 28.75–7, 97–8 = Crawford 1996: 404–5, 408–9).[3] Both laws place on magistrates the obligation to hold games at their own expense during their year of office, but under the LexTarentina, they were allowed to pay for the construction of a public building or monument instead (*CIL* I^2.32–8). The *Digest* also reveals concern about the maintenance of public buildings. Abandonment or decrepitude of buildings was regarded as unacceptable, as derelict structures were thought to affect the appearance and general dignity and reputation of a city (*Dig.* 39.1.20.11). One of the specified functions of the *curatores rei publicae* was a responsibility for ensuring that derelict houses and buildings were rebuilt (*Dig.* 39.2.46.1). Clearly, the integrity of the physical fabric of a city was an important issue, which was expected to be of concern to the city's magistrates, and any decrepitude or lack of embellishment was believed to reflect adversely on the status of the community.

The evidence for public building in Italy is plentiful but problematic. Few individual cities have been preserved in a state which allows detailed study – Pompeii, Herculaneum, Ostia, and to a lesser extent, Paestum, are very much the exceptions rather than the rule. For the most part, the body of evidence consists of inscriptions and archaeological remains of public buildings scattered throughout the cities of Roman Italy, and rarely allowing an evaluation of more than an individual structure or a small part of the urban fabric of any given city.[4] In some cases, literary evidence gives a context for the archaeological remains, or adds additional information about a specific structure, but this sort of corroboration is all too infrequent and in most cases we only have an inscription, a reference or the physical structures, not all three (Gros 2000: 307–12). Dating can sometimes be only approximate, due to constraints of excavation and recording, or to identification of buildings by references much later than the putative date of construction. The primary problem, however, for present purposes is that it is frequently uncertain who constructed a building, and even where we do know the identity, the motivation behind the choice of structure and the level of benefaction. Thus we are frequently left with an incomplete picture of why particular individuals or groups paid for this type of benefaction, but we can, nevertheless, reach some conclusions.

Even a cursory glance at the statistical breakdown of this material (Tables 2.1 and 2.2) reveals a marked change in patterns of public building in the early empire. Republican building was heavily biased towards construction and maintenance of walls, towers and gateways – structures which had a vital function as the defences of the city but were also a powerful statement of communal identity (Gabba 1971; Poccetti 1988) – and towards the building of temples. There was an upsurge in the building of structures for public entertainment in the period after the Hannibalic war, as well as construction of baths. Many of these structures seem to tie in with the influx of wealth into Italy in the later second century BC, and are also geographically specific in their distribution (Jouffroy 1986: 18–26; Cébeillac-Gervasioni 1990: 715–22, 1998: 126–33). In most regions of Italy, but in particular in Latium and Campania, the high point of the construction of public buildings falls between *c.*100BC and the reign of Augustus, a period in which there is also a demonstrable change in patterns of euergetism and the funding of these building projects.

The pattern of public building in early imperial Italy indicates a rather different set of priorities. Constructions of new defences and rebuilding of existing ones were much less prevalent, and where they took place, they were heavily, although not exclusively, weighted towards imperial patronage and activity. They were also

Table 2.1 Public building in Italy, fourth–first centuries BC (figures from Jouffroy 1986)

Type of building	*fourth/third century BC*	*second century BC*	*first century BC*	*Undated*
Fortifications	48	19	56	0
Temples	40	53	46	14
Major public works	0	15	20	15
Macella	0	4	7	0
Basilicas/curiae	3	12	10	3
Baths	2	4	14	0
Theatres and amphitheatres	1	5	27	1

Table 2.2 Public building in early imperial Italy (figures from Jouffroy 1986)

Type of building	*Augustan*	*Julio-Claudian*	*Flavian*	*Undated*
Fortifications	16	4	0	0
Temples	40	28	17	23
Major public works	33	14	5	11
Arches	7	5	1	0
Macella	3	3	1	2
Basilicas/curiae	10	5	5	1
Baths	11	9	4	1
Theatres	35	15	4	3
Amphitheatres	11	17	10	2

different in character. Wholesale reconstructions of city walls, such as had occurred after the Social War (Gabba 1971; Poccetti 1988), became much less frequent. Instances in which city walls were repaired or replaced seem to have been primarily activities undertaken and paid for by the council or magistrates of cities, rather than acts of private benefaction. There are also a number of examples of repairs to walls and fortifications as imperial benefactions or paid for by members of the imperial family. At Saepinum and Laus Pompeia, for instance, the walls were rebuilt by Tiberius and Drusus in 2BC and AD14–23 respectively (*CIL* IX.2443, *CIL* V.6358), those of Fanum Fortunae by Augustus (*CIL* XI.6218–19, Vitruv. *Arch.* 5.1.6–10, Jouffroy 1986: 65), and those of Ravenna by Claudius in AD43 (*CIL* IX.5). Triumphal arches and monumental gateways and entrances to cities were something which seems to have become entirely an imperial prerogative. Most know examples were built by Augustus or members of his family. Many were constructed as part of imperial road-building programmes, or in commemoration of military events, and carried inscriptions to make this clear (Laurence 2000). Examples include the arch of Augustus at Brundisium (Dio 51.19.1), the arch of Augustus at Ariminum (*CIL* XI.365),[5] an arch of Augustus at Ticinum (*CIL* V.6416), and arches dedicated to Drusus and Germanicus at Spoletium (*CIL* XI.4776–7), Nero and Drusus at Bergamum, Tiberius at Ravenna (*CIL* XI.5) and G. and L. Caesar at Pisa (*CIL* XI.1421).

Construction and embellishment of temples still flourished, stimulated to some extent by the establishment of the imperial cult and also by the need to repair structures damaged during the civil wars (Jouffroy 1986: 73–85; Gros 2000: 308–12). A large number of the temple constructions, and particularly those which were new rather than additions and repairs to existing sanctuaries, were dedicated to various manifestations of the cult of Augustus. A shrine to the *gens* Julia containing statues of Augustus was established at Bovillae on his death in AD14 (Tac. *Ann.* 2.41.1, Suet. Aug. 2) and at Ferentum, an *Augusteum* with statues was constructed during the last years of his reign or under Tiberius (*CIL* XI.7431, *AE* 1911, 184). Elsewhere, there are cult buildings dedicated to the *Lares Augusti*, such as those at Tusculum (*Eph. Epig.* 9.679), Acerrae (*CIL* X.3757), and Pola (*CIL* V.18). Other Augustan cults include *Salus Augusti* at Ariminum (*CIL* XI.361), *Concordia Augusta* at Minturnae (Johnson 1933), *Fortuna Augusta* at Pompeii (*CIL* X.820), and the frequent combination of Roma and Augustus as found at Ostia (*CIL* XIV.73, 353, 4642), Terracina (*CIL* X.6305) and Superaequum (*AE* 1898, 79). Other elite building activity which involved temples, such as the extensive rebuilding of the temple of Apollo at Cumae (Gabricì 1913), was directed towards restoration of the damage caused by the civil wars or towards temples of cults non-indigenous to Italy, such as those of Mithras or Isis (Jouffroy 1986: 73–82). The overwhelming impression, however, is of a focusing of public activity on shrine to the imperial cult in its various manifestations.

The period between the Social War and the death of Augustus was also the era in which many Italian cities underwent major remodelling and gained a whole suite of new amenities, although in some parts of Campania, this process begins as early as 150BC. The category listed as 'major public works' covers a range of building projects, all of large scale and most involving more than one structure. It ranges from the construction of aqueducts, cisterns and drains, through paving roads and altering street patterns, to wholesale reconstruction of entire areas of a city. At Aletrium, for instance, L. Betelienus Varus (*CIL* I^2.1529 = X.5807) was responsible in 130–120BC for the reconstruction of all the city's streets, a portico, a macellum, a basilica, a public sundial and various aspects of the water supply. At Praeneste, the duoviri rebuilt the city's baths and restored the water supply to them (*CIL* XIV.3013) in the post-Sullan era, and at Volsinii, the late Republican local dignitary and magistrate L. Caecina repaved the city's streets at his own expense (*AE* 1916.115). In the early empire, there were some equally ambitious projects afoot. The forum of Terracina seems to have been rebuilt in the Augustan period, largely by A. Aemilius (*CIL* X.6306), and there were major reconstructions of the forum at Minturnae, Herdonia and Volaterrae. New aqueducts were built at Venafrum, Brundisium, Teate, Bononia, Capena and a number of other cities.

A number of new building types became very prominent in the cities of Italy towards the end of the Republic and under Augustus. Some have a clear connection with systematisation of administrative structures in newly founded colonies or newly enfranchised *municipia*. There is an upsurge of constructions of basilicas and *curiae*, both of which housed important aspects of civic government, and of *macella*, which provided a facility for trading the sort of luxury goods for which the main market was the elite (De Ruyt 1983; Frayn 1993). Many of these may be connected with the process of municipalisation and Romanisation of the structures of government in the aftermath of the Social War, although this does not provide a full explanation for the phenomenon. Most of these structures are known from archaeological, rather than epigraphic, evidence and it is in many cases not known who paid for them, or on what basis. However, it is clear that there is a wide spectrum of possibilities. Examples from Latium and Campania dating to the second or first centuries BC are constructed primarily by local notables, mainly but not invariably in their capacity as magistrates (Jouffroy 1986: 44–51, 85–8; Cébeillac-Gervasioni 1990: 712–4).[6] During the Principate, the pattern is more varied. The monumental centre of Fanum Fortunae, which was an Augustan colony, seems to have been carefully planned and financed from Roman resources (Vitruv. *Arch.* 5.1.6–10).[7] Elsewhere, however, basilicas, *curiae* and *macella* are paid for by civic patrons, such as the Flavian proconsul who built a basilica at Herculaneum and the civic patron who did likewise at Veleia (*CIL* X.1425, XI. 1185–6), or as acts of local euergetism such as that of a freedman of the Augustan period who paid for repairs to the basilica at Pompeii (*CIL* X.807). There is also a distinction in terms of how these projects were funded, with many *macella* being built at private expense, while most basilicas and *curiae* were built by civic magistrates in their official capacity (Jouffroy 1986: 44–51, 85–8; Cébeillac-Gervasioni 1990: 712–4, 1998: 113–5).

The major change in the early Empire is the big increase in the building of structures related to leisure and entertainment, such as baths, theatres and amphitheatres. There was a significant phase of bath-building in the first century BC but it was regionally specific, with over half the known examples concentrated in southern Latium and Campania (Jouffroy 1986: 52–3). The building activities of Betelienus Varus at Aletrium, for instance, included a *lacus balnearius* (*CIL* X.5807), and by 80BC, Pompeii had no fewer than three baths (Zanker 1998: 32–52; *CIL* X.829, 817). There was a further flourishing of bath construction under Augustus, and then a fall-off in activity until the Antonine period, when members of the elite once again began to pay for building, reconstruction or embellishment of baths (Jouffroy 1986: 93–6, 125–9). Here again, we run into the problem that most structures do not have surviving inscriptions, and therefore no information about who constructed them. Where details have survived, they again show a mixture of external patrons, local magistrates and eminent private citizens, with the finance for most projects coming from local sources.[8]

The main field of expansion, however, is in the construction of buildings for public entertainment – mainly theatres and amphitheatres, but including a small number of circuses and other structures such as the covered theatre at Pompeii and the *odeion* at Naples. A considerable number of stone-built theatres, and some amphitheatres, are known from Republican Italy as a whole,[9] but the distribution of them is very limited. There is a particularly high concentration of both types of building in Campania and to a less marked extent, in Latium (Jouffroy 1986: 53–8, Frézouls 1983) and at some sites in Samnium.[10] It is notable that some pre-Augustan theatres form part of religious sanctuaries, sometimes entirely divorced from an urban context, as at Pietrabbondante. Outside this central Italian area, stone theatres and amphitheatres are much fewer in number and are mainly associated with colonisation. It is probable that until the Augustan period, a significant number of theatres were constructed in wood, as they continued to be at Rome, and so did not survive. Games, in particular, were frequently staged in the forum of a city, which would be adapted with wooden seating and partitions for the occasion. Vitruvius notes that a forum should be designed explicitly to take into account the need to be able to set up these structures (Vitruv. *Arch.* 5.1.2; *cf* Welch 1994 on the development of stone amphitheatres). During the Augustan period the number of stone theatres constructed rises throughout Italy, as does the number of amphitheatres – a factor which represents a major investment in public building by the benefactors who were footing the bill, given that buildings of this size and elaboration represented a major outlay of resources by either a state or an individual.

The bare statistical evidence, presented as tables or distribution maps, gives a sharp indication that there were major changes afoot in the Italian city during the late Republic and the early empire, both in number and in type of benefactions. This indicates that serious money was being invested in the infrastructure, despite the economic strain imposed on the country by almost a century of civil war, and also that there are changes going on within the cities in the way that social relations operated and in the ways in which civic identity was both defined and expressed. What is less clear, however, is where the money was coming from, precisely why these particular building types were selected, and what the underlying pattern of euergetism and benefaction signified.

The shift in choice of building types – which shows a clear move away from temples and defensive works towards an emphasis on structures for public entertainment – seems to coincide roughly with the reign of Augustus. Much of the public building activity of the Augustan period shows a pattern similar to that of the late Republic, in what was being constructed and in the considerable scale of building activity. From the middle of the first century AD onwards, there is a distinct falling-away of willingness to invest in public building, both by communities and individuals (Whittaker 1994). The underlying reasons for these changes and for this peak of activity between the Social War and the death of Augustus, have been much debated (Gabba 1971; Eck 1984; Zanker 1988; Patterson 1991: 149–57), as have the significance of some of the changes in the form of urban development in this period of Italian history. In part, the prevalence of public building can be attributed to the growing urbanisation of some areas of Italy which had not had a strong tradition of urban development before the second century BC, but it is noticeable that in fact, the greatest amount of activity took place in the cities of Latium, Campania, southern Etruria and parts of Umbria (Jouffroy 1986) – precisely the areas of Italy which were already most densely urbanised. This seems to argue less for a phase of development in less urbanised regions that for a change in ways of conceptualising the city. Changes to the structures of the forum and the upsurge in construction of theatres are perhaps the most visible and large-scale changes, and both of these seem to reflect a combination of the Augustan cultural agenda of the late first century BC, a shift in euergetic behaviour by the municipal elites, and a fundamental change in ideas of what a city should consist of. They are also accompanied by a shift – which is most notable in the financing of buildings for public entertainment, and in additions, embellishments and repairs to existing structures – from building undertaken by magistrates to private initiatives, and from publicly-funded projects to private benefactions.

The changes to the form – and by extension the function – of the forum is something which is very marked in the Augustan period. From being an area which was, typically, surrounded by tabernae and the offices of civic officials and was both the centre of political activity and the commercial hub of the community, it became a very much more ceremonial area dominated by temples, and buildings associated with the imperial cult, and marked off from the rest of the city with monumental entrance. Probably the best known, and most complete, example is that of Pompeii (Zanker 1998: 78–106; Laurence 1994: 20–7; Gros 2000: 311–14), from which the *tabernae* were cleared and replaced by temples of the Lares Augusti, the Eumachia building and the *macellum*, both of which contained additional shrines to the imperial cult. Other examples of monumentalised *fora* include those of Terracina, Volterrae, Minturnae, and Herdonia all of which seem to have been based closely on Augustan developments in Rome.[11]

The prominence of theatres in the list of new constructions in the early Empire may have a political and ideological slant as well as reflecting changes in euergetic behaviour by local elites.

Augustus made skilful use of public spectacle to communicate with, and present himself to, the people of Rome (Rawson 1987; Coleman, Chapter 4 of this volume). It has been suggested that that the emphasis on theatre building in the Augustan era was directly connected with the *Lex Julia Theatralis* and was a conscious attempt to corral public entertainment into a building in which the populace could be systematised into a physical map of the Augustan social hierarchy (Bejor 1979: 126–38; Rawson 1987), with due prominence given to the decurions and visiting dignitaries, special recognition to other favoured groups such as priests and Augustales, and women and underage youths decently segregated. The sudden prevalence of permanent stone theatres, some of them with inscriptions defining the status of each block of seating, can be interpreted as an attempt to rationalise a potentially unruly populace into its appropriate social parts. The theatre was also a prominent building in the cult and representation of the emperor during the Julio-Claudian period (Bejor 1979; Frézouls 1983; Gros 1994, 2000: 311–15; Lomas 1997: 30–9). Probably the most complete example of this is Minturnae,[12] where the north side of the forum was reconstructed after the foundation of the Augustan colony. A complex of a theatre, porticoes, and temples to Divus Julius and to *Concordia Augusta* was constructed around the existing temple of Jupiter, turning the whole of one side of the forum into an Augustan monument. In form, it is closely paralleled by the forum of Augustus in Rome, in that a closed precinct is an integral part of it, and is also similar in structure to the theatre of Pompey, which also incorporated a theatre and portico complex.[13]

The new emphasis on the forum as formalised ceremonial space, and on the prominence of stone-built theatres seems, therefore to have a close link with the development of the imperial cult, and in particular with the cult of Augustus and his family,[14] but it may also have other implications. The impetus behind this apparent change in the conceptualisation of what a city should be is difficult to define, but examination of euergetic behaviour may provide some way into the problem. The change broadly coincides with the beginnings of a shift from publicly-funded building projects controlled by civic magistrates to a greater degree of privately-funded buildings. It is notable that theatres and other structures connected with leisure and entertainment were the types of building which were most frequently paid for as an act of private benefaction (Jouffroy 1986: 96–108; Cébeillac-Gervasioni 1998: 128–33). The other notable factor is that while new buildings may be funded by the community or a magistrate, additions, embellishments, reconstruction and refurbishment of existing structures[15] were more frequently paid for by private benefaction (Cébeillac-Gervasioni 1998: 128–33). It is tempting, therefore, to see the distinction between building and urban development by the community and building and urban development by private benefaction both as a chronological development and as a distinction between two different types of building activity – utilitarian structures on the one hand and embellishments to buildings or structures connected with leisure on the other.

It is, however, all too easy to look at the overview of statistics for the whole of Italy and overlook the fact that there may be significant regional variations buried in them. Even at the high point of public building as a focus of private benefaction and civic activity, there are considerable regional variations in the extent of this activity, in what was being constructed, and in the mechanisms by which these projects were funded. Examination of Latium and Campania, the regions with the most prolific evidence, indicates that there were been significant differences even between neighbouring regions, while patterns of euergetism and building seem to be different again in Apulia. The high point of public building in Latium – particularly that which was demonstrably paid for from private funds – dates to the second century BC and the very early first century, and begins to tail off in the period after Sulla. In Campania, by contrast, there was an upsurge in public building in the Sullan period and again under Augustus, with a gradual tailing off in the middle and later years of the first century AD. The is also a difference in the buildings erected, with more utilitarian structures built in Latium, but a greater proportion of buildings for leisure and entertainment constructed in Campania (Cébeillac-Gervasioni 1990: 715–22, 1998: 130–5). Elsewhere, with much smaller quantities of evidence, it is much more difficult to analyse regional variations. In Apulia, for instance, there is a much lower level of public building throughout the period in question, and that which does take place is focused mainly on utilitarian structures such as street paving, water supplies, defensive works and remodelling of *fora*, with very few baths, theatres or amphitheatres (Chelotti 1996: 55–60). A similar pattern can be found for Picenum (Delplace 1996: 71–5).

The role of colonisation in the urban changes which took place in the last century of the Republic and the first century of the Principate has been much debated. In the case of some communities, there is a clear phase of reconstruction and reshaping of the urban environment coinciding with the foundation of a veteran colony by Sulla, Caesar or Augustus, but in others, this was less marked. In Picenum and Apulia, there is a strong correlation between construction of public buildings and foundation of colonies (Delplace 1996; Chelotti 1996; see Welch 1994 for a possible connection between colonisation and specific building types). Even in affluent Campania, where there is evidence of a dynamic culture of public benefaction which found its outlet in building, there are instances of major building projects triggered by the foundation of a colony. At Pompeii, the Sullan settlement involved the entire restructuring of the monumental centre of the city (Laurence 1994: 20–7), and there is corroborating evidence (Cic. *Sull.* 60–2) that control of public space was a highly contentious issue between the colonists and the indigenous Pompeians, along with changes to the political process.[16] However, the link between public building activity and colonisation is not a secure one and seems to have varied from region to region. The is much less evidence for public building as the direct result of a colonial foundation in Latium, Campania and Samnium than there is in Picenum and Apulia. Augustus asserted that he had provided his colonies not only with economic resources but also with the public buildings they needed (Suet. *Aug.* 46, *RG* 16, 20, Appendix 4; Keppie 1983: 114–22), but this is only partly borne out by the evidence. There are some spectacular examples of Augustan public building which seems to have taken place as a cohesive programme and is contemporary with a colonial foundation. The best-known example is Fanum Fortunae, where Vitruvius was the architect in charge of the forum, and was much concerned to construct it so as to maximise the effect of the shrine of Augustus housed in the basilica (Vitruv. *Arch.* 5.1.7, Gaggiotti *et al.* 1980, 207–9). However, other major building programmes appear to have been prompted from within the colonial elite rather than by outside intervention. There is no evidence for who paid for the rebuilding of the forum at Minturnae, or why, but we have more information about the building of the amphitheatre at Luceria. It was built by L. Vecilius Campanus (*AE* 1937, 64) who was clearly highly placed in the hierarchy of the colonists sent there, having been military tribune, *praefectus fabrum*[17] and duumvir of the colony. Although Campanus was a magistrate, the amphitheatre was a private benefaction, paid for *de sua pecunia*. It was explicitly dedicated in honour of the emperor and the city[18] but the impetus and finance for building it came not from Campanus himself, not from a centrally-funded or controlled source. Clearly colonisation could prompt building activity, particularly activity which was designed to honour the emperor, but it was carried out by just as much of a mixture of public activity and private initiative and benefaction as it was in non-colonial communities.

The crucial problem, when considering public buildings as a form of benefaction, is the identification of why they were constructed, who by, and how they were funded. In order to use public building as a means of gaining an insight into these transformations taking place in the urban development of Italy, it is important to define which social groups were responsible and to attempt to examine their motives. It is clear from the epigraphic evidence available, that not all public building activity took place on the same basis. Much of it was conducted by magistrates – acting either individually or as a college of magistrates – as part of the obligations of their year of office. Some buildings are constructed '*de pecunia publica*' and can thus be securely identified as being public projects, undertaken at civic expense rather than acts of benefaction. Conversely, the formula *de sua pecunia* indicates that the project was financed by a private individual and was therefore an act of euergetism in the fullest sense. There is, however, a considerable grey area between these categories which is less clear-cut. Many inscriptions – particularly those which pre-date Augustus – carry an indication that work was authorised by a decree of the decurions or senate of the city[19] and it has been argued (Pobjoy 2000) that inscriptions of this type – the majority of those of Republican date – indicate construction programmes which were controlled by the state and therefore reflect the development of an 'official' civic identity rather than being a reflection of euergetic behaviour by private individuals. An alternative approach may indicate that these two categories may not be mutually exclusive. Even a private benefaction, particularly if it involved large-scale construction in a public area of the city, would have required permission from the senate, decurions or magistrates. A municipal decree from Caere (*CIL* XI.3614) grants permission to Julius Vesbinus, an imperial freedman, to build a meeting-house for the Augustales at his own expense, and also records correspondence between the decurions and the patron of the city about this decision. It is, therefore, not impossible that private benefactions needed official permission from the decurions. Building projects undertaken by civic magistrates are also a grey area unless there is epigraphic evidence that the money came from public sources. Many such projects were no doubt undertaken as part of a magistrate's official duties or were funded by *summa honoraria* (Duncan-Jones 1965; Cébeillac-Gervasioni 1998: 66–105), but there is also the possibility that some magistrates elected to fund more lavish buildings or entertainments, over and above the requirements of *summa honoraria*, as an act of benefaction.[20] It is therefore difficult to be prescriptive about the dividing line between public activity and euergetism, and it must be recognised that even projects undertaken by magistrates, or at the behest of the decurions, may have involved some measure of private benefaction.

The motivations of those who undertook public building projects have frequently been examined, but the underlying process which drove this upsurge in civic development between 150BC and AD100 is still a matter of speculation. It has frequently been attributed to external factors such as colonisation, or to the displacement of elite euergetism from Rome by the establishment of the Principate (Eck 1984), but these can provide, at best, only a partial explanation. Colonisation was undoubtedly a factor in some regions of Italy, but it cannot explain the dramatic upsurge in building activity in regions such as Latium and Campania, and it does not address the reason for the shift from projects controlled by magistrates and/or paid for by public funds towards a culture of civic euergetism.

The main initiators of public building projects are the local elites, acting either as magistrates or (increasing frequently) in a private capacity. Some were senators or their families who continued to invest in their home cities. Examples include Ummidia Quadratilla, who paid for the theatre and amphitheatre at Casinum, and whose love of the theatre was recorded by Pliny (*AE* 1946, 174, Pliny *Epist.* 7.24). L. Arruntius, consul in 22BC, was responsible for the reorganisation of the urban plan of Atina (*CIL* X.5055), L. Volusius Saturninus, who also held the consulship, built the temple of Augustus at Lucus Feroniae (Jouffroy 1986: 79), and L. Caecilius Secundus, probably the father of Pliny, who built the temple of the imperial cult at Comum (Alföldy 1983). The bread and butter of urban reconstruction was, however, done by the local elites – men such as Q. Plautius Iustus of Ariminum, aedile and constructor of the temple of Salus Augustus (*CIL* XI.361), the Lucceius family who restored the temple of Demeter at Cumae (*CIL* X.3685), L. Naevius Pansa, duumvir, who built a basilica at Saepinum (*CIL* IX.6308), Gn. Satrius Rufus, quattuorvir, who did extensive reconstruction on the theatre and forum of Iguvium (*CIL* XI.5820), or the Holoconius brothers who rebuilt the theatre at Pompeii. If colonisation or other centrally-determined events (for instance, the construction of the Via Traiana, which heralded considerable activity at cities on its route) provided a focus around which changes in civic identity crystallised, much of the impetus for change came from within the local communities, not via centrally-organised construction programmes.

The relationship between local elites who gave visible support to the ruling regime and reflected this in the way they reconstructed their communities and access to power is an obscure one. Patterson (1991: 149–57) constructed a model for Apennine Italy in which visible symbols of loyalty to Rome and the emperor were succeeded by increasing access to senatorial power. *Gentes* which supported Rome after the Social War and demonstrated this by shifting the focus of their euergetic activity from the *pagus* and the indigenous sanctuaries such as Pietrabbondante to the new Roman municipia began, during the late Republic and under Augustus, to be absorbed into the senatorial elite. It is an attractive model, and fits well with Augustus' known willingness to turn to Italian notables for support, but a preliminary examination of the inscriptions listed above suggests that it may be regionally specific. Comparison between a list of municipal benefactors who are clearly from within the city, either as colonists, local magistrates or private benefactors, and municipal families which are known to have gained senatorial rank during the late Republic and early Empire show that few of these *gentes* were raised in rank or had a significant senatorial career. For instance, L. Betilienus of Aletrium reconstructed the centre of Aletrium virtually single-handed *c.*130–120BC (donations included baths, basilica, *macellum*, rebuilding of city walls and various other public works around the forum), creating a powerful statement of Romanised identity for the city. The Betilieni flourished under Sulla but produced two minor senators, only one of whom held significant office (P. Betilienus Bassus, quaestor in AD40). Equally, contact between *gentes* who had already been advanced and their native cities is variable, although in some circumstances it could be financially significant, and it is clear that senators who took on the role of patron had an obligation to offer some benefactions (Pliny *Epist.* 3.4, 4.1, 10.8, for earlier examples cf. T. Labienus, benefactor of Cingulum, the Ummidii Quadrati at Casinum, L. Seius Strabo at Volsinii and Asinius Gallus at Teate). Cicero's view (Cic. *Offic.* 2.60–1) is that much euergetic behaviour is to be deplored. He draws a distinction between useful benefactions to friends and clients, defined as payment of debts and ransoms, provision of dowries or low-interest loans, and extravagance – deeply disapproved of – which included the traditional bread and circuses. Public buildings form an intermediate category, in which useful items such as harbours, aqueducts and fortifications are praiseworthy, while buildings devoted to entertainment – theatres and porticoes – are not. Significantly, it is precisely these categories of building which are most frequently paid for by private benefaction, while utilitarian structures were more likely to be overseen by magistrates and paid for by public funds.

Perhaps the most revealing piece of evidence is an incident related by Tacitus (*Hist.* 2.21) during the first battle of Cremona in AD69. During the initial skirmishes before the battle, Caecina attacked the neighbouring city of Placentia and burnt down the wooden amphitheatre situated outside the walls. Tacitus comments that of all the events of this time, this was the one which caused the most outrage amongst the citizens. Two reasons are given – that it was one of the largest and finest amphitheatres in Italy, and that the destruction was therefore widely assumed to be the work of people from other cities in the region who, motivated by envy, had taken advantage of turbulent events to set fire to it. The strong implication is that the size and elegance of the public buildings was a major element in establishing the status of a city in the local hierarchy, and that status could be undermined if the building was compromised or destroyed, point further reinforced by the *Digest* (*Dig.* 39.1.20.11), and by the Augustales' meeting-house at Caere, which was approved by the city's patron on the grounds that a new building would enhance the city's prestige (*CIL* XI.3614).[21] It also implies that in order to achieve this effect, attacks on structures by neighbouring cities were not unknown.

The dynamics behind urban reconstruction and public building activity may, therefore, lie less in explicit power relations or elite social mobility, than in competition for local and regional status, both between cities and individuals. Magistrates and private individuals who build are not so much looking to enhance their personal status in the tangible legal sense of social promotion to equestrian or senatorial rank, but are driven by the need to maintain their own status and that of their city within the local hierarchy. Even outside the ranks of the municipal elite, this impulse towards building programmes as a form of civic benefaction was strong. During the second century AD, there was a lower level of elite benefaction, but the gap was filled by non-elite groups or individuals such as *collegia*, or wealthy freedmen (Patterson 1994). Whatever the process by which municipal families infiltrated into the senatorial elite – and they undoubtedly did so in significant numbers – it was not, on the prosopographical evidence available, closely connected with patterns of benefaction and euergetism within local communities. The dynamic for this appears to lie much more in the field of peer polity interaction – the need for communities to maintain or enhance their place in the local hierarchy, either by out-building their neighbours, by undermining the efforts of others, or in extreme cases by attacking them.[22] Senatorial activity within communities was mediated much more by the formal relations of municipal patronage – sometimes with local connections, sometimes not – than by close family ties. Local origins were not taken seriously but there can be no easy assumptions about the relationship between behaviour of municipal elites and access to central power. What is clear is that there was a powerful change of urban identity throughout Italy, beginning with Sulla but reaching its highest point under Augustus, which resulted in most communities being not just Romanised but also having their public areas saturated with imperial imagery and building types with imperial significance. This does not, however, have any straightforward connection with the social and political advancement of Italian senators in the early Empire, or even with the massive programmes of colonisation in the first century BC, although these clearly played a part. The explanation for rapid dissemination of these changes seems to lie in the powerfully competitive instincts of both local notables and communities, which prompted them to adopt new features of urban life with alacrity as a means of maintaining the position of their cities in the local hierarchy and of ensuring their own prominence by initiating and/or paying for these projects.

Acknowledgement

This paper was first delivered at the conference on 'Euergetism and public patronage in ancient Italy' at the Institute of Classical Studies, and subsequent versions have been delivered to research seminars in Durham, Exeter and Newcastle. I would like to thank Prof. M. Millett, Mr J.J. Paterson and Prof. T.J. Cornell for their comments on various aspects of this paper.

Notes

1 For the range of public building costs in Italy, and for a comparative set of costs from North Africa, see Duncan-Jones 1965 and 1962.

2 For example, Rykwert 1976, Laurence 1994. For a more theoretical discussion of urban space, see Lefebvre 1991, Duncan and Ley 1993.

3 The *Lex Genetiva* also specifies that the magistrates must ensure adequate seating for citizens and visitors at the games (ll.126), and places restrictions on their use of public space (ll.73–81).

4 A comprehensive collection of the data for public building in Italy and in Roman North Africa has been compiled by Hélène Jouffroy (Jouffroy 1986), from inscriptions, literary sources and archaeological evidence, and forms basic data-set for this chapter.

5 The structure commemorated the repair of the Via Flaminia by Augustus, paid for by spoils of war. *cf RG* 20.5,

6 e.g. Spurius Rufus (*macellum*, Puteoli – *CIL* I2. 1625), Betilienus Varus, at Aletrium (*macellum* and portico, *CIL* X.5055), L. Paccius (*Formiae*, portico and *curia*, Columbini 1966: 137–41).

7 Details of other basilicas and *curiae*. On Augustan colonisation more generally, see Keppie 1983: 112–22.

8 For example, *CIL* IX.1466 (Ligures Baebiani, patron), *CIL* XI.3932 (Capena, benefaction by imperial freedman), *CIL* XI.6360 (Pisaurum, building by duumvir quinquennalis).

9 On amphitheatres, see Golvin 1988: 25, 33–42, and for their possible connections with colonisation, Welch 1994. An overview of theatres and amphitheatres in Republican Italy is also presented by Holleran, this volume.

10 On Pietrabbondante, see Strazulla and De Marco 1982.

11 Opinions vary as to which area of Rome served as the prototype for forum developments in Italy. Zanker (1988: 79–85) suggested the Forum of Augustus as the most likely model, but Gros (2000: 315–7) has argued that Agrippa's redevelopment of the Campus Martius may have been the inspiration for some of the forum/theatre complexes, such as that of Minturnae.

12 Gros (1994) identifies possible parallels at Saepinum and Aquinum.

13 The close relation between theatres and temples is also a feature of Apennine Italy, as represented in the theatre and Temple B at Pietrabbondante and at the sanctuary of Fortuna at Praeneste. However, cf, Vitruv. *Arch.* 5.3, 5.9.1–9 for a purely secular connection between theatres and porticoes.

14 Gros 2000: 311–13. See also Lefebvre, 2000 for the extent to which Augustus and his family predominate in dedications to the imperial cult in the first century AD.

15 *cf* Thomas and Witschel 1992 for the difficulties of securely establishing the extent of restorations and rebuilding from epigraphic evidence.
16 The location referred to as the *ambulatio* in this passage, and its political significance has been much debated, but it is likely that it refers to a structure in which voting took place. Wiseman 1977: 21–2, Berry 1996: 35–6, 250–7.
17 On the possible role of *praefecti fabrum* in public building in Italy, see Verzàr-Bass 2000: 213–24; Welch 1995: 131–45.
18 '*In honor. imp. Caesaris Augusti coloniaeque Luceriae*' ('in honour of the emperor Caesar Augustus and the colony of Luceria'). A similar example is found at Beneventum, where the Caesareum was funded by P. Veidius Pollio and dedicated using the same formula (*CIL* IX.1556).
19 Typically, *DD* (de *decreto decurionum*), *SS* (*de senatu sententia*), *DSC* (*de senatu consultu*).
20 Cébeillac-Gervasioni 1998: 103–8 suggests that the games put on at Pompeii by A. Clodius Flaccus (*CIL* X.1074d) fall into this category, and it is very possible that some building projects also exceeded the specified *summa honoraria.*
21 A similar effect may have been felt if buildings were abandoned or cities were prevented from using them. Although the fabric of the building was not destroyed, it seems likely that Pompeii lost status when use of the amphitheatre was banned after the riots of AD59.
22 The amphitheatre riot at Pompeii in AD59 (Tac. *Ann.* 14.17) indicates the extent to which local tensions could boil over, and a local grievance between Capua and Puteoli spilled over into open warfare (Tac. *Hist.* 3.57) in AD69.

References

Alföldy, G. (1983) 'Ein Tempel des Herrscherkultes in Comum', *Athenaeum* 61: 362–73.

Bejor, G. (1979) 'L'edificio teatrale nell'urbanizzazione Augustea', *Athenaeum* 57: 126–38.

Berry, D.H. (1996) *Cicero Pro P. Sulla Oratio*, Cambridge: Cambridge University Press.

Cébeillac-Gervasioni, M. (1990) 'L'Evergetisme des magistrats du Latium et de la Campanie des Gracques à Auguste à travers les témoignages épigraphiques', *MEFRA* 102: 699–722.

Cébeillac-Gervasioni, M. (1998) *Les magistrats des cités italiennes de la seconde guerre punique à Auguste*, Rome: École Française de Rome.

Cébeillac-Gervasioni, M. (ed.) (2000) *Les Élites municipales de l'Italie péninsulaire de la mort de César à la mort de Domitien: Classes sociales dirigeantes et pouvoir central*, Rome: École Française de Rome.

Chelotti, M. (1996) 'Programma edilizio, magistrati, evergetismo in Apulia tra guerra sociale ed età neroniana'. In M. Cébeillac-Gervasioni (ed.), *Les Élites municipales de l'Italie péninsulaire des Gracques à Néron*: 55–60, Naples and Rome: Centre Jean Bérard and École Française de Rome.

Crawford, M.H. (ed.) (1996) *Roman Statutes* (*BICS* Supplement, No. 64), London: Institute of Classical Studies.

De Ruyt, C. (1983) *Macellum. Marché alimentaire des Romains*, Louvain-la-Neuve: Institut supérieur d'archéologie et d'histoire de l'art, Collège Érasme.

Delplace, C. (1996) 'Les élites municipales et leur rôle dans le développement politique et économique de la region V Auguste'. In M. Cébeillac-Gervasioni (ed.), *Les Élites municipales de l'Italie péninsulaire des Gracques à Néron*: 71–80, Naples and Rome: Centre Jean Bérard and École Française de Rome.

Duncan, J. and Ley, D. (eds) (1993) *Place, Culture, Representation*, London: Routledge.

Duncan-Jones, R. (1962) 'Costs, outlays and summae honorariae in Roman Africa', *PBSR* 17: 42–115.

Duncan-Jones, R. (1965) 'An epigraphic survey of costs in Roman Italy', *PBSR* 20: 189–306.

Eck, W. (1984) 'Senatorial self-representation: developments in the Augustan period'. In F. Millar and E. Segal (eds), *Caesar Augustus: Seven Aspects*: 129–68, Oxford: Clarendon Press.

Frayn, J.M. (1993) *Markets and Fairs in Roman Italy*, Oxford: Clarendon Press.

Frederiksen, M.W. (1976) 'Changes in patterns of settlement'. In P. Zanker (ed.), *Hellenismus in Mittelitalien*: 341–55.

Frézouls, E. (1983) 'Le théâtre romain et la culture urbain'. In *La città come fatta di cultura*: 105–30, Rome: École Française de Rome.

Gabba, E. (1971) 'Urbanizzazione e rinnovamenti urbanistici nell'Italia centro-meridionale del sec. I a.C.', *Studi Classici e Orientali* 20: 73–112.

Gabrici, E. (1913) 'Cuma', *Monumenti Antichi dei Lincei* 22.

Gaggiotti, M., Manconi, D., Mercando, L. and Verzár, M. (1980) *Umbria–Marche* (*Guide archeologiche Laterza*), Bari: Laterza.

Golvin, J.-C. (1988) *L'Amphithéâtre romain*, Paris: Diffusion de Boccard.

Gros, P. (1994) 'Les théâtres en Italie au Ier siècle de notre ère: situation et fonctions dans l'urbanisme impérial', In *L'Italie d'Auguste à Dioclétien. Actes du colloque international de l'École Française de Rome*: 285–307, Rome: École Française de Rome.

Gros, P. (2000) 'L'Évolution des centres monumentaux des cités Italiennes en fonction d'implantation du culte imperiale'. In M. Cébeillac-Gervasioni (ed.), *Les Élites municipales de l'Italie péninsulaire de la mort de César à la mort de Domitien: Classes sociales dirigeantes et pouvoir central*: 307–26.

Johnson, J. (1933) *Excavations at Minturnae I. The Republican Magistri*, Philadelphia: University of Pennsylvania Press.

Jouffroy, H. (1986) *La construction publique en Italie et dans l'Afrique romaine*, Strasbourg: AECR.

Keppie, L.F. (1983) *Colonisation and Veteran Settlement in Italy, 47–14 B.C.*, London: British School at Rome.

Laurence, R.M. (1994) *Roman Pompeii. Space and Society*, London: Routledge.

Laurence, R.M. (2000) *The Roads of Roman Italy: Mobility and Cultural Change*, London Routledge.

Lefebvre, H. (1991) *The Production of Space*, Oxford: Blackwell.

Lefebvre, S. (2000) 'Les hommages publics rendus à la famille impériale'. In M. Cébeillac-Gervasioni (ed.), *Les Élites municipales de l'Italie péninsulaire de la mort de César à la mort de Domitien: Classes sociales dirigeantes et pouvoir central*: 267–305, Rome: École Française de Rome.

Lomas, K. (1997) 'The idea of a city: elite ideology and the evolution of urban form in Italy, 200BC–AD200'. In H. Parkin (ed.), *Roman Urbanism: Beyond the Consumer City*: 21–41, London: Routledge.

Millar, F.G.B. (1986) 'Italy and the Roman Empire: from Augustus to Constantine', *Phoenix* 46: 295–318.

Patterson, J.R. (1991) 'Settlement, city and elite in Samnium and Lycia'. In J. Rich and A. Wallace-Hadrill (eds), *City and Country in the Ancient World*: 147–68, London: Routledge.

Patterson, J.R. (1994) 'The *collegia* and the transformation of the towns of Italy in the second century AD'. In *L'Italie d'Auguste à Dioclétien: Actes du colloque international de l'école Française de Rome*: 228–38, Rome: École Française de Rome.

Pobjoy, M. (2000) 'Building inscriptions in Republican Italy: euergetism, responsibility and civic virtue'. In A. Cooley (ed.), *The Epigraphic Landscape of Roman Italy*: 77–92, London: Institute of Classical Studies.

Poccetti, P. (1988) 'Riflessi di strutture di fortificatizioni nell'epigrafica Italica tra il II e il I secolo a.C.', *Athenaeum* 66: 303–28.

Rawson, E.D. (1987) '*Discrimina Ordinum*: *The Lex Julia Theatralis*'. *Papers of the British School at Rome* 55: 83–114.

Rykwert, J. (1976) *The Idea of a Town: The Anthropology of Urban Form in Rome, Italy and the Ancient World*, Cambridge, MA: MIT Press.

Strazzulla, M.J. and De Marco, B. (1982) *Il santuario sannitico di Pietrabbondante*, Rome: Centenari.

Thomas, E. and Witschel, C. (1992) 'Constructing reconstruction: claim and reality of Roman rebuilding inscriptions from the Latin West', *PBSR* 60: 135–78.

Verzár-Bass, M. (2000) 'Il *Praefectus Fabrum* e il problema dell'edilizia pubblica'. In M. Cébeillac-Gervasioni (ed.), *Les Élites municipales de l'Italie péninsulaire de la mort de César à la mort de Domitien: Classes socials diregeantes et pouvoir central*: 197–224, Rome: École Française de Rome.

Welch, K.E. (1994) 'The Roman arena in late-Republican Italy: a new interpretation', *JRA* 7: 59–79.

Welch, K.E. (1995) 'The office of *Praefectus Fabrum* in the late republic', *Chiron* 25: 131–45.

Whittaker, C.R. (1994) 'The politics of power: the cities of Italy'. In *L'Italie d'Auguste à Dioclétien: Actes du colloque internationale de l'École Française de Rome*, 127–43, Rome: École Française de Rome.

Wiseman, T.P. (1977) 'Cicero *Pro Sulla* 61–2', *LCM* 2: 21–2.

Zanker, P. (1988) *The Power of Images in the Age of Augustus*, Ann Arbor: University of Michigan Press.

Zanker, P. (1998) *Pompeii: Public and Private Life*, Cambridge MA: Harvard University Press.

3

THE DEVELOPMENT OF PUBLIC ENTERTAINMENT VENUES IN ROME AND ITALY

Claire Holleran[1]

Introduction

Despite political discord, the late Republic was a period of prosperity for many. Town life was obviously thriving in Italy, and the archaeology of a town such as Pompeii displays the increasingly luxurious lifestyle of the wealthy. Private spending on residential opulence was coupled with an increase in public spending, and a number of public structures were erected in the cities of south-central Italy; for example, theatres were erected at Pompeii, Sarno, Teanum and Capua (Dyson 1992: 31–2). In Pompeii a large stone theatre was constructed in the second century BC, with tiered seating resting on a natural slope in the Greek style. It seems most likely that donations from wealthy locals financed this construction, by the mechanism known as *euergetism*.[2] Indeed, when Pompeii became a Roman colony in 80BC, the original theatre was further supplemented by the *Odeion*, built by two members of the local elite, the *duumviri* Gaius Quinctius Valgus and Marcus Portius (*CIL* I^2.126).

Capua was another Italian town embellished with a theatre in this period. As the town prospered, the elite of Capua wanted to show their new wealth and raise their status within the town and the local region. As was customary, this was done through the donation of public buildings, and much of this was done at the local shrine. Religious magistrates not only cared for the shrine but also oversaw the construction of related buildings, including a theatre; inscriptions record improvements made to this theatre by the magistrates from 108–94BC (Dyson 1992: 32, 46). This pattern of theatres found within religious areas is repeated elsewhere in Italy, for example in Latium. Here the great sanctuary of Fortuna Primigeneia at Praeneste included a theatre as part of the monumental complex constructed in the late second century BC. Also in Latium was the sanctuary of Diana Nemorensis, a religious centre for cities of the Latin league. Archaeological evidence shows that the first temple on the site was built in the late fourth century BC, but was rebuilt in the second century with a theatre later added to the complex.

The wealth achieved by some Italians in the late Republic is further displayed by the construction that took place in the tribal sanctuaries of non-urban areas. The greatest of the Samnite sanctuaries – Pietrabbondante – was the religious gathering place of the Pentri and presumably served as a central meeting place for the area. Pietrabbondante was destroyed during the Hannibalic war and was subsequently rebuilt with a new theatre and an axially placed temple overlooking the seating. Both the sanctuary and the fort are completely detached from any trace of urbanisation but a theatre is still found here, ostensibly in the middle of nowhere. Yet Rome, the city whose power and influence dwarfed that of all other Italian towns, was to be without a theatre until 55 BC. Obviously this is not an exhaustive list of all the theatres to be found in late Republican Italy, but simply illustrates the fact that such structures were far from rare. This lack of such an amenity in Rome – almost commonplace in the towns of Italy – contrasts sharply with the natural expectations one might have of such a large and dominant city.

This contrast between expectation and reality is also true of the distribution of amphitheatres in Roman Italy. Such structures have become synonymous with the spread of Roman culture, yet the earliest datable permanent amphitheatre in Italy is to be found at Pompeii, predating that at Rome itself by almost fifty years. There are at least fifteen other amphitheatres in Italy that can be dated to the period before the principate of Augustus by a combination of historical circumstances and comparison with the amphitheatre at Pompeii; all are small, functional and simple in construction, making extensive use of the natural terrain (Welch 1994: 65). Golvin (1988: 25, 33–42) gives a list of Republican amphitheatres and many appear in Campania – not only in Pompeii but in places such as Puteoli, Cumae and Capua – and elsewhere, for example at Paestum in Lucania.

Thus entertainment venues such as theatres and amphitheatres were found across late Republican Italy and in fact beyond, as most Greek cities already possessed a theatre. A town such as Pompeii had what almost amounts to an entertainment district, and when we consider that Pompeii also had facilities such as monumental bath complexes, we can see that in the early first century BC the town was way ahead of Rome in its urban development. It is easy to misjudge the importance of Pompeii because of the wealth of evidence of town life and urban planning that we get from the justifiably famous archaeological remains, but in reality the town – although thriving economically – was probably not one of major importance. Yet the town's amenities far outstripped those of Rome. This raises the obvious question as to why Rome was still haphazard and disorganised in appearance, with little evidence of rational planning (Cornell 2000: 42, 51); the city lacked a permanent stone theatre, amphitheatre or even monumental public baths. It cannot be an accident that Rome lacked any entertainment venues other than the ancient Circus Maximus, particularly considering how quickly Rome was provided with such facilities at the very end of the Republic and the early days of the Empire. Thus I plan to begin with an examination of the reasons for the deliberate decision to deprive Rome of certain amenities, before looking at the rapid development of public entertainment venues in the city.

The stilted development of the city of Rome

The backward nature of Rome's outward appearance was undoubtedly due to artificial constraints and pressures, which prevented the city from developing naturally. Indeed, attempts were made to build stone theatres in the city as early as the middle of the second century BC, but these were always thwarted by the conservative reactions of the Senate. The *Epitomator* of Livy (Livy *Per.* 48), for example, tells us that in 154BC a permanent theatre which the censors[3] had started to erect was demolished by a senatorial decree. A similar story is told by Appian (Appian *BC* 1.28), regarding a further attempt to build a theatre in 106BC which was again blocked. This opposition was said to be due to a fear of decadent Greek influences and the effect that these might have on the strong moral character of Rome (Tac. *Ann.* 14.20). Some modern authors (for example, Brothers, 1989: 101) have accepted this explanation at face value – viewing theatres as part of a Greek world – and have suggested that structures such as those built at Pompeii were constructed as a result of Greek influence in Italy. However, this idea that towns to the south of Rome were corrupted by Greek entertainment whilst Rome remained staunchly moral does not seem to be a plausible reason for the lack of theatres in Rome. Rather this reflects the traditional prejudice of the Roman upper classes against what they saw as the effeminacy of the Greeks.

Furthermore, the town of Paestum yields evidence of an amphitheatre but not a theatre. Paestum began life as the Greek colony of Poseidonia, before coming under Lucanian (after 410BC) and then Roman influence (after 273BC). To what extent the influence of Greek culture persisted is unclear, but it is obvious that the town was open to the sphere of Hellenistic influence, and the dominance of theatres as entertainment venues in towns of the Greek world. Thus Pedley suggests that the entertainment in Paestum was carefully selected as part of a deliberate plan to place the town alongside Rome (Pedley 1990: 113). This idea of amphitheatres being constructed in Italian towns for political reasons is taken up by Welch, who suggests that there is a connection between gladiatorial games and veteran colonisation (Welch 1994: 61). For instance, the earliest datable monumental amphitheatre appears at Pompeii, a city which underwent the imposition of a large Sullan colony in 80BC. Welch also states that Republican amphitheatres appear in places that had close ties to Rome, particularly in Campania (Welch 1994: 67). However, whilst it is true that the majority of Republican amphitheatres appear in Campanian towns – in either old Latin colonies or new Sullan colonies – the link between these amphitheatres and Rome is tenuous. Indeed, although Welch believes that the amphitheatre at Pompeii made a statement of the power of Rome, and the construction of the building established a particularly Roman architectural presence in the town (Welch 1994: 79), this makes little sense as Rome had no amphitheatre of its own until the time of Augustus. It is far more likely that the amphitheatre developed in Campania independent of Roman influence, just as gladiatorial combat in fact spread from Campania to Rome. Although we may now see such combat as a peculiarly Roman form of entertainment, such games grew up amongst the native tribes of Italy. The Romans believed that they had inherited gladiatorial games from Etruscans,[4] but earlier than any Etruscan artistic representations of these fights are Samnite paintings depicting them, which date from around 400BC (Grant 1978: 89). The Samnites arrived in Campania in the fifth century, and the area was in turn annexed by Rome in the fourth century; gladiatorial combat, therefore, came to Rome through Campania. Thus the preponderance of early amphitheatres in the area is due to the popularity of gladiatorial style entertainment in Campania, rather than the influence of Rome.[5]

Veyne has sought to explain the discrepancies between the facilities in Rome and those found in other Italian towns by a supposed difference in the mentality of their respective upper classes. He argues that the motive for *euergetism* at Rome was political ambition rather than social zeal (Veyne 1990: 232 ff). Thus acts of public generosity were perpetrated in the city solely by politicians hoping to further their own careers, rather than by the rich in general. However, he suggests that the amphitheatre at Pompeii was built in a genuine spirit of philanthropism. Veyne argues that buildings were less useful for a political career than games or distributions of money, thus the lack of public amenities in Rome is simply due to a difference in the donations of the upper classes. Whilst it seems correct that senators in Rome used *euergetism* as a means of gaining popularity, it seems unlikely that the two *duumviri* responsible for the construction of the *Odeion* and amphitheatre in Pompeii were merely motivated by a spirit of generosity. Indeed, although it is obviously impossible to prove, it is almost certain that they were motivated by the desire for popularity and an elevation of their social and political status within the town. Furthermore, there was incredible competition between the cities in a particular region, and citizens naturally wanted to elevate the status of their city locally by constructing increasingly elaborate public buildings. A further flaw in Veyne's argument is the idea that a public building would be of no use in gaining popularity, as it seems more likely that the donation of a permanent entertainment venue to the people would create powerful and lasting support for an individual and his descendants in the politically charged climate of Rome.

It is possible that the Greek experience of theatres was a cause of fear to the senatorial aristocracy of Rome, because they were found at the centre of political life in Greek cities. They were often used for popular gatherings and public assemblies, where people would sit down in order to listen to political speeches; thus theatres had associations with democracy (Cic. *Flacc.* 16). They could also be the venue for encounters between rulers and subject-citizens in the Hellenistic period. For example, after the surrender of Athens following a siege in 294 BC, Demetrius Poliorcetes '... ordered all the people to assemble in the theatre ... while he himself, like the tragic actors, came into view through one of the upper-side entrances' (Plut. *Demetrius* 34.3). Perhaps the political uses of Greek theatres contributed to the senatorial reluctance to allow permanent structures to be erected in Rome, especially as temporary theatres in the city were often the scene of popular demonstrations by the spectators. In 59BC, for example, Cicero tells us that at the Games for Apollo, an actor, Diphilus, recited a line from a tragedy that was seen as reflecting adversely on Pompey – 'To our misfortune are you great' – and the people demanded a dozen encores (Cic. *Att.* 2.19.3). On the same occasion the temporary theatre witnessed the opponents of Caesar being greeted with cheers whilst Caesar and his party were met with silence (Cic. *Att.* 2.19.3).

In fact, for Cicero at least, the public opinions expressed at the games represented a far truer voice of the Roman populace than that expressed at the assemblies. In a speech delivered in 56BC, he expresses a belief in the theatre as 'the true and incorruptible judgement of the whole people' (Cic. *Sest.* 119). At the games people were less vulnerable to manipulation and the audience closely replicated Roman society as a whole; the segregated seating allowed for a wide cross section of the community to be present. Yet this suggestion that a crowd at the spectacles represented all sections of the community and were totally free of manipulation seems a little naïve; the simple fact that the audiences were being entertained at the expense of somebody else renders this impossible, as does the system of ticket distribution. It is unclear exactly how this worked but it is probable that admission was to some extent determined by the sponsors. Based on the evidence of Cicero's speech in defence of Murena,[6] it appears that traditionally the ruling class, acting as individuals, controlled access to games by handing out passes to their clientele (Futrell1997: 162). Cicero asks if anybody can 'ever remember a time when there has not been this wish … to provide a seat in the circus and the Forum for our friend and fellow-tribesmen?'(Cic. *Mur.* 72). Members of the upper class must have received blocks of seating to distribute,[7] possibly from the magistrate who was sponsoring the show. Murena was accused of giving tickets out indiscriminately, not just to his friends or associates, and in this way making a show of providing seats. This would have helped his political career, as many Romans who gained tickets through Murena would be likely to vote for him in elections. Although the exact workings of the system of ticket distribution remain far from clear, the people were obviously reliant on their connections rather than on any fair method of ticket distribution. Thus the audiences were easily exploited by wealthy politicians.

Games were significant in political terms because they enabled the masses to gain an audience with the men who held the power; without the interaction between the audience and the editor, the political meaning of the display would have been lost. In imperial Rome, the theatre was one of the few places where loss of political liberty was not complete.[8] Indeed, Claudius was forced to issue 'edicts sternly rebuking audiences for their unruliness' after they insulted a 'former consul and playwright Publius Pomponius Secondus and high-ranking ladies' (Tac. *Ann.* 11.13). On other occasions the audiences offered praise; for example, when the words 'O just and gracious lord' were said in the theatre, the people applauded this as though it referred to Augustus and rose to their feet to show their agreement with the statement (Suet. *Aug.* 53.1). In the imperial period the games played a crucial role in establishing a relationship between the masses and their emperor. At the shows the crowd could honour the ruler, but demand from him also; these demands must have ranged from the personal matters of individuals to widespread concerns such as the price of corn. This idea that the people were able to voice their concerns directly to the emperor, and make their opinions clear to him, was part of the symbolism of their status.

The 'special relationship' which the people and the *princeps* of Rome enjoyed, presented the city to the rest of the empire as its 'uniquely favoured capital' (Purcell 1996: 806). At the games the emperor was most answerable to his people, as a request made in front of thousands of citizens is always potentially political and difficult to resist (Cameron 1976: 162). At first glance it may seem strange that an emperor who acted as an absolute ruler of such a vast territory, should put himself in such a position. However, the games gave emperors the opportunity of personal contact and the ability to ingratiate themselves with the assembled people – the more they aimed at popularity, the more frequently they attended their own spectacles (Friedländer 1909: 4). The emperor was in theory the 'first citizen' of the empire and it was an important myth that he appeared at the head of a free people; the Roman past and the notion of freedom in the capital contrasting with subjugation across the empire as a whole meant that the games became part of an elaborate act. By appearing with the people, the emperor could demonstrate that he was one of them, with a feel for popular tastes, whilst also gauging the mood of the masses. Perhaps the senatorial aristocracy were right in their reluctance to allow huge entertainment venues to be erected, as the importance that these took on in the empire clearly shows their place in a monarchical system. If an individual[9] had been allowed to construct his own theatre or amphitheatre under the Republic, there would have been little to stop him acting in the same way as an emperor during the shows he held, and thus gaining disproportionate power amongst the people. Although this assumes a certain amount of foresight on the part of the Senate, it must have been fairly plain to them how important public entertainment had become in the political game.

Indeed, the shows that were being staged by senators towards the end of the Republic show all too clearly the fight for individual glory and the fierce competitiveness which was coming to characterise Roman politics. Games grew ever more expensive and lavish, and politicians disliked taking the post of *aedile* at the same time as a richer colleague, whose games would eclipse their own. When Caesar was *aedile* in 65BC, for example, he 'exhibited wild-beast hunts and stage-plays; some at his own expense, some in co-operation with his colleague, Marcus Bibulus – but took all the credit in either case, so that Bibulus remarked openly: "The temple of the Heavenly Twins in the Forum is always simply called 'Castor's'; and I always play Pollux to Caesar's Castor when we give a public entertainment together"' (Caelius, in Cic. *Fam.* 8.3). The *aediles* who staged the games were men who had a career to make, and public entertainment was a way of securing votes for later magistracies; without magnificent games as *aedile* a politician stood little chance of ever being elected *praetor* or *consul*, and thus lost the opportunity to earn huge riches through provincial government or military command. Originally *munera* (gladiatorial combats) were associated with the funeral games of important Romans but gradually, as the opportunity for political manipulation was realised, these associations became looser and looser. *Munera* became a useful tool in obtaining public support, but as a politician could not count upon a death at the necessary time, the associations between these spectacles and funerals were stretched to extreme limits (Futrell 1997: 30, Veyne 1990: 212 ff.). Candidates began to postpone games until the year of their candidature; for example, whilst *aedile* Caesar added a *munus* to his public games in memory of his father who had died twenty years earlier (Plut. *Caesar* 5.9, Pliny *NH* 33.16, Dio, 37.8.1).

It was not merely the lavishness of the spectacles themselves that was important, but the setting itself was also crucial. Traditionally entertainments were held in temporary open-air structures, either near a temple associated with the deity to whom the games were dedicated or in an area such as the Forum.[10] By the late Republic, however, some of these temporary structures were incredibly elaborate and it made little economic sense to build them and then demolish them. Yet this practice continued and reached a peak with the lavish theatre of M. Aemilius Scaurus in 58BC, which boasted a stage building three storeys high. In 52BC C. Scribonius Curio relied on technical innovation in order to impress the masses. He built two theatres back to back that revolved to form an amphitheatre, although how this worked in practice is unclear (Pliny *NH* 36.116–20). Thus we can see how senators tried to outdo each other not only with the content of the games that they staged, but with the venues they created also. In this competitive system the only barrier to glory and elevated status was financial, and as it was the wealthy who ultimately controlled Roman politics, they were happy to allow the economic folly of erecting temporary theatrical structures to continue. Once a permanent venue had been constructed, bearing the name of an individual, then the competition would have been over. It is therefore unlikely that senators would endorse a proposal that would rob them of a chance to better their colleagues. Compliance with the accepted system meant that there was always an opportunity for a politician to stage an even greater set of games in a far more fantastic venue the following year.

Indeed, the competitiveness of Roman politics in the late Republic holds the key to the stilted development of public entertainment venues in the city. As the Roman empire grew, and the elite became wealthier, the competitive nature of Roman politics increased to such an extent that the Republic began to disintegrate; power became more and more concentrated in the hands of a few great men and the competition was no longer fair. In an attempt to halt this disintegration of the political system the senate tried to ensure that no one man was able to provide the people with a permanent entertainment venue. Even when Pompey created the first stone theatre in Rome,[11] he still needed to maintain the legal fiction that the seats of his theatre were merely the steps of a monumental entrance to his temple of Venus Victrix (Aul. Gell. *NA* 10.1.7). The entire complex was dedicated as a sanctuary (Tertullian, *On Spectacles*, 10.5) and although it is doubtful that anyone believed this fiction, Pompey was thus able to place his building firmly within the Republican tradition. The most common victory monument under the Republic was the votive temple, generally vowed to a deity during a campaign and financed from the spoils of war. Piety was not the principal motive behind the temples, and their main function was really to confer prestige on generals and their descendants. These victory temples quickly became associated directly in the public mind with the men who had built them, and in some cases even bore their names, at least informally. For example, the temple of Honour and Virtue built by Gaius Marius after his victory over the Germans in 101 BC became known simply as the 'Monument of Marius' (Cic. *Sest.* 116 , Vitruv. *Arch.* 3.2.5). Thus the dedication of a victory monument was a way of creating a permanent reminder of your achievements. In contrast to this, public benefactions such as games and shows gave an individual fleeting prestige that only lasted as long as people remembered the spectacles. However, a permanent entertainment venue would forever be associated with an individual and this is ultimately why temporary structures continued to be used in Rome long after this was practical and economically sound.

At the end of the Republic the change in the political structure of the city meant that Rome finally got the entertainment venues that the city required. Admittedly, the ancient venue of the Circus Maximus had been in use throughout much of Roman history, and the sheer size of this valley may lead to the conclusion that Rome had no need for any other entertainment venue until the population rose in the late Republic. However, the fact that so many venues were built in such a short space of time, all associated with an individual or a dynasty, suggests otherwise. Indeed, the transformation of Rome that began in the late Republic and continued under the empire with Augustus' great building programme, was made possible by the removal of the artificial boundaries that had kept Rome haphazard and almost archaic in appearance. The power that the building of public amenities bestowed upon their instigators became clear under the empire and from Augustus onwards there are very few references to senatorially financed building activity in Rome, despite the fact that this had been common in the Republic. This was not because the senatorial families were financially incapable – indeed, large theatres were built by senators at Volaterrae and Herculaneum in the Augustan period (*AE* 1957. 229, *CIL* X.1423) – but because public building activity, at least unofficially, was regarded as the job of the emperor. Indeed, the glory to be gained in the city from benefactions to the public was to be reserved for the emperor and the emperor alone.

Theatres

Once the city began to be embellished by all sorts of public entertainment venues, some of the most spectacular monuments of the Roman empire were created. However, of the first stone theatre in Rome – the theatre of Pompey – very little survives, despite the enormous size of the structure and the impact that it had upon the late Republican city. It remained the only stone theatre in Rome for forty years, and coupled with the surrounding porticoes and gardens, it was a showpiece of the city (Hanson 1959: 43). The theatre was commissioned by Pompey, one of the richest and most powerful men the Roman world had ever seen. Yet he still acknowledged the ban of the Senate by dedicating the complex in 55 BC not as a theatre but as a temple, claiming that the theatre was merely a monumental staircase to the temple of Venus Victrix at the top of the *cavea* (Aul. Gell. 'NA' 101.7/Tertullian 'On Spectacles' 10.5). By ostensibly dedicating the complex to a deity, Pompey could claim, however superfluously, that he was building a victory monument following his triple triumph in 61BC. This would be in keeping with Republican tradition and Pompey in fact positioned his complex behind a whole line of earlier victory temples (in the modern Largo Argentina), thus associating himself with past achievements and the triumphal route (Coleman 2000: 222). However, the fact that the complex was known not as the sanctuary or temple of Pompey, but quite clearly as his theatre, makes it clear that his disguise fooled nobody. Indeed, if Pompey had merely wanted to thank the gods for his victories, or even merely to preserve his family name for generations to come, he would have built a simple temple that would have quickly come to bear his name.

Pompey was never really popular with the urban masses in the way that Julius Caesar was, and whilst Caesar portrayed himself as the friend and protector of the plebs, Pompey lagged behind in the popularity stakes. By constructing the first permanent theatre in the city, Pompey was undoubtedly attempting to win popularity, whilst also demonstrating his power. Furthermore, during his travels in the east, Pompey may have observed that the theatre was often used to glorify rulers; Plutarch tells us that the ceremonies which Pompey witnessed in the theatre at Mytilene were in fact a glorification of his own deeds (Plut. *Pomp.* 42.4). The personal adulation that he received in this Greek theatre may well have shown him the value of a theatre for personal propaganda and glorification (Hanson 1959: 54). He certainly took advantage of the opportunity to display himself as conqueror of the east, including a Hellenistic style monumental garden in his theatre complex, with a curated collection of art with specific references to Pergamon and the Eastern Mediterranean (for example, Pliny *NH* 36.4.41). The complex may have been built ostensibly to honour Venus, but the project was in truth a strategically planned attempt to display the political and military power of Pompey at the height of his rivalry with Julius Caesar. Successive restorations probably increased the magnificence of the theatre and throughout the empire it remained one of the most celebrated and most visited attractions of the city.

Julius Caesar's reaction was not only to begin the Forum Iulium in 54BC and to provide the Circus Maximus with permanent structures, but also to plan a theatre adjacent to the temple of Apollo. He began to clear the area (Suet. *Iul.*, 44), but following his death the project was taken over by Augustus and dedicated to his nephew Marcellus, who died in 23BC (Suet. *Aug.* 29). The theatre was officially inaugurated in either 13BC (Dio 54.26.1) or 11BC (Pliny *NH* 8.65), with splendid games given by Augustus, a man who was often treated with suspicion and caution by the crowd. As Pompey before him, he turned to the capital city of the empire and tried to win the popularity and awe of the people by providing them with a splendid environment to live in, at least publicly (Yavetz 1969: 57). However, unlike Pompey, Augustus made no attempt to disguise his intentions with traditional religious practices; he built a free-standing theatre decorated with dramatic masks, blatantly advertising his intention to entertain the masses.

A further theatre was constructed in this period, the theatre of Balbus, which was built by L. Cornelius Balbus after his triumph for a campaign in Africa in 19BC. This represents the last of the great projects funded by *manubiae* awarded to Augustus' generals, and was dedicated in 13BC with lavish games (Suet. *Aug.* 29.5). Rome also had an *Odeum*, which was situated in the Campus Martius at the south-east corner of what is now the Piazza Navona. This was begun by Domitian, who also built a stadium nearby, perhaps with the intention of creating an area of 'Greek-style' entertainment. Thus we can see that within a relatively short time Rome went from having no theatres at all to possessing three permanent stone structures and an *Odeum*. Perhaps this development of permanent theatres can act as a measure of the increasing importance of theatrical entertainment by the late first century BC, but it seems a little naïve to believe that these venues appeared at this point merely because they suddenly became necessary. Indeed, it is hardly likely that the idea of theatre building simply suddenly occurred to the upper classes, and the rash of building that took place supports the argument that this development had previously been constrained by artificial factors which disappeared with the breakdown of the Republic.

Amphitheatres

Although it should be remembered that there was always an element of cross-over between the spectacles held in the different venues – beast hunts were held in the Circus Maximus, for example, and gladiatorial combats in the theatres – Rome needed a permanent amphitheatre, not only to stage specific forms of entertainment but also to bring the city in line with many of the towns in Campania (see p. 47, above). Previously, gladiatorial combats had been held in temporary amphitheatres or in the Forum Romanum, but eventually Rome's first permanent amphitheatre was built by Statilius Taurus – a general of Augustus – in 29BC using triumphal money (Dio 51.23.1, Suet. *Aug.* 29.5). A second amphitheatre begun by Caligula (Suet. *Cal.* 21) was soon abandoned, but Nero built a huge wooden structure in AD57 (Tac. *Ann.* 13.31.1, Suet. *Nero*, 12.1) which was obviously intended to be a showpiece (Pliny *NH* 16.200, 19.24). However, this was presumably destroyed in the fire of AD64, along with the amphitheatre of Statilius Taurus. Thus when Vespasian emerged victorious from the succession struggle of AD69, he saw a gap in Rome's amenities and the opportunity to ingratiate himself with a public who were still in mourning for their beloved Nero. Despite his reputation, the populace had a deep-rooted and lasting affection for Nero, who provided them with an 'immense variety of entertainments' (Suet. *Nero* 11–12). Many people refused to believe he had died, and 'false Neros' appeared all over the empire, whilst others laid flowers on his grave and had statues made of him (Suet. *Nero* 57). Nero's ancestry, his youth, his tastes and his courting of the populace, made him a favourite (Levick 1999: 63), yet Vespasian was a usurper, emerging as emperor from the bitter anarchy of AD69. Vespasian, therefore, had to win over the populace and he began by rebuilding the city of Rome. He not only rebuilt the Capitol,[12] but also built a temple of Peace, a sanctuary dedicated to Claudius, and of course, the Flavian amphitheatre, or Colosseum, which he began in AD70. Although this represents one of the most impressive building projects of the Roman empire, the amphitheatre was not merely a grandiose and extravagant gesture but a carefully calculated move. Nero had built himself a luxurious private residence, the *Domus Aurea*, across the heart of Rome; by draining the lake that was at the centre of Nero's palace and building a venue for the populace, Vespasian was symbolically giving the area back to the people.[13]

The Colosseum was the largest amphitheatre in the Roman world, and modern estimates have put the capacity in the region of 50,000 spectators.[14] If we accept that the population of Rome was around one million during the Flavian era, then only one in twenty would be able to attend a performance at any one time. Thus it can be assumed that tickets to events at the Colosseum were as difficult to get hold of as tickets to prestigious sports finals are now. Indeed, although the amphitheatre may have ostensibly been a gift to the people, it is likely that many never saw the inside; the building of such a huge imposing structure might well have been more about exclusion than inclusion.[15] Originally gladiatorial combats were held in the open and were available to all. This can be shown by Gaius Gracchus' demand that temporary seats erected in the Forum in 123BC be torn down, as they were being rented out at prices which the poor of the city simply could not afford (Plut. *C. Gracc.* 12.3). Seats in the Colosseum would have been free originally, as it was important that the games were seen as a gift, rather than as a profit-making venture. Yet seats must have changed hands at extortionate prices, in much the same way as touts today still profit from the unofficial sale of tickets. If tickets were distributed through connections, as was the case in the Republic,[16] then it would have been the plebs who were involved in the client–patron system that found it easiest to get seats at the games, receiving tickets distributed by their patron. Possibly the shopkeepers and craftsmen of Rome could afford to occasionally purchase tickets on some sort of 'black market', but the unemployed poor rarely, if ever, got a glimpse inside the great amphitheatre of Rome. Much of this is obviously mere speculation – and it could equally be supposed that as the games always went on for days most citizens got an opportunity to attend the spectacles at least once – but it can be imagined that there was a healthy trade in tickets.

In building the Colosseum, Vespasian was legitimising his power by affiliating himself with Augustus; Augustus was the great rebuilder of Rome and the founder of a dynasty, and Vespasian was presenting himself as his successor, as a founder of a new dynasty and a new city. Indeed, the Colosseum is said to have been originally planned by Augustus, but completed by Vespasian (Suet. *Vesp.* 9), although this is far more likely to be propaganda than a true plan of Augustus. Indeed, propaganda is the obvious motive behind the amphitheatre, as the structure guaranteed immortality to the Flavian dynasty and their achievements, most notably the crushing of Jerusalem. Attempts have been made to restore the original dedication of the amphitheatre which suggests that the building was constructed out of the spoils of war (Claridge 1998: 278), presumably the riches that Vespasian took from the temple at Jerusalem in AD70. This reflects the Republican tradition of sharing the wealth of imperial conquest with the people through manubial building projects. The Colosseum must have provided continuous employment for many skilled craftsmen and labourers alike, contributing to a general feeling of prosperity and regeneration in the city. Such a magnificent building displayed the power of the imperial family and the Roman empire to the population of Rome and to any visitors or foreign ambassadors in the city; a government that had the power to produce such an awe-inspiring construction should surely be feared and obeyed. The sheer size and solidity of the structure showed an emperor confident in the stability and permanence of his empire. Furthermore, the amphitheatre was a living monument to the benevolence of the emperor, his gift to the people to show them that he shared their interests and would continue to provide for them in the way that Nero had. Even today the ruin of the building remains one of the most famous symbols of the power of the Roman empire, and represents not merely the brutality of the regime but the ingenuity and intelligence of Vespasian's political vision.

Conclusion

Life was certainly no endless round of free entertainment for the mass of the populace in Rome, but it can be imagined that festival days were a riot of colour and noise, with entertainment not merely confined to the official venues, but found all over the city. If you could not manage to obtain a ticket for an official performance, then the streets themselves must surely have been almost as entertaining, thronged as they were with busking musicians, storytellers, tightrope walkers, bear-baiters, jugglers, conjurers and all manner of performers. There was the opportunity to make money also, and these entertainers must have jostled for space with temporary stalls and hawkers selling all sorts of goods. Much of this is obviously conjectural, as temporary entertainers and stall-holders leave no trace, but it only takes a glance at any modern city festival to see the people which such events will attract.

However, what we can be certain of is the importance of official entertainment in the city, as the sheer number and grandeur of the buildings dedicated to leisure in Rome show us the central place which games had in this society. The entertainment that has left its mark in Rome originally had a religious function but quickly acquired a secular and political function that the street theatre did not fulfil. Public building had always been an important part of the role of the elite in ancient society, as it gave the upper classes the opportunity to glorify themselves and display their commitment to public service by means of permanent memorials. However, in Republican Rome the situation was different to that in many of the cities of Italy and the Mediterranean. An individual may have been able to put his name to a manubial temple, or a road or some other functional structure such as an aqueduct, but not to any building that benefited the masses in a 'frivolous' or 'social' sense. This is the key to the stilted development of the city of Rome; the state as a whole never erected a building for leisure, and no individual would have financed such a venture anonymously without expecting any credit for his benefaction. Thus individuals ploughed their money into the games themselves and lavish temporary structures to house them, as this way they were not prevented from self-glorification.

The gradual evolution of permanent structures designed to accommodate spectators reflects the ambitions of wealthy and powerful politicians and eventually emperors, and the finance involved was huge. In the late Republic the power of entertainment as a political tool for furthering a magisterial career was recognised and began to be to be abused. As the empire of Rome grew and the wealth of the oligarchy in the city increased, individuals began to grasp power from the senate. Once individuals began to dominate politics, the Republic lived on in name only, and these dominant individuals were able to donate buildings for the enhancement of the city and the benefit of the masses, whilst also furthering their own political careers. Entertainment was monumentalised by the last generation of the Republic, and we see Pompey giving the city its first stone theatre in 55BC, an act which began the process that changed the face of Rome.

Once the imperial system had superseded the Republic, the emperor became the supreme benefactor of Rome and he shaped the nature of the entertainment in the city and the physical form of the buildings that contained the games. The emperor may have been an absolute ruler, but there was a public aspect to his role in the city; he acted as protector and patron of the plebs of the city, most obviously when he attended the shows. The ideology of public building under the empire remained largely unchanged across Italy, but in Rome such building became the preserve of the emperor who acted as the sole benefactor of the city. His buildings were generally immense and their solidity was used to show that the state was durable and permanent; the ruler could also achieve what no private individual in the city ever could. Only the emperor had the resources to build a structure as immense as the Colosseum for his people, and the games themselves were on a scale in Rome that could not be seen in the provinces.

In the late Republic and early Empire Roman politics was very much about individuals, and we have seen that politics, the games and public building were all inter-linked in such a way that one could not be separated from the other. The speed with which entertainment venues sprang up in the city of Rome is striking. In less than 50 years Rome went from having no theatres at all to possessing three permanent stone structures. The Flavian dynasty produced perhaps the greatest surviving of all Roman monuments, the Colosseum, along with the stadium and Odeum of Domitian. The Circus Maximus – which is the oldest of all the venues in Rome and tellingly does not carry the name of any named individual – was enhanced and added to by subsequent emperors[17] and became one of the most magnificent structures in the ancient world. It is hardly likely that the idea of building entertainment venues suddenly occurred to the upper classes; rather it is more likely that the power that such structures had on the city was recognised early and thus artificial factors prevented their development. With the breakdown of the Republic these artificial constraints disappeared and a rash of building occurred that made Rome into the sort of city that should be found at the head of such a huge empire.

Notes

1 This chapter is based upon an unpublished dissertation, 'The development of public entertainment venues in the city of Rome', Claire Holleran (University of Manchester, 2000).

2 See Chapter 4 by Coleman and Chapter 2 by Lomas in this volume.

3 Censors oversaw the building work in the city and were appointed every five years from the most distinguished ex-consuls.

4 Nicolaos of Damascus recorded this in the time of Augustus (Athen. *Deip.* 153f.).

5 A study of the origins of gladiatorial games is beyond the scope of this chapter but it is interesting to note that neither the Etruscans nor the Samnites practised gladiatorial combat before they invaded Campania; it is possible that the inhabitants of the area played an important role in the invention and development of gladiatorial games (Mouratidis 1996: 116). For a study of the origins of the games see Mouratidis, 1996.

6 The *Pro Murena* of Cicero discusses whether Murena's habit of seat distribution at spectacles constituted electoral bribery or not.

7 '... our leading citizens ... have provided whole blocks of seats' (Cic. *Mur.* 73).

8 In AD15 the people lost the right to elect praetors and consuls, although even under Augustus the popular assembly had been a mere formality. Indeed, the loss of election privileges was merely symbolic, as by this time the people turned directly to the emperor on matters that concerned them.

9 Pompey was able to build his theatre during the breakdown of the Republic simply due to the personal power that he wielded. That one of the first great individual leaders of the Roman empire constructed such a theatre serves to illustrate the place that such structures had in a monarchical system.

10 Coleman argues that the fact that various plays were associated with various gods and should be held in the vicinity of specific temples meant that a theatre structure would have been superfluous whilst entertainment retained a strong religious connection. It was necessary for entertainment venues to be flexible in their location, because games dedicated to Apollo should be held near the Temple of Apollo etc. This perhaps goes some way towards explaining the Roman temple design; the elevated podium and number of steps at the entrance could be used for performances (Coleman 2000: 220). See also, Hanson, 1959, 9–26, who has established that each temporary theatre erected during the Republic was placed as close as possible to the temple of the deity in whose honour the festival was given.

11 See below, pp. 53–4.

12 This had been burnt during the Civil War.

13 See Martial, *On the Spectacles*, 2, for the emphasis on this contrast.

14 To give a modern comparison, this is equivalent to the capacity of a large football stadium. The largest stadium in Britain – Old Trafford – has a maximum capacity of around 67,000.

15 In contrast to this, up to a quarter of the population of Rome would be able to attend the races in the Circus Maximus at any one time, making this the true heart of public entertainment in the city. With a venue of this size it would have been impossible to regulate entrance to any great extent, but there are anecdotal references which imply that spectators had to pay to enter the circus in the imperial period. For example, a crowd, including

some equestrians, burst in at midnight in order to secure free seats (Suet. *Cal.* 26). However, it is probable that few people in Rome could afford to pay to attend the races, and this story refers to some of the best seats in the circus, perhaps those controlled by the black market.

16 See above, p. 50.

17 In particular Trajan, who undertook a massive reconstruction of the building and commemorated his work on bronze coinage issued in AD103, providing us with the earliest known representation of the entire circus.

References

Brothers, A.J. (1989) 'Buildings for entertainment'. In I.M. Barton (ed.), *Roman Public Buildings*: 97–126, Exeter: Exeter University Press.

Cameron, A. (1976) *Circus Factions*, Oxford: Clarendon Press.

Claridge, A. (1998) *Rome: An Oxford Archaeological Guide*, Oxford: Oxford University Press.

Coleman, K.M. (2000) 'Entertaining Rome'. In J. Coulston and H. Dodge (eds), *Ancient Rome: The Archaeology of the Eternal City*: 210–45, Oxford: Oxford University School of Archaeology.

Cornell, T.J. (2000) 'The city of Rome in the Middle Republic (400–100BC)'. In J. Coulston and H. Dodge (eds), *Ancient Rome: The Archaeology of the Eternal City*: 42–56, Oxford: Oxford University School of Archaeology.

Dyson, S. L. (1992) *Community and Society in Roman Italy*, Baltimore and London: Johns Hopkins University Press.

Friedländer, L. (1909) *Roman Life and Manners under the Early Empire*, London and New York: Routledge.

Futrell, A. (1997) *Blood in the Arena: The spectacle of Roman Power*, Austin: University of Texas Press.

Gebhard, E.R. (1996) 'The theatre and the city'. In W. Slater (ed.), *Roman Theatre and Society*: 113–27, Ann Arbor: University of Michigan Press.

Gleason, K.L. (1994) 'Porticus Pompeiana: a new perspective on the first public park of ancient Rome', *Journal of Garden History* 14: 13–27.

Golvin, J.-C. (1988) *L'Amphithéâtre romain*, Paris: Diffusion de Boccard.

Grant, M. (1978) *History of Rome*, London: Weidenfeld and Nicholson.

Hanson, J. (1959) *Roman Theater-Temples*, Princeton: Princeton University Press.

Levick, B. (1999) *Vespasian*, London: Routledge.

Mouratidis, J. (1996) 'On the origin of the gladiatorial games', *Nikephoros* 9: 111–34.

Pedley, J.G. (1990) *Paestum*, London: Thames and Hudson.

Purcell, N. (1996) 'Rome and its development under Augustus and his successors'. In A.K. Bowman, E. Champlin and A. Lintott (eds), *Cambridge Ancient History*, 2nd edn, Vol. 10: 782–811, Cambridge: Cambridge University Press.

Richardson, L. (1992) *A New Topographical Dictionary of Ancient Rome*, Baltimore and London: Johns Hopkins University Press.

Spina, L. (1997) *L'Anfiteatro Campano di Capua*. Napoli: Electa Napoli.

Toner, J.P. (1995) *Leisure and Ancient Rome*, Cambridge: Cambridge University Press.

Veyne, P. (1990) (O. Murray, trans. and ed.) *Bread and Circuses* (abridged translation of *Le pain et le cirque* (1976) Paris: Seuil), London: Penguin.

Ward-Perkins, J.B. (1981) *Roman Imperial Architecture*, New Haven: Yale University Press.

Welch, K. (1994) 'The arena in late-Republican Italy: a new interpretation', *JRA* 7: 59–80.

Yavetz, Z. (1969) *Plebs and Princeps*, Oxford: Clarendon Press.

4

EUERGETISM IN ITS PLACE

Where was the amphitheatre in Augustan Rome?

Kathleen M. Coleman

Vespasian was to style himself Augustus' spiritual heir by claiming that the first Princeps had cherished the ambition of building a monumental amphitheatre in the centre of Rome (Suet. *Vesp.* 9): '[fecit Vespasianus] amphitheatrum urbe media, ut destinasse compererat Augustum' ('[Vespasian built] an amphitheatre in the middle of the city, as he had discovered had been Augustus' intention'). Seduced as we are by the magnetism of the Colosseum, it is almost impossible for us to conjure up a Rome in which plans to build it needed justification. It may prove impossible to establish the veracity of Vespasian's claim; yet it draws attention to the fact that for more than a century after Actium the topography and amenities of Rome remained devoid of a permanent amphitheatre of monumental dimensions. It has recently emerged that the amphitheatre as a permanent fixture was a feature of Roman colonies at least one hundred and fifty years before the Colosseum was built, and that the design appears to have been predicated on the temporary structures erected in the Forum Romanum at Rome.[1] We may well ask why it is that the city of Rome, where the design of the amphitheatre originated, did not acquire a monumental stone amphitheatre of grand dimensions long before the Flavian era. Why, specifically, was such an opportunity not realised by Augustus, that great benefactor who both changed the face of the city and exploited the provision of public spectacle as a major tool of self-promotion?[2]

The *Appendix* to the *Res Gestae* summarises Augustus' personal expenditure in the public interest. Only his *congiaria* are given a monetary value: 2,400 million sesterces (*App.* 1). For buildings the author of the *Appendix* (who was not Augustus himself) is content with a list of twenty-one projects that Augustus undertook *ab initio*, including four connected with the provision of recreation facilities: the *pulvinar* in the Circus Maximus, the theatre of Marcellus, the *porticus Octavia*, and the *nemus Caesarum* across the Tiber (*App.* 2). Among five categories of general structures that Augustus repaired (including 'sacred buildings to the number of eighty-two', 'sacras ... aedes numero octoginta duas'), the theatre of Pompey is specifically mentioned (*App.* 3). The *Appendix* concludes with a list of shows sponsored and grants-in-aid to communities and individuals in order to demonstrate that Augustus' generosity was beyond reckoning (*App.* 4): 'impensa praestita in spectacula scaenica et munera gladiatorum atque athletas et uenationes et naumachiam et donata pecunia colonis, municipiis, oppidis terrae motu incendioque consumptis aut uiritim amicis senatoribusque quorum census expleuit innumerabilis' ('The expenditure that he devoted to dramatic shows, to gladiatorial exhibitions and athletes and hunts and the sea battle, and the money granted to colonies, *municipia*, towns destroyed by earthquake and fire or to individual friends and senators whose property qualification he made up, was beyond counting'). Hence the profile of euergetism in the *Res Gestae* conforms exactly to the standard pattern, in which the construction of buildings and the provision of entertainment are key elements.

This chapter will focus on the overlap between these two areas of euergetism by examining the provision of venues for 'arena-type' spectacles in Augustan Rome (i.e. gladiatorial combat, beast-shows, and massed battles on land and water). The aim is to understand why Augustus did not build the equivalent of the Colosseum. This enquiry raises various questions. Did different types of spectacle-building entail a hierarchy of cachet for the people who built them? And since, in any case, few benefactors are able to sponsor spectacles in buildings that they themselves have built, what were the options in the Augustan age? Did the available venues confer differing status on the events held there? To examine these questions it is necessary to establish the known venues for arena-type spectacles in Augustan Rome. Hence summary evidence for such spectacles between 31 BC and AD 14 is collected in chronological order in the Appendix; in the discussion, cross-references are given according to the enumeration adopted there. Almost every one of these spectacles has numerous attendant problems, of which the barest hint is given in the notes. I am focussing instead upon the venues where these spectacles were performed, in the hope of discovering why the most powerful contemporary benefactor, Augustus himself, did not construct the most magnificent of all Roman buildings.

Julius Caesar: ephemeral innovation

At Rome under the Republic, *munera* (gladiatorial displays) were associated with the Forum, since they had originated in the *fora* of Rome (first the Forum Boarium, then the Forum Romanum) as funerary celebrations in honour of deceased aristocrats. *Venationes* (staged hunts) were an adjunct to *ludi*,[3] and may not have been so strictly associated with a single venue. They were definitely held in the Circus Maximus;[4] they may also have been held in the Forum, although secure evidence is lacking. But the Circus remained the sole permanent structure for public spectacle at Rome until the very end of the Republic. Rome's first permanent theatre was built by Pompey on the Campus Martius in 55 BC. Three years later Curio experimented with his pair of theatres that revolved to form an amphitheatre.[5] It is clear that in the period of the civil wars and their aftermath the notion of permanent spectacle-buildings at Rome was still being negotiated by the elite, and simultaneously the repertoire of spectacle performed in the city was expanding. The half-century (virtually) between the battle of Actium and the death of its victor saw radical developments in the staging of spectacles at Rome, and the provision of buildings in which to mount them. Both spheres offered opportunities for euergetism that would rapidly become concentrated into the hands of the Princeps and his trusted associates.

As in so many other areas of public life, significant developments in the staging of spectacle began under Julius Caesar. On the occasion of his quadruple triumph in 46BC he can be seen to have been innovating both in the events that he staged and in the venues that he employed. The games of 46BC were apparently triumphal *ludi uotiui* that incorporated five days of *uenationes*. The programme culminated in a massed battle involving a thousand infantry, forty elephants, and sixty cavalry. This spectacle definitely took place in the Circus Maximus, since the track was specially equipped for such an event by the removal of the *metae* at either end of the *spina*.[6] The *munus funebre* for Caesar's daughter Julia, however, who had died eight years earlier in 54, was evidently quite separate from these *ludi uotiui*, despite Dio's conflation of both of them with the dedication of the Forum Iulium; it is significant that Dio credits Caesar with the construction of a wooden amphitheatre on this occasion (43.22.2–3):

> *ταύτην [τὴν ἀγοράν] τε οὖν καὶ τὸν τῆς ᾿Αφροδίτης, ὡς καὶ ἀρχηγέτιδος τοῦ γένους αὐτοῦ οὔσης, ποιήσας καθιέρωσεν εὐθὺς τότε καὶ πολλούς γε ἐὴ αὐτοῖς καὶ παντοδαποὺς ἀγῶνας ἔθηκε, θέατρόν τι κυνηγετικὸν ἰκριώσας, ὃ καὶ ἀμφιθέατρον ἐκ τοῦ πέριξ πανταχόθεν ἕδρας ἄνευ σκηνῆς ἔχειν προσερρήθη. καὶ ἐπὶ τούτῳ καὶ ἐπὶ τῇ θυγατρὶ καὶ θηρίων σφαγὰς καὶ ἀνδρῶν ὁπλομαχίας ἐποίησεν.*

> When he had built this forum and the temple to Venus, as the founder of his family, he dedicated them straight away on that occasion. He instituted many contests of all sorts in their honour, constructing a hunting-theatre out of wood which was also called an amphitheatre because it had seats all the way round without any stage. In honour of this and of his daughter he sponsored beast-hunts and gladiatorial displays.

Where was the amphitheatre that Dio ascribes to Caesar? There are at least three possibilities: the Forum Romanum, the Forum Iulium, and the Campus Martius. Caesar held at least one *munus* in a *forum*, evidently the Forum Romanum.[7] His amphitheatre is usually assumed to be the traditional type of structure erected there;[8] Dio's emphasis on its shape might suggest otherwise, except that this is the first time that the word 'amphitheatre' occurs in his extant work, and this explanation is therefore in the nature of an etymological gloss. Conceivably, however, Caesar's structure was in his new Forum Iulium instead. In the Forum Romanum between the Basilica Aemilia and the Basilica Iulia there was room to erect temporary stands around a space with the same dimensions as the arena at Pompeii (68 × 35 m).[9] Hence in the Forum Iulium the piazza in front of the Temple of Venus Genetrix, measuring 124 × 45 m, would have been large enough to accommodate a comparable structure; we can be reasonably confident that the statuary displayed there would not have been in the way.[10]

Without the sub-structures that had been installed in the Forum Romanum, however,[11] beasts would have had to be introduced at ground-level. Yet it is by no means certain that Caesar held *uenationes* in his wooden amphitheatre, since the only evidence is the statement of Dio, who is untrustworthy precisely because he has confused Caesar's *munus funebre* for Julia with the *ludi uotiui* on the occasion of his triumph. Furthermore, Dio's term θέατρον κυνηγετικόν, which was employed as a periphrasis for an amphitheatre, need not imply that every such structure accommodated *uenationes*. And it is understandable that he should associate *munera* with *uenationes*, which was the standard pairing in his own day. Finally, the juxtaposition that Dio achieves between the dedication of the Forum Iulium and the construction of the amphitheatre does not prove that there was any connection between them. So, after all, Caesar's amphitheatre may have been no more than a very elaborate version of a traditional construction in the Forum Romanum, the time-honoured site for a *munus funebre*.[12] A third possibility remains, however: the Campus Martius.[13] This area was already strongly associated with entertainment-buildings. It is where Caesar constructed his temporary stadium and perhaps also his *stagnum*; to these I will now turn.

Although Suetonius does not refer to Caesar's amphitheatre, he does mention the temporary stadium (i.e. presumably also of wood) that Caesar erected on the Campus Martius for three days of athletic contests (*Iul.* 39.3):[14] 'athletae stadio ad tempus extructo regione Marti campi certauerunt per triduum' ('Athletes competed for three days in a temporary stadium that had been erected in the area of the Campus Martius'). This supplied a precedent for the temporary stadium constructed by Octavian and Agrippa in 28 BC (Appendix item 3, discussed below). And both Suetonius and Dio describe the *stagnum* that Caesar excavated in order to stage a naval battle. Its location seems to lie hidden beneath a corruption in Suetonius' description (*Iul.* 39.4): 'nauali proelio in morem cochleae (ϒ: minore [minori *T*] Codeta [cocleta *G*] *Turnebus*) defosso lacu biremes ac triremes quadriremesque Tyriae et Aegyptiae classis magno pugnatorum numero conflixerunt' ('He dug out a lake in the shape of a shell [ϒ: in the lesser Codeta *Turnebus*], and a battle was waged between biremes, triremes and quadriremes of the fleets of Tyre and Egypt involving a large number of combatants').[15] Dio locates the *stagnum* in the Campus Martius (43.23.4), and Suetonius includes it immediately after mentioning the stadium there (*Iul.* 39.4). Suetonius also remarks that Caesar intended to fill in the basin afterwards and level the site for a temple to Mars (*Iul.* 44.1). Hence Dio's location of the *stagnum* in the Campus Martius seems to be correct, and Caesar evidently did not intend this structure to be permanent. In fact, it was filled in the year after his death on suspicion of having contributed to an outbreak of plague (Dio 45.17.8). It therefore seems that although Caesar constructed three spectacle-venues in the city of Rome, they were all conceived as temporary structures. This was the precedent that Octavian inherited.

The Julio-Claudians: unfulfilled ambitions

Rome acquired her first amphitheatre within two years of the victory at Actium, although it was not Octavian who built it. In the late Republic, buildings for the staging of mass entertainment were part of the bounty bestowed upon the people of Rome by prominent *triumphales*. Once Augustus restricted triumphs to members of the imperial house, this avenue of self-aggrandising munificence was closed off to the rest of the upper class. But between the death of Caesar and the death of Augustus, construction by *uiri triumphales* (including Augustus himself) transformed the city of Rome.[16] In the immediate aftermath of Actium the *triumphales* were an obvious resource for the realisation of the programme of urban renewal initiated in Agrippa's tenure of the aedileship in 33BC. T. Statilius Taurus, himself the commander of the land forces at Actium, had been awarded a triumph in 34BC after securing the province of Africa for Octavian.[17] In using his share of the spoils of war to donate to Rome a building that would preserve his name, he was investing his *manubiae* in a traditional sphere of *gloria*.[18]

The building that Taurus erected was the first permanent amphitheatre at Rome (Dio 51.23.1):

> *τοῦ δὲ δὴ* Καίσαρος *τὸ τέταρτον ἔτι ὑπατεύοντος ὁ* Ταῦρος *ὁ* Στατίλιος *θέατρον τι ἐν τῷ* 'Αρείῳ *πεδίῳ κυνηγετικὸν λίθινον καὶ ἐξεποίησε τοῖς ἑαυτοῦ τέλεσι καὶ καθιέρωσεν ὁπλομαχίᾳ, καὶ διὰ τοῦτο στρατηγὸν ἕνα παρὰ τοῦ δήμου κατ' ἔτος αἱρεῖσθαι ἐλάμβανε.*

> When Caesar was still in his fourth consulship Statilius Taurus built a stone hunting-theatre on the Campus Martius at his own expense, and he dedicated it with a gladiatorial display [Appendix item 2]. Because of this the people granted him the right to choose one of the praetors every year.

Possibly only the outer shell was of stone and the interior wooden, since all trace of this building was lost in the great fire of AD64.[19] Its function and upkeep remained within the purview of Taurus' descendants, as is evident from the number of funerary inscriptions in the *monumentum Statiliorum* commemorating slaves of the Statilii who performed tasks associated with the building and its spectacles.[20] Its exact location in the Campus Martius is still in dispute, though it probably stood at the southern end beside the river.[21] The privilege that Taurus received from the Roman people as a result of this benefaction confirms that it was conceived as a structure for staging public events. Notably, however, it was not used on occasions of major political importance like the *munus* to commemorate Agrippa in 7BC (Appendix item 19).[22]

Apart from the dedicatory games (Appendix item 2), the only secure occasion during the reign of Augustus when Taurus' amphitheatre is known to have been used is the *munus* that Tiberius held in memory of his grandfather at a date after 23 April 27BC (Appendix item 5). Augustus, however, appears to have used it too. Whereas he does not specify the venue for his *munera*, he mentions a range of locations, including *amphitheatra*, for the twenty-six occasions on which he held *uenationes*; perhaps this specificity is because *uenationes*, being unfettered by associations of propriety, are more flexible in location than funerary celebrations (*RG* 22.1, 3):

> Ter munus gladiatorium dedi meo nomine et quinquiens filiorum meorum aut nepotum nomine, quibus muneribus depugnauerunt hominum circiter decem millia ... uenationes bestiarum Africanarum meo nomine aut filiorum meorum et nepotum in circo aut in foro aut in amphitheatris populo dedi sexiens et uiciens, quibus confecta sunt bestiarum circiter tria millia et quingentae.
>
> I gave three gladiatorial games in my own name and five in that of my sons or grandsons; at these games some 10,000 men took part in combat ... I gave beast-hunts of African beasts in my own name or in that of my sons and grandsons in circus, forum or any amphitheatre on twenty-six occasions, on which about 3,500 beasts were destroyed.

This latter statement raises fresh questions: our current body of evidence allows us to identify fewer than half the occasions on which Augustus claims to have staged *uenationes* (see Appendix);[23] and the enigmatic expression *in amphitheatris* demands discussion.

The plural form in Augustus' phrase *in amphitheatris* is significant. Juxtaposed with *forum*, it suggests something other than the temporary structures in the Forum Romanum. Since Taurus' amphitheatre is the only structure of this type known to have existed in Rome at this time, elaborate explanations have been devised to ascribe the plural form to this single building: either it is said to be 'etymologizing', reflecting the shape of an amphitheatre as a double theatre,[24] or it is explained as plural by analogy with the term *spectacula*, which was the word for an amphitheatre before the Greek term *amphitheatrum* was adopted.[25] But Augustus' usage seems more likely to be a true plural, as appears to be the case with the earliest extant use of the term (Vitruv. *Arch.* 1.7.1, discussing the siting of sacred buildings): 'Herculi, in quibus ciuitatibus non sunt gymnasia neque amphitheatra, ad circum' ('in cities where there are no gymnasia or amphitheatres, a shrine to Hercules should be built at the circus'). Since Vitruvius is apparently thinking of a structure that might be duplicated within a single city, he is perhaps using the term *amphitheatrum* to describe a general category of buildings of the stadium variety, i.e. with seating on both sides, rather than conceiving of an amphitheatre in the formal sense.

Two of Vitruvius' Greek contemporaries seem to use the term ἀμφιθέατρον in this way. Dionysius of Halicarnassus describes the Circus Maximus as a στοὰ ἀμφιθέατρος (3.68.3) and an ἀμφιθέατρος ἱππόδρομος (4.44.1); in both cases ἀμφιθέατρος is clearly adjectival.[26] And Strabo uses the term ἀμφιθέατρον both *stricto sensu* (5.3.8, of Taurus' amphitheatre) and in instances where he is more likely to be referring to a stadium (14.1.43, of Nysa on the Maeander, where Strabo was educated; and 17.1.10, of Nicopolis at Alexandria). As late as the Flavian era the adjectival use of ἀμφιθέατρος is still current: the stadium at Laodicea on the Lycus, which has two curved ends and was clearly designed to accommodate gladiatorial combat as well as athletics, was dedicated in AD79 under the designation of στάδιον ἀνφιθέατρον (*sic*).[27]

One of the candidates falling under Augustus' rubric of *amphitheatra* could perhaps be the hybrid wooden stadium (Appendix item 3) that Octavian and Agrippa constructed on the Campus Martius in 28BC to accommodate gladiatorial combat as well as athletics (see note 70). If, as seems likely, *amphitheatris* in the *Res Gestae* includes Taurus' amphitheatre, its use by Augustus for *uenationes* may suggest that it was equipped with a *hypogeum*, a facility that would have been at a premium after the Forum Romanum was paved over, perhaps in 12BC.[28] It is also possible, however, that Augustus used Taurus' amphitheatre for small-scale events for which the introduction of animals at ground-level would not have posed too many logistical difficulties; obviously it would be methodologically unsound to suppose that on all twenty-six occasions Augustus deployed an equal proportion of the approximately 3,500 beasts that he claims to have dispatched in total.

Subsequently Caligula used Taurus' amphitheatre (Suet. *Cal.* 18.1), though Dio records an occasion in AD38 when it was passed over in favour of the Saepta, which Caligula excavated and filled with water for the display of a single ship (59.10.5). The implication is that Taurus' amphitheatre was rather small. Already under Augustus the Saepta had been the site of gladiatorial displays, first in 7BC for the *munus* in memory of Agrippa (Appendix item 19) and then again in 2BC for the *munus* at the dedication of the Temple of Mars Ultor (Appendix item 20). In 7BC the Forum was unavailable because of fire-damage; and in a sense the Saepta functioned as a sort of annex to the Forum anyway, since Agrippa had built it as a voting-enclosure, an extension of the activities associated with *fora*.[29] Also, the Saepta was deemed appropriate for Agrippa's memorial display precisely because he had built it (see note 95). Neither damage to the Forum nor the explicit connection with Agrippa, however, would be applicable to the *munus* of 2BC, so for the choice of venue on this occasion we should perhaps look to scale, symbolism, and propriety. Obviously the Saepta (310 × 120 m) was far bigger than the Forum Augusti (125 × 90 m), and could therefore accommodate more spectators and perhaps a more lavish display. Nevertheless, the Forum Augusti might have been considered the appropriate venue for the dedicatory *munus*, on the grounds that it was dominated by the Temple of Mars Ultor; but the association of the Campus Martius with Mars would have favoured the choice of the Saepta equally well. And the fact that the Saepta was chosen suggests that the only *forum* that Augustus thought suitable for gladiatorial displays was the Forum Romanum.

In trying to assess the impetus towards custom-built venues for 'arena-type' displays, there is one last structure from the reign of Augustus that deserves consideration. It is one for which he was himself responsible: his *stagnum*. He documented its inauguration in his own words (*RG* 23):

> naualis proeli spectaclum populo dedi trans Tiberim in quo loco nunc nemus est Caesarum, cauato solo in longitudinem mille et octingentos pedes, in latitudinem mille et ducenti, in quo triginta rostratae naues triremes aut biremes, plures autem minores inter se conflixerunt; quibus in classibus pugnauerunt praeter remiges millia hominum tria circiter.
>
> I produced a naval battle as a show for the people at the place across the Tiber now occupied by the grove of the Caesars, where a site 1,800 feet long and 1,200 broad was excavated. There thirty beaked triremes or biremes and an even larger number of smaller vessels were joined in battle. About 3,000 men, besides the rowers, fought in these fleets.

This massive project[30] testifies to Augustus' eagerness to be associated with the provision of outsize, permanent venues for public spectacles; the Naumachia Augusti (as it is usually known) remained in use until at least the reign of Titus, and traces of it were still visible early in the third century (Dio 55.10.7).[31] The *stagnum* was clearly a top priority in the planning for the spectacles of 2BC, since there was no other venue in Rome capable of sustaining an aquatic display on the scale of Augustus' replay of Salamis, in which – oarsmen apart – approximately 3,000 men were involved.[32] A clean water supply and a regular through-flow were carefully planned: the basin was fed by the Aqua Alsietina, an aqueduct that Augustus had built partly for that purpose, and it drained into the Tiber by means of a canal. Seating was apparently not incorporated, since Titus is recorded as having erected stands when he covered part of the surface with planks to stage a land-engagement during the festivities to mark his inauguration of the Colosseum in AD80.[33] All in all, the structure was nowhere near the order of complexity of an amphitheatre, and although the scale of excavation must have been enormous, in a slave-powered economy digging is not expensive. Relative to the construction of an amphitheatre large enough to supersede Taurus' (which, though it may have been small, was not negligible), Augustus' *stagnum* certainly cost far less. And it paid dividends in terms of the number of casualties achieved in Augustus' naval display.

Augustus' attention to arena-spectacles was matched by all his Julio-Claudian successors except Tiberius. But if Augustus did not build a monumental stone amphitheatre, neither did any of the other members of his dynasty. Caligula at first held gladiatorial combat in the Saepta, and then transferred to a venue that he had cleared of buildings in order to erect wooden stands, allegedly because he despised Taurus' amphitheatre (Dio 59.10.5). It is not clear whether this structure was related to Caligula's nascent amphitheatre next door to the Saepta that was aborted by Claudius.[34] Caligula's doomed project may in turn have provided the site for Nero's amphitheatre. Although extremely elaborate, this too was wooden.[35] Nero may have been in a hurry to erect it; the whole project was completed within a year in AD57. But instead, or additionally, he may have been unable to afford a stone construction. Eighty-six years after Taurus built his amphitheatre, modest as it appears to have been, there was still no permanent amphitheatre at Rome of a size consonant with the status of the capital of the Empire. This situation would prevail for another decade and more.

The Flavians: victory and propaganda

It was almost exactly a century after Taurus completed his project that Vespasian, in the early seventies AD, initiated Rome's next stone amphitheatre. The lengthy dedication that was probably inscribed on the podium wall was replicated in abbreviated form on the architrave over at least one of the main entrances, since traces of this version have survived underneath a fifth-century inscription on a slab found inside the south entrance. This inscription, recently reconstructed by a brilliant feat of scholarly detective-work, confirms that the amphitheatre was funded out of the spoils of a military campaign:[36] 'I[mp(erator)] T(itus) Caes(ar) Vespasi[anus Aug(ustus)] / amphitheatru[m novum (?)] / [ex] manubi(i)s (vac.) [fieri iussit (?)]' ('The emperor Titus Caesar Vespasian Augustus ordered the new amphitheatre to be constructed out of the spoils of war'). The campaign conducted by Vespasian and Titus that culminated in the sack of Jerusalem in AD70 brought to Rome the fabulous treasure that is symbolised on the reliefs inside the Arch of Titus (Josephus *BJ* 148–51). The annual tax of half a shekel levied on all Jews over the age of twenty ('auri illa inuidia Iudaici', Cic. *Flacc.* 66) was destined for the Temple at Jerusalem, which was the repository of enormous wealth and functioned in some respects as a banking operation for the whole of the Near East.[37] The Roman troops are said to have seized so much plunder that the value of gold in Syria dropped by half.[38]

A mere fraction of the wealth invested in the Temple can be estimated from the stash of Essene treasure itemised on one of the Qumran scrolls (hCU = 3Q15).[39] The more significant items listed include: 62 large silver jugs and 609 vessels of silver and gold; the equivalent of 250 kg of gold and 14,585 kg of silver; and approximately 48,000 kg of bronze.[40] Nothing like such wealth had accrued to Rome since the annexation of Egypt after Actium. It is significant that Vespasian still had to employ strict fiscal measures to achieve financial stability for Rome after the civil wars of AD69–70. Clearly there was an old expectation that an increase of revenue accruing from a national victory should be spent upon a memorial of that victory rather than being used to make up an existing deficit or build up future capital investment. The wealth seized from the Jews was not to be swallowed up on state house-keeping; instead, the portion that was transmuted into *manubiae* (an archaising term under the Empire) could be used simultaneously to aggrandise its trustees and to supply games and buildings, which have aptly been called 'the perquisites of the victorious Roman people'.[41]

A recent study of the Baths of Caracalla concludes that the annual cost over the period of construction was beyond the means of almost any private individual other than the emperor himself. The cost was equivalent to the emperor's annual expenditure on *congiaria*, suggesting that handouts and public buildings provided alternative methods for distributing the same sums of money.[42] The investment that the Colosseum represented is perhaps best approached through comparison of the cost of different types of public building. In the second century AD a medium-sized temple in Africa cost 60,000–70,000 sesterces; a small paved forum with porticoes, 200,000 sesterces; a theatre, upwards of 600,000 sesterces, depending upon the size.[43] An amphitheatre would represent an investment many times larger than any of these public buildings. The Colosseum, moreover, was unprecedented in both scale and complexity of design. Unique logistical difficulties were posed by the hoisting of travertine blocks to construct a four-storey building that towers 48 m above ground-level. The stark ruin of today was originally clothed in sumptuous decoration, of which a few astonishing traces survive.[44] Skilled artisans must have been recruited for specialised tasks such as applying stucco and mosaic. Still, the raw construction must have required vast quantities of unskilled labour, noteworthy perhaps for more than its scale alone; it would have been consonant with the Roman penal principle of combining hurt with humiliation if Jewish prisoners-of-war had provided the staple work-force in the construction of the amphitheatre that was funded by the plunder from their own nation.[45]

Furthermore, if funds and workforce favoured the Flavian project, so did location: the site of the *stagnum* in the grounds of the Domus Aurea enabled the Flavians to promote themselves as the champions of a people's facility in the place of a tyrant's selfish pleasance.[46] And it also provided enough space to realise such an ambitious project. Despite the presence of water, the area was not a swamp; it was well-drained, and the Roman techniques for laying foundations, as described by Vitruvius, were perfectly adequate for supporting such a massive structure in this terrain.[47] Nero's artificial pond, once drained, was excavated down to the Republican levels beneath, exposing a stable base of sand and clay upon which the Flavian engineers constructed the pair of colossal concrete rings, occupying a depth of more than 12 m, that formed the foundations of the amphitheatre.[48] The surrounding park will have provided an area for the delivery of supplies and equipment, and for the manoeuvring of the spans of oxen that hauled the carts carrying the stone and other materials.[49] Space was also required for storage, and for the workshops that dressed timber for scaffolding, and for the smithies that repaired tools in the course of construction.[50] Normally a built-up area simply could not accommodate all these facilities; for Vespasian and Titus the Domus Aurea was a windfall.

Augustus: impetus and restraint

When Vespasian claimed that Augustus had intended to build a monumental amphitheatre in the centre of Rome (Suet. *Vesp.* 9, quoted at the beginning of this chapter), he may have been ascribing to his revered predecessor a spurious ambition in order to legitimate his own project of building the Colosseum. Yet it is not implausible that Augustus would have been planning a large amphitheatre at Rome, though the impetus and hence his motivation may have varied with circumstances. When Augustus was building energetically during the early part of his reign, his projects divided almost equally between sacred and secular,[51] an amphitheatre may not have seemed an urgent priority. But later on, when the Forum was damaged by fire in 7BC (Appendix item 19), one might have supposed that the necessity of finding an alternative venue would have spurred him to consider a monumental amphitheatre of his own. In evaluating a range of possible incentives and disincentives that may have influenced Augustus in the course of his reign, four key considerations require discussion: prestige; ideology; space; and funds.

First: prestige. It is highly unlikely that Augustus remained willing for one of his own partisans to be permanently and exclusively associated with the amenity of an amphitheatre for the city. Elsewhere in Italy at this period cities were acquiring clusters of entertainment buildings located peripherally or extra-murally in clear imitation of the Campus Martius. Of seventeen cities in Cisalpine Gaul, sixteen acquired a theatre (Pola indeed acquired two), nine an amphitheatre, and one a stadium.[52] The amphitheatre at Pola has been directly attributed to the example of Statilius Taurus, whose descendants are well attested in Istria; he is surmised to have been from Istria himself, and to have maintained close ties with his native community.[53] In this atmosphere it seems very unlikely that Augustus would have been content to allow an increasingly popular building type to remain associated with a name in the metropolis other than his own. Caesar had planned a theatre on the slopes of the Capitoline to rival Pompey's on the Campus Martius. Augustus was effectively responsible for the Theatre of Marcellus, which bore a name associated with the imperial house and displayed considerable elegance despite its modest dimensions. Yet Pompey's theatre remained the dominant structure in Rome, in both concept and scope. All the more reason for Augustus to build an amphitheatre that would simultaneously eclipse the magnificence of the theatre built by his hereditary enemy, Pompey, and surpass the prestige that Taurus' amphitheatre represented for the *triumphales* of the Second Triumvirate.

Second: ideology. In excavating their *stagna*, Caesar and Augustus were not constrained by the associations of a traditional venue for *naumachiae*, since Caesar's *naumachia* in 46BC was the first in the city of Rome. For *munera* and *uenationes*, however, metropolitan conservatism would favour the retention of the traditional locations of the Forum and the Circus Maximus. And Augustus was not a man to sweep away the *status quo*, except to restore an earlier tradition.[54] But Taurus had paved the way in constructing his own amphitheatre; so why did Augustus not cap his achievement with a more glorious one of his own? It has been suggested that he was restrained from building an amphitheatre by the absence of sacral associations that were deployed to validate the construction of theatres.[55] Clearly, however, such scruples did not keep him from building his *stagnum*. Moreover,

Pompey's example shows that sacral associations were devised precisely to legitimise the construction of a permanent theatre in the teeth of strong senatorial opposition;[56] it is perfectly credible that comparable justification could have been deployed for an amphitheatre, a building-type that developed strong religious associations.[57] Hence ideology does not satisfactorily explain why Augustus did not construct a monumental amphitheatre of his own.

Third: space. Here both symbolism and practical restraints need to be considered. For one thing, a monumental amphitheatre might seem to offer limited amenities. It was obviously Augustus' intention that his *stagnum* should be the focal point of a park, the future Nemus Caesarum (though presumably he could not have foreseen that it would commemorate his lamented grandsons). Such a purpose was consonant with the extensive *horti* that graced the right bank of the Tiber. Theatres, too, had amenities attached to them that served a similar recreational purpose to that of a park. The *porticus* that stretched behind the theatres of Pompey and Balbus, though differing considerably in scale, afforded the audience opportunities to stroll in the shade during intermission, and provided a recreational space for city-dwellers whether the theatre was in use or not. Pompey's *porticus*, in particular, was a combination of a botanical garden and an art gallery, and constituted a major cultural amenity.[58] For the Theatre of Marcellus, its *scaenae frons* squashed against the bank of the Tiber, the porticoes of Octavia and Philippus across the street would have fulfilled the same function. Admittedly, if the association were felt to be necessary and appropriate, attempts could have been made to locate an amphitheatre near a pre-existing amenity of this type. But a cultural agenda comparable to that associated with theatres does not seem to have developed in association with the amphitheatre. And in any case the only place where a second, larger amphitheatre could have been constructed in Augustan Rome was the Campus Martius. Maybe Augustus questioned the wisdom of sequestering a large amount of space in Rome's cherished recreation ground for a structure that offered limited amenities and would, furthermore, be scheduled for infrequent use by comparison with a venue for staging *ludi scaenici*. And, besides, the magnificent complex of Augustan monuments focussing upon the Horologium should perhaps brook no competitors.

Fourth: funds. There is no knowing whether Augustus would have conceived of a project of the magnitude of the Colosseum, nor can we reliably reconstruct the amphitheatre of Taurus that he would have had to surpass. But in relative terms the Colosseum provides us with a model of what was deemed a suitable benefaction a century after Taurus' amphitheatre was built and some sixty years after the death of Augustus. How do Vespasian's circumstances compare with those of Augustus at different phases of his reign? Augustus' personal fortune, swollen by the spoils of Egypt, has been estimated at 1,000 million sesterces.[59] He spent part of it, at least, on public buildings. Significantly, the pattern of datable building projects at Rome during his reign shows a dramatic decline after 2BC: thirty-four projects or project clusters have been counted between Actium and 2BC, and only six in the rest of Augustus' lifetime.[60] In the two decades after

Actium Augustus had not restrained Taurus and his peers from dedicating their *manubiae* and other financial resources 'as an adornment to enhance the city forever' (note 18 above). But the Theatre of Balbus in 13BC was the last such enterprise. It is not that entertainment venues alone became too important to be associated with anyone other than the emperor; rather, it is that any public monument brought publicity that was perceived by the emperors to belong properly to the imperial house.[61] And yet in the second half of his reign Augustus' own sponsorship of building projects declined as well, perhaps because there was no source available that was comparable to the coffers of Egypt.[62] It seems eminently plausible that he should have wished to build an amphitheatre in the centre of Rome, but plausible also that such a project might have attracted odium from a people who were growing restless with a regime whose glamour had been eclipsed by shortages and taxation at home, and military and diplomatic setbacks abroad.[63] Augustus, consummate politician to the end, may have won respect precisely by denying himself the monument that would symbolise to posterity the ambiguities of Roman civilization.

Conclusion

The reign of Augustus bears witness to a sea-change in the sphere of euergetism, as in almost everything else. The example of Taurus' amphitheatre testifies to a co-operative spirit in which the sponsors of public spectacles could enjoy a productive symbiosis with those who provided the entertainment-buildings in which to stage them. Gradually these two roles would converge in the single person of the emperor, as he devised more extravagant spectacles and constructed more complex buildings to accommodate them. The age of Augustus reveals the amphitheatre as a building type that was not yet synonymous with the wealth and power of the supreme *euergetes* of the Roman world. And it also shows that euergetism – even the euergetism of the emperor – met restraints both symbolic and practical. The case of the amphitheatre in the city of Rome fits the model in which space was defined by custom as much as by pragmatism. Perhaps Augustus ultimately found it expedient to be lacking the practical resources that would translate a grand ambition into an appropriate monument.

Appendix: arena spectacles at Rome in the reign of Augustus, 31BC–AD14[64]

NB: The regular occurrence of *ludi sollemnes* is not noted below except for those specific occasions upon which 'arena-type' spectacles are known to have been performed. One documented instance of a display involving beasts is not included in this catalogue, since no date or occasion can be ascertained: the execution of the bandit Selouros from Sicily in the Forum (presumably the Forum Romanum) that was witnessed by Strabo.[65]

1. Occasion: inauguration of Aedes Divi Iulii
   Date: 18 August 29BC[66]
   Location: not specified[67]
   Sponsor: Octavian
   Programme: Lusus Troiae; *ludi circenses*; *uenatio*; *munus* (in pairs and *gregatim*)
   Source: Dio 51.22.4–6, 9: cf. Ville no. 48, 65
2. Occasion: inauguration of Taurus' amphitheatre
   Date: 29BC[68]
   Location: Taurus' amphitheatre
   Sponsor: T. Statilius Taurus
   Programme: *munus*
   Source: Dio 51.23.1: cf. Ville no. 49
3. Occasion: *ludi pro ualetudine Caesaris*[69]
   Date: 28BC
   Location: Circus Maximus (?), and custom-built stadium on Campus Martius[70]
   Sponsors: Octavian and Agrippa, i.e. consuls and *quindecimuiri*
   Programme: *ludi circenses*; gymnastic contest; *munus*
   Source: Dio 53.1.4–6: cf. Ville no. 50[71]
4. Occasion: in honour of Tiberius' father, Ti. Claudius Nero, died between 34 and 32BC
   Date: after 23 April 27BC[72]
   Location: Forum
   Sponsor: Tiberius
   Programme: *munus*
   Source: Suet. *Tib.* 7.1: cf. Ville no. 51
5. Occasion: in honor of Tiberius' grandfather Drusus, died 42BC
   Date: after 23 April 27BC
   Location: Taurus' amphitheatre
   Sponsor: Tiberius
   Programme: *munus*
   Source: Suet. *Tib.* 7.1: cf. Ville no. 52
6. Occasion: praetorian games (Ludi Apollinares?)[73]
   Date: 25BC

Location: Circus Maximus?[74]
Sponsor: P. Servilius, praetor
Programme: *uenatio* (300 bears and 300 *Africanae* killed)[75]
Source: Dio 53.27.6: cf. Ville no. 66

7. Occasion: aedilician games[76]
Date: 23BC
Location: uncertain[77]
Sponsor: M. Marcellus
Programme: *ludi scaenici* (and *munus*?)
Source: Prop. 3.18.11–20, Vell. Pat. 2.93.1, Dio 53.31.2–3: cf. Ville no. *53]

8. Occasion: Augustus' birthday[78]
Date: 23 (and 24?) September 20BC[79]
Location: Circus Maximus?[80]
Sponsors: aediles
Programme: *ludi circenses*; *uenatio*
Source: Dio 54.8.5: cf. Ville no. 67

9. Occasion and date: uncertain[81]
Location: Circus Maximus, and individual *uici*[82]
Sponsor: L. Domitius Ahenobarbus, grandfather of Nero
Programme: *uenationes*; *munus*
Source: Suet. *Nero* 4: cf. Ville no. 54, 68–69

10. Occasion: *ludi honorarii* at Ludi Saeculares
Date: 12 June 17BC
Location: Circus Maximus?[83]
Sponsors: *quindecimuiri*
Programme: *uenatio*; *pompa circensis*; *quadrigae*
Source: *CIL* vi.32323: cf. Ville no. 70

11. Occasion: dedication of Temple of Quirinus
Date: 29 June 16BC
Location: not specified[84]
Sponsors: Augustus, in name of Tiberius (praetor) and Drusus[85]
Programme: *munus*
Source: Dio 54.19.5: cf. Ville no. 55

12. Occasion: Augustus' birthday
Date: 23–24 September 13BC
Location: Circus Maximus (?), with a banquet on the Capitoline[86]
Sponsor: Antonius Iullus, praetor
Programme: *epulum*; *uenationes*; *ludi circenses*
Source: Dio 54.26.2: cf. Ville no. 71

13. Occasion: Quinquatrus[87]
Date: 20–23 March 12BC
Location: not specified
Sponsor: Augustus, in name of Gaius and Lucius

Programme: *munus*
Source: Dio 54.28.3: cf. Ville no. 56

14. Occasion: *munus* after the death of Agrippa[88]
Date: 12BC
Location: not specified[89]
Sponsor: Augustus
Programme: *munus*
Source: Dio 54.29.6: cf. Ville no. 57
15. Occasion: dedication of Theatre of Marcellus
Date: disputed[90]
Location: various, including Theatre of Marcellus[91]
Sponsor: Augustus
Programme: Lusus Troiae; *uenatio*; display of tiger
Source: Dio 54.26.1, Plin. *NH* 8.65 (tiger): cf. Ville no. 72
16. Occasion: Augustus' birthday
Date: 23–24 September 11BC
Location: Circus Maximus, and individual *uici*[92]
Sponsor: praetor
Programme: *ludi circenses*; *uenatio*
Source: Dio 54.34.1–2 : cf. Ville no. 73
17. Occasion: annual praetorian *munus*[93]
Date: 11BC
Location: not specified
Sponsors: 2 praetors chosen by lot
Programme: *munus*
Source: Dio 56.25.7–8: cf. Ville no. 62
18. Occasion: uncertain[94]
Date: 8BC
Location: unspecified
Sponsors: C. Asinius Gallus and C. Marcius Censorinus, consuls
Programme: *πανήγυρις*, including *munus* involving prisoners of war
Source: Dio 55.5.2, *ILS* 8894: cf. Ville no. 58
19. Occasion: to commemorate Agrippa
Date: 7BC
Location: Saepta Iulia[95]
Sponsor: Augustus[96]
Programme: *munus*, in pairs and *gregatim*
Source: Dio 55.8.5: cf. Ville no. 59
20. Occasion: dedication of Temple of Mars Ultor
Date: 1 August 2BC[97]
Location: Circus Maximus; Circus Flaminius; Saepta Iulia; Stagnum Augusti[98]
Sponsor: Augustus[99]
Programme: *ludi circenses*; Lusus Troiae; *uenationes*; *munus*; *naumachia*

Source: Dio 55.10.6–8, Vell. Pat. 2.100.2, Hieron. *ab Abr.* 2013: cf. Ville no. 60, 74, 75

21. Occasion: in honor of Drusus, father of Germanicus and Claudius, died 9BC
Date: AD6
Location: unspecified (*munus*); theatre (animal displays)
Sponsor(s): Augustus, or Germanicus and Claudius[100]
Programme: *munus*; performing animals[101]
Source: Dio 55.27.3, Suet. *Claud.* 2.2, Plin. *NH* 2.96, 8.4–5. Ael. *Nat. Anim.* 2.11: cf. Ville no. 61, 76
22. Occasion: Ludi Martiales
Date: 12 May AD12[102]
Location: Forum Augusti[103] (in lieu of Circus Maximus, temporarily flooded by the Tiber) and (after flooding subsided) Circus Maximus
Sponsor: Germanicus, consul[104]
Programme: *ludi circenses* and *uenatio* (200 lions)
Source: Dio 56.27.4–5: cf. Ville no. 77
23. Occasion, date, and location unknown[105]
Sponsor: Augustus
Programme: *uenatio* (420 *Africanae*)
Source: Plin. *NH* 8.64: cf. Ville no. 78

Acknowledgements

I am very grateful to Horst Blanck, Betsy Gebhard and Rabun Taylor for bibliographical assistance, and to Bettina Bergmann, Guy Chamberland, Barbara Kellum and William Slater for close reading, stimulating comments and generous guidance.

Notes

1 Welch (1994); Gros (1996: 318–23).
2 On the role of architecture in Augustus' legacy to Rome see Zanker (1988); Favro (1996); Walker (2000), with bibliography. On his treatment of public spectacle see Wiedemann (1992: *passim*, esp. 11, 60, 176); Edmondson (1996). The imprint of festivals upon the changing face of Augustan Rome is emphasised by Benoist (1999: 298–316).
3 Ville (1981: 98–9, 123).
4 For example, in 99BC by C. Claudius Pulcher, curule aedile (Plin. *NH* 8.19); in 93 by L. Sulla, *praetor urbanus* (Sen. *Breu. Vit.* 13.6); in 61 by L. Domitius Ahenobarbus, curule aedile (Plin. *NH* 8.36); and in 55 by Pompey as part of the celebrations at the dedication of his theatre (Plin. *NH* 8.53).
5 Plin. *NH* 36.116–20. For possible reconstructions see Golvin (1988: 31–2 and pl. IV).
6 Suet. *Iul.* 39.3; cf. Dio 43.23.3 and Ville (1981: 93–4).
7 Suet. *Iul.* 39.1 'munere in foro', Dio 43.23.3 *τοὺς δ' ἄνδρας συνέβαλλε μὲν καὶ ἕνα ἑνὶ ἐν τῇ ἀγορᾷ, ὥσπερ εἴθιστο, συνέβαλλε δὲ καὶ ἐν τῷ ἱπποδρόμῳ πλείους* ('As for the men, he not only pitted them against one another individually in the Forum, as was customary, but he also made them fight together in troupes in the Circus').
8 Ville (1981: 70); Golvin (1988: 48–9).
9 Welch (1994: 72–6).

10 Despite Golvin (1988: 48), the fact that the Forum Iulium was unfinished in 46BC does not preclude the possibility that games were staged there; indeed, it could strengthen the likelihood that there was space for them. The date at which Caesar installed the statue of his horse is unknown: cf. Suet. *Iul.* 61 'utebatur autem equo insigni … cuius etiam instar pro aede Veneris Genetricis postea dedicauit' ('He had a remarkable horse … Afterwards he dedicated a life-size statue of it in front of the Temple of Venus Genetrix'). Even if the Equus Caesaris was already *in situ* in 46BC, its position in the middle of the piazza would not have interfered with the erection of temporary stands around the perimeter, and it need not have prevented the staging of gladiatorial combat and *uenationes* around it; we have subsequent testimony that scenery might be erected in the arena, at least for the staging of *uenationes* (Calp. Sic. *Ecl.* 7.69–72, Suet. *Claud.* 34.2, Apul. *Met.* 4.13, 10.34.2). Similarly, the fountains formed by the statue-group known as the Appiades (*LTUR* i.59–60 s.v. Appiades [F. Coarelli]) were located immediately below the podium of the Temple of Venus Genetrix and thus did not encroach on the open space of the Forum. In any case they are likely to be Augustan, since they are first attested by Ovid, who mentions them three times (*Ars* 1.81–2, 3.451–2, *Rem.* 660): see Ulrich (1986: 419–21).

11 Carettoni (1956–8); Ville (1981: 380 n. 76).

12 For a detailed discussion of Caesar's *munus funebre* see Ville (1981: 68–71).

13 See Coarelli (2001: 43). A relief depicting a wooden amphitheatre, which is to be dated no later than the Augustan period, is preserved beneath the Cancelleria; hence Coarelli (2001: 47) suggests that it probably comes from a building on the Campus Martius and might depict Caesar's amphitheatre.

14 Perhaps on the site that Domitian was to use for his own Stadium more than one hundred years later, i.e. beneath Piazza Navona: see *LTUR* i.291 s.v. Codeta Minor (F. Coarelli).

15 The reading of Υ is defended at *LTUR* iii.338 s.v. Naumachia Caesaris (A. M. Liberati). *Contra*: Coleman (1993: 50); Coarelli (previous note).

16 For an overview of this impact see Benoist (1999: 276–98).

17 *RE* 2.iii.2199–203 s.v. Statilius 34 (Nagl).

18 The ancient sources do not say explicitly that Taurus' structure was a manubial building, though Tacitus' phrasing allows that inference to be drawn (*Ann.* 3.72.1): 'nec Augustus arcuerat Taurum, Philippum, Balbum hostiles exuuias aut exundantis opes ornatum ad urbis et posterum gloriam conferre' ('Augustus had not prevented Taurus, Philippus, and Balbus from employing enemy spoils or abundant resources as an adornment to enhance the city forever'). But Dio states that Taurus built the amphitheatre at his own expense (τοῖς ἑαυτοῦ τέλεσι), whereas *manubiae* are not the general's property but strictly spoils entrusted to him to use for the common good: see Churchill (1999: 100). By Dio's day, however, this distinction may have been a matter of strictly antiquarian interest that was lost on him; the fact that the Statilii Tauri remained responsible for the upkeep of the building is entirely consonant with the obligations inherited by a *triumphator*'s heirs: see Eck (1984: 141).

19 Dio 62.18.2: see Golvin (1988: 52–3).

20 *CIL* vi.6226–8 = *EAOR* i.38–40. A *uelarius* in the household of the Statilii (*CIL* vi.6258) may conceivably have been connected with the amphitheatre as well.

21 The consensus that Gros (1996: 323) ascribes to the site of the Palazzo Cenci has been challenged by its recent identification as the Temple of the Dioscuri: see *LTUR* i.37 s.v. Amphitheatrum Statilii Tauri (A. Viscogliosi). This temple, however, has in turn been identified further east: see Tucci (1994). It is both tantalising and suggestive that a cinerary urn inscribed with the names of two Statilii stands inside the sacristy of San Tommaso ai Cenci (not recorded in *CIL*): see Tucci (1996: 748 n. 11).

22 I can find no trace of the naval battle that Taurus' amphitheatre is alleged to have been unable to accommodate on the occasion of Agrippa's funerary celebration: see Golvin (1988: 53), with the phantom citation of Dio 55.7.

23 Neither of the *uenationes* attested between the death of Caesar and the battle of Actium is thought to have been given by Octavian. Both are recorded in the context of the Ludi Apollinares. C. Antonius presided over these Ludi in the absence of Brutus in July, 44BC: see Ville (1981: 106–8 no. 63). The Ludi Apollinares attributed to the year 41BC (for which the identity of the *praetor urbanus* is unknown) should perhaps be re-dated to 40BC and identified with the Ludi Apollinares conducted by Agrippa: see Ville (1981: 108).

24 Mommsen *ad loc.* Ovid's definition, 'theatrum utrimque structum' (*Met.* 11.25), is etymologically precise, since *ἀμφί* in compounds carries the root meaning 'on both sides' and the nominal element therefore retains the singular form: cf. *ἀμφίθυρος* = *ἀμφὶ αἱ θύραι*, 'with a door on both sides', and see Petersen (1986: 211–13).

25 Étienne (1965: 217–18). *Spectacula*, the regular word for 'seating' (Cic. *Mur.* 72, Liv. 1.35), was what Festus called the balconies used by spectators during gladiatorial displays in the Forum (120 L). It is also the term for the amphitheatre at Pompeii on the dedicatory inscription (*CIL* x.852 = *ILS* 5637), which is datable to 70 or 65BC (or conceivably earlier: see Welch [1994: 61]).

26 Drexel (1921: 209).

27 *IGRR* iv.845, 861.

28 L. Naevius Surdinus completed the paving during his praetorship, which is tentatively dated to 12 or 10 BC: *CIL* vi.1468, 31662, 37068 (= *AE* 1968, 24), Eck (1984: 136 and n. 59), Giuliani and Verduchi (1987: 93–4, with figs. 119 and 120).

29 There is no documented occasion on which the Saepta was used for the purpose for which it was designed. Apart from its use for spectacles, it housed a meeting of the Senate in 17BC (*CIL* vi.32323.50), and in 9BC Tiberius addressed the people there in the presence of the Senate on his return from Illyricum (Suet. *Tib.* 17.2). Later on it seems to have taken over the function of a shopping mall (Mart. 9.59.1–2, 10.80.4).

30 1,800 × 1,200 Roman feet (*RG* 23) = 536 × 357 m, approximately the size of a modern city block.

31 Taylor (1997: 482).

32 Coleman (1993: 54).

33 Dio 66.25.3. With respect both to Caesar's *stagnum* and to Augustus', the emphasis in the sources is on excavation rather than construction (Suet. *Iul.* 39.4 'defosso lacu', *RG* 23 'cauato solo'). Construction of some sort, however, must have been required, as is suggested by the diction describing the subsequent projects of Domitian and Philip the Arab (Suet. *Dom.* 4.1 'effosso et circumstructo … lacu', 5 'naumachiam, e cuius postea lapide maximus circus ... extructus est', Aur. Vict. *Caes.* 28.1 'exstructoque ... lacu'). Travertine blocks (some cut to a curve) and extensive fragments of mosaic have been found in Trastevere between S. Francesco a Ripa and S. Cosimato. These are believed to have delineated part of the edge of Augustus' *stagnum* itself and of the island in the middle (Dio 66.25.4): see Taylor (1997: 482).

34 Suet. *Cal.* 21: 'incohauit autem aquae ductum regione Tiburti et amphitheatrum iuxta Saepta, quorum operum a successore eius Claudio alterum peractum, omissum alterum est' ('He began an aqueduct in the vicinity of Tibur and an amphitheatre next door to the Saepta; of these works one was completed by his successor Claudius and the other abandoned'). See Golvin (1988: 54); *LTUR* i.35 s.v. Amphitheatrum Caligulae (D. Palombi). Because the Diribitorium was to the south, the complex of Agrippa's Pantheon and Baths to the west, and possibly the precursor of Domitian's restored Iseum and Serapeum to the east, Caligula's amphitheatre must have been located to the north of the Saepta. This location is supported by an inscription of Claudius recording repairs to arches of the Aqua Virgo that had been damaged by Caligula (*CIL* vi.1252); the portion of this aqueduct running north of the Saepta may have been adapted by Caligula to accommodate his amphitheatre: see Coarelli (2001: 45).

35 Plin. *NH* 16.200, 19.24, Tac. *Ann.* 13.31.1, Suet. *Nero* 12.1, Dio 61.9.5. If Calpurnius Siculus in *Eclogue* 7 is describing Nero's amphitheatre, he furnishes additional details of

its lavish decoration, and implies a site overlooking the Capitol, i.e. on the edge of the Campus Martius to the east of the Saepta (Calp. Sic. 7.24). See Golvin (1988: 55–6); *LTUR* 1.36 s.v. Amphitheatrum Neronis (D. Palombi).

36 Alföldy (1995) = *AE* 1995, 111b = *CIL* vi.40454a.

37 Jos. *BJ* 6.387–91, Stegemann (1994: 105).

38 Jos. *BJ* 5.550, 6.317 (repeated almost verbatim at Zon. 6.25): cf. Jos. *BJ* 7.15 (gold, silver and textiles awarded to soldiers of distinction).

39 Stegemann (1994: 104–8).

40 Beyer (1994: 224–33). Alföldy's total of 8,360 kg for the weight of silver recorded in the scroll is an underestimate (1995: 218 n. 53).

41 Quotation: Levick (1999: 97). Vespasian's financial measures: Levick (1999: 95–106).

42 DeLaine (1997: 222–3).

43 Duncan-Jones (1990: 175–7).

44 For sculptural details (chiefly column capitals and balustrades) see Pensabene (1988), and for stucco relief on the barrel vaults of the annular corridors see Paparatti (1988), with bibliography.

45 For the use of prisoners in construction projects and mines see Millar (1984). Of the Jews taken prisoner (even granted that Josephus' figure of 93,000 is inflated), some starved to death in detention; thousands were sent to the mines in Egypt or employed in the *uenationes* and re-enacted battles that Titus celebrated on his way home; and 700 were reserved for his triumph at Rome (*BJ* 6.417–19). I have been unable to trace the 'antica notizia' to which Cozzo ascribes the claim that 15,000 prisoners were taken to Rome to work on the construction of the amphitheatre (1928: 215). Detailed estimates for the manpower required to build the Colosseum are, alas, not yet available, although some valuable preliminaries were covered by Cozzo (1928: 203–51). Fortunately, however, very careful calculations have been done for the Baths of Caracalla. It is estimated that in AD213, when the project was most labour-intensive, a maximum workforce of 13,100 men was engaged on the building (DeLaine 1997: 193–7). Although the total footprint of the Baths (including the precinct) was larger than that of the Colosseum, they had a much lower elevation and therefore did not present comparable problems in, for example, the hoisting of materials or the manoeuvring of cranes on narrow terraces. So with the Colosseum we are probably dealing with a project of an even greater order of magnitude.

46 Mart. *Spect.* 2.5–6, 11–12: 'hic ubi conspicui uenerabilis Amphitheatri / erigitur moles, stagna Neronis erant. / … / reddita Roma sibi est et sunt te praeside, Caesar, / deliciae populi, quae fuerant domini' ('Here, where the awesome bulk of the Amphitheatre soars before our eyes, there used to be Nero's pools. … Rome has been restored to herself, and, with you at the helm, Caesar, what used to be the pleasure of a master is now the pleasure of the people').

47 Vitruv. *Arch.* 3.4.2, 5.12.5–6: see Rea (2001: 69).

48 Mocchegiani Carpano (1977); Rea (2001: 77).

49 DeLaine (1977: 191) has calculated that it would take upward of 40 yoke of oxen to move an average-sized entablature block (10 tonnes) for the Baths of Caracalla. For the risks involved in hauling heavy loads to construction-sites, including collapse of sections of the road surface and traffic congestion due to mechanical breakdown, see the vivid evocation in Korres (1995: 40).

50 DeLaine (1977: 131–2).

51 Cf. the chronological list compiled by Bourne (1946: 17–20).

52 Verzár-Bass (1995: figs. 1–17).

53 For the Statilii Tauri in Istria see Tassaux (1984: 211–13), for the amphitheatre at Pola Verzár-Bass (1995: 105).

54 See the penetrating assessment by Crook (1996b).

55 Gros (1996: 319–20).

56 For a summary of senatorial opposition to the construction of a permanent theatre, and Pompey's expedient of styling his theatre an approach to the Temple of Venus Victrix, see Coleman (2000: 220–1).
57 Le Glay (1990).
58 Kuttner (1999).
59 Shatzman (1975: 357–71 no. 153), emphasising the Egyptian contribution.
60 Bourne (1946: 17–20).
61 After the reign of Tiberius, the emperor alone was credited with the construction or renovation of all public buildings: see Eck (1984: 136).
62 Bourne (1946: 16).
63 Crook (1996a: 102–12).
64 For a summary of the locations attested in the reign of Augustus see Ville (1981: 380–4). My tabulation is indebted to the catalogue of *munera* and *uenationes* in his book.
65 Strabo 6.273: see Coleman (1990: 53). Note that it is rash to assume that, just because this event took place in the Forum, it must have pre-dated the construction of Taurus' amphitheatre.
66 *Inscr. It.* xiii.2.497.
67 The Aedes Divi Iulii was located in the Forum, at the east end opposite the Regia, on the site of Julius Caesar's funeral pyre. The physical location, and the association with a funerary context, makes it doubly likely that those parts of the *munus* involving single combat, at least, were held in the Forum. *Circenses* were regularly held in the Circus Maximus. The *Lusus Troiae*, requiring space for equestrian manoeuvres, was presumably held there too, and perhaps also the displays of massed gladiators. Cf. Julius Caesar's massed battle in 46BC, which formed the climax to a series of *uenationes* and involved 1,000 infantry. For this event the turning-posts in the Circus were removed, *quo laxius dimicaretur* (Suet. *Iul.* 39.3); Dio specifically distinguishes between Caesar's display of individual pairs in the Forum, as was customary, and his use of the Circus as a venue for combat *gregatim* (43.23.3). A small *uenatio* could have been held in the Forum, availing of the sub-structures installed for that purpose; the Circus would have accommodated a *uenatio* on a larger scale, such as is implied on this occasion: cf. Dio 51.22.5 *καὶ θηρία καὶ βοτὰ ἄλλα τε παμπληθῆ ... ἐσφάγη* ('Animals both wild and tame were slaughtered in huge numbers'). If Taurus' amphitheatre had already been dedicated by 18 August (cf. Appendix item 2), one of the *uenationes* could conceivably have been held there (cf. *RG* 22.3).
68 The inauguration must have taken place either very early or very late in the year, since Taurus was fighting in Spain during the campaigning season (Dio 51.20.5).
69 For careful discussion of the problematic series of games *pro ualetudine* (or *salute*) *Caesaris* see *Diz. Epigr.* iv.2018 s.v. Ludi (L. Polverini); Cavallaro (1984: 154–60); Caldelli (1993: 21–4); Gurval (1998: 120–3). In 30 BC the Senate decreed that vows were to be undertaken every four years by the consuls and priests for the health of Octavian (*RG* 9.1: cf. Dio 51.19.2). These vows were usually accompanied by *ludi* presided over in turn by the four chief colleges of priests (*pontifices*, augurs, *septemuiri* and *quindecimuiri*) or by the consuls (*RG* 9.1, Dio 53.1.5). In 28BC the presidents were Octavian and Agrippa, who were the consuls for that year but also *quindecimuiri*, as noted by Cavallaro (1984: 156 and 157 n. 29). These games are perhaps to be identified with the *ludi pontificales* of 24BC (Suet. *Aug.* 44.3). In 20BC the presidents were augurs (*CIL* vi.877a.4), in 16BC *quindecimuiri* (Dio 54.19.8). The games of 28BC are the only occasion on which the basic programme of *circenses* is known to have included a *munus* (Dio 53.1.5, cited in next note); hence the subsequent celebrations down to 16BC, whether hypothetical or certain, are not included in the Appendix here. Although Dio mentions the celebration of 28BC immediately after he has described the dedication of the temple of Palatine Apollo, there is no certainty that the games were part of the dedicatory festival. Nevertheless, *ludi* are frequently associated with the dedication of temples, and Apollo's

association with healing would make the connection with *ludi pro ualetudine* appropriate: see Gurval (1998: 122).

70 Dio does not say where the *ludi circenses* were staged, but presumably it was the usual venue of the Circus Maximus. For the gymnastic contest he specifies the construction of a wooden stadium on the Campus Martius, and immediately thereafter reports the staging of the *munus* (53.1.5): *τότε δὲ καὶ γυμνικὸς ἀγὼν σταδίου τινὸς ἐν τῷ ᾿Αρείῳ πεδίῳ ξυλίνου κατασκευασθέντος ἐποιήθη, ὁπλομαχία τε ἐκ τῶν αἰχμαλώτων ἐγένετο* ('Then an athletic contest was held, a wooden stadium having been constructed on the Campus Martius, and there was a gladiatorial combat between captives'). It is plausible to infer that the *munus* took place in the stadium as well. At least three stadia in the Greek East that were constructed around the turn of the era (at Laodicea [note 27 above], Aphrodisias, and Nicopolis) were designed to accommodate both athletics and gladiatorial combat: see Welch (1998: 563).

71 Ville (1981: 100 no. 50) connects these games with those vowed at Actium, but fails to identify them with the *ludi pro ualetudine Caesaris*; he therefore assumes that they were sponsored exclusively by Octavian, and that Agrippa only became involved when he was co-opted to preside over them while Octavian was ill (Dio 53.1.6).

72 But not simultaneously with Appendix item 5 above: cf. Suet. *Tib.* 7.1 'diuersis temporibus'.

73 Servilius may have been *praetor urbanus*: see Ville (1981: 109). The occasion (*πανήγυρις*: Dio 53.27.6) was presumably the Ludi Apollinares, which at this stage were the only *ludi* under praetorian control. Three years later, in 22BC, responsibility for the five *ludi* that had previously been entrusted to the aediles was transferred to the praetors, i.e. the Megalenses, Ceriales, Florales, Romani, and Plebeii (Dio 54.2.3–4): see Ville (1981: 120), Rich (1990: 173).

74 The Ludi Apollinares were traditionally associated with the Circus Maximus: cf. Liv. 25.12.14 (212BC), 30.38.10–12 (202BC).

75 For a *uenatio* on this scale the Circus Maximus would be the most likely venue.

76 It is uncertain precisely which games Marcellus sponsored. Curule aediles gave the Ludi Megalenses (4–10 April) and the Ludi Romani, also known as Ludi Magni (4–19 September, by which time Marcellus may already have died). They may also have given the Ludi Florales (28 April–3 May).

77 The uncertainty over the location is closely tied to uncertainty over the nature of the event. Dio specifically locates it in the Forum, on the grounds that Marcellus had erected awnings there throughout the summer for the comfort of the spectators (53.31.2–3): *καὶ τὴν ἑορτὴν ἣν ἐκ τῆς ἀγορανομίας ἐπετέλει συνδιαθεὶς λαμπρῶς, ὥστε τήν τε ἀγορὰν ἐν παντὶ τῷ θέρει παραπετάσμασι κατὰ κορυφὴν διαλαβεῖν* ('He collaborated with him brilliantly at the festival that he held as aedile, sheltering the Forum all summer long with awnings stretched overhead'). But Pliny specifies that this was done for the sake of people involved in litigation (*NH* 19.24): 'deinde et sine ludis Marcellus ... a kal. Aug. uelis forum inumbrauit, ut salubrius litigantes consisterent' ('At that stage, and in the absence of any games, from the first of August Marcellus shaded the Forum with awnings, so that litigants could stay there more comfortably'). Pliny's phrase *et sine ludis* could perhaps admit the interpretation that the awnings were there for the sake of *ludi* as well; but the context clearly undermines the reliability of Dio's testimony. If he is using *theatrum* in the narrow sense, the evidence of Propertius is unambiguous, locating the event in the theatre (3.18.13): 'aut modo tam pleno fluitantia uela theatro' ('awnings fluttering in the packed theatre'). Velleius Paterculus, however, describes this occasion as a *munus* (2.93.1): 'magnificentissimo munere aedilitatis edito decessit admodum iuuenis' ('Having given a most magnificent gladiatorial show during his tenure as aedile, he died while he was still a young man'). But since both Propertius and Dio specify only *scaenici*, Ville (1981: 101) suggests that Velleius' use of *munus* here harks back to its original meaning

of 'spectacle' in general rather than 'gladiatorial spectacle' in particular; for the evolution of this term see Ville (1981: 72–8). Hence I have enclosed this entry in square brackets to indicate that it may not qualify for inclusion as an 'arena-type' spectacle at all.

78 Rich (1990: 183) suggests that in holding games on Augustus' birthday the aediles may have been responding to his measure of 22BC, whereby responsibility for holding games was transferred from the aediles to the praetors (Dio 54.2.3). Later the praetors regularly celebrated Augustus' birthday with games: Dio 54.26.2 (= Appendix item 12), 54.34.1–2 (= Appendix item 16). In AD14 responsibility for these games was transferred to the consuls: Dio 56.46.4.

79 It is uncertain when the notorious 'double' celebration of Augustus' birthday on two successive days started (i.e. 23 September, which was his actual birthday, and 24 September as well). It is first securely attested in an inscription from Narbonne from AD12 or AD13 (*CIL* xii.4333 = *ILS* 112): see König (1972: 8). The origins of this practice are most plausibly attributed to a spontaneous gesture by the Equites (Suet. *Aug.* 57.1), perhaps exploiting the confusion arising from alternative ways of expressing the date in pre- and post-Julian terminology after Caesar's calendar reform: see Suerbaum (1980: 335).

80 Dio 54.8.5 *ἰδίᾳ δὲ δὴ οἱ ἀγορανόμοι ἱπποδρομίαν τε ἐν τοῖς τοῦ Αὐγούστου γενεθλίοις καὶ θηρίων σφαγὰς ἐποίησαν* ('On their own initiative the aediles sponsored races and a *uenatio* on Augustus' birthday').

81 As praetor (19BC) and consul (16BC) Domitius put on *scaenici*, but his *munus* and *uenationes* need not have been associated with either of these magistracies. Ville (1981: 101) suggests that the date of 19 BC for the *munus* can be excluded, on the grounds that a single praetor is unlikely to have been simultaneously responsible for *scaenici* and *munera*.

82 Suet. *Nero* 4 'uenationes et in circo et in omnibus urbis regionibus dedit, munus etiam gladiatorium' ('He gave beast-hunts in the Circus and in all the districts of the city, and a gladiatorial show'). It is hard to envisage *uenationes* 'in all the districts of the city', since secure facilities were lacking: cf. Appendix item 16.

83 These three events, forming the closing sequence of the Ludi Saeculares, may have taken place in the same venue. The *quadrigae* at least must have raced in the Circus Maximus.

84 The exact location of the temple of Quirinus on the Quirinal is still uncertain: see *LTUR* iv.185–7 s.v. Quirinus, Aedes (F. Coarelli). Before theatres began to be constructed at Rome, the relevant temple precinct had been the traditional location for *ludi scaenici* connected with individual deities. It is not inconceivable that a token *munus* could have been performed in the temple-precinct on this occasion, but it seems more likely that these dedicatory games were performed in the Forum, where a large audience was traditionally accommodated. Pragmatism allows that dedicatory games need not be celebrated exclusively at the location being dedicated; at the inauguration of the Colosseum (AD80), aquatic spectacles were divided between the Colosseum itself and the *stagnum Augusti*, according to the scale required: see Coleman (1993: 60–8). For spectacles at multiple venues to celebrate the dedication of a single building cf. Appendix items 1, 15, 20.

85 Cf. Dio 54.19.5 *μονομαχίας ἀγῶνας διά τε τοῦ Τιβερίου καὶ διὰ τοῦ Δρούσου ... ἔθηκε* ('He put on gladiatorial contests through the agency of Tiberius and Drusus').

86 Dio specifies that an *epulum* was given on the Capitoline, and his juxtaposition of *circenses* and *uenationes* allows the inference that they were held in the Circus Maximus, which would be the obvious venue (54.26.2): *τά τε γενέθλια τοῦ Αὐγούστου ... καὶ ἱπποδρομίᾳ καὶ σφαγαῖς ἑώρτασε, καὶ ἐν τῷ Καπιτωλίῳ καὶ ἐκεῖνον καὶ τὴν βουλὴν ... εἱστίασεν* ('He celebrated Augustus' birthday with a circus race and beast hunts, and entertained both him and the Senate on the Capitol').

87 Rich (1980) suggests that this gladiatorial display may have been intended to celebrate Augustus' appointment as *pontifex maximus* on 6 March (*RG* 10.2, Ov. *F.* 3.415–28).

88 Dio reports this occasion in the chapter in which he sums up the significance of Agrippa's death. Hence this *munus* has traditionally been interpreted as the first of two funerary celebrations, the second following in 7BC (Appendix item 19): see Ville (1981: 102–3).

But Dio's report of the event in 12BC alleges that leading men wanted to boycott it (54.29.6): *οὐ μέντοι οὔτε τοῖς ἄλλοις ἐκλιπεῖν τι τῶν πατρίων, καίπερ μηδενὸς τῶν πρώτων ἐς τὰς πανηγύρεις ἀπαντῆσαι ἐθέλοντος, ἐπέτρεψε, καὶ αὐτὸς τὰς μονομαχίας διετέλεσε· πολλάκις τε καὶ ἀπόντος αὐτοῦ ἐποιοῦντο* ('However, he did not allow the rest of them to omit any of the traditional observances, even though none of the leading citizens wanted to attend the games, and he supervised the gladiatorial combats himself; actually, they often took place during his absence'). Such an allegation, however, is in stark contrast to Dio's adulatory treatment of Agrippa, and a public manifestation of dislike for Augustus' late-lamented colleague is unthinkable under the circumstances. Hence a transposition or lacuna was suspected as early as 1865, though no alternative occasion for the *munus* was canvassed (see Ville 1981: 102). Rich (1980: 219) has further objected that the repetition of the funerary *munus* is unprecedented, and suggests that the *munus* immediately after Agrippa's death was not funerary but a resumption of the gladiatorial display that Augustus had been holding at the Quinquatrus when he departed in a hurry for Agrippa's bedside (Appendix item 12). Although Dio does not say that the *munus* on that occasion was suspended, this is a plausible inference: see Rich (1980: 220). Hence Rich conjectures that Augustus resumed this *munus* in the context of one of the regular *ludi* held in April, i.e. the Megalenses, Cereales, or Florales. Since the praetors were normally responsible for the celebrations at the Quinquatrus, Augustus was not obliged to resume the presidency after their interruption, hence Dio's concluding remark (quoted above). The spectators' unwillingness to attend the regular games would thus be a sign of their respect for Agrippa, not the opposite; and Augustus would be showing him respect in a different way, by insisting that the observances that had been interrupted at his death should be completed all the same.

89 Ville (1981: 117) interprets the phrase *τι τῶν πατρίων* to mean that, in accordance with Republican tradition, this *munus* was performed at Agrippa's graveside. This interpretation is predicated on the assumption that it was a funerary celebration: see previous note.

90 Pliny's date (4 May 13BC) is contradicted by Dio (11BC). Ville (1981: 110) notes that if Pliny preserves the correct month, Dio's year must be a mistake, since in May 13BC Augustus was still in the East.

91 Dio mentions the *lusus Troiae* and the *uenatio*, but does not specify the venue for either. The *uenatio* was probably held in the Circus Maximus (cf. note 67 above), though the Forum and Taurus' amphitheatre are also possibilities (cf. *RG* 22.3). The Lusus Troiae was presumably held either in the Circus Maximus or in the Circus Flaminius, which was adjacent to the Theatre of Marcellus. Despite an ambiguous phrase in the record, the tiger seems to have been exhibited in the theatre itself (Plin. *NH* 8.65): 'theatri Marcelli dedicatione tigrim primus omnium Romae ostendit in cauea mansuefactam' ('At the dedication of the Theatre of Marcellus he was the first person at Rome to exhibit a tame tiger in a cage/in the auditorium').

92 Dio 54.34.1 *καὶ ἐν τῷ ἱπποδρόμῳ καὶ ἐν τῇ ἄλλῃ πόλει πολλαχόθι* ('in the Circus and in a number of places in the rest of the city'): cf. Appendix item 9 above.

93 Ville (1981: 119–21) identifies this annual praetorian *munus* with the *munus* at the Quinquatrus, over which Augustus presided in lieu of the praetors in 12BC (cf. Appendix item 13 above).

94 Dio associates this *munus* with the return of Augustus early in 8BC from the German campaign in which Drusus had been killed on 14 September 9BC. Games in fulfilment of a vow for Augustus' safe return were also celebrated by the consuls of 13BC, Tiberius and Varus (Dio 54.27.1, *ILS* 88) and by those of 7BC, Tiberius and Piso, the former represented by Gaius (Dio 55.8.3, *ILS* 95). On the latter occasions Dio refers to the games as *πανήγυρις*; in the epigraphic testimony all three events are called *ludi uotiui*. Dio makes it clear that the inclusion of a *munus* was supernumerary to the events that were normally celebrated on such an occasion, and implies that the *munus* was in lieu of the triumph that Augustus had refused out of mourning for Drusus (55.5.2): *καὶ αὐτὸς μὲν οὐδεμίαν ἐπὶ τούτοις ἑορτὴν ἤγαγε, πολὺ πλεῖον ἐν τῷ τοῦ Δρούσου ὀλέθρῳ ἐξημιῶσθαι*

ἢ ἐν ταῖς νίκαις ὠφελῆσθαι νομίζων· οἱ δὲ δὴ ὕπατοι τά τε ἄλλα ὅσα ἐπὶ τοῖς τοιούτοις γίγνεται ἐποίησαν, καὶ ἐκ τῶν αἰχμαλώτων τινὰς ἀλλήλοις συνέβαλον ('He did not perform any celebration in honour of these achievements, thinking that he had lost much more in the death of Drusus than he had gained in his victories, but the consuls performed the ceremonies that customarily happen on those occasions, and they pitted some of the captives against one another'). Ville (1981: 103) notes that Augustus never celebrated a formal triumph with a *munus*, and suggests that the *munus* on this occasion honoured Drusus, whose funeral had been celebrated at the end of 9BC. A *munus* at the graveside (cf. Appendix item 14) involving prisoners of war would conform to traditional Republican funerary practice: see Ville (1981: 118).

95 The Forum had been damaged by fire, and the Saepta, as one of Agrippa's own buildings, was deemed an appropriate substitute (Dio 55.8.5): ἐν τοῖς σέπτοις διά τε τὴν ἐς τὸν Ἀγρίππαν τιμὴν καὶ διὰ τὸ πολλὰ τῶν περὶ τὴν ἀγορὰν οἰκοδομημάτων κεκαῦσθαι ('in the Saepta to honour Agrippa and because many of the buildings around the Forum had burnt down').

96 Ville (1981: 104) notes that as Augustus had already sponsored three *munera* in his own name (*RG* 22.1: Appendix items 1, 3, 14), this one must have been in the name of Gaius and Lucius.

97 These games must be distinguished from the Ludi Martiales that were inaugurated at the opening of the Forum Augusti two and a half months earlier on 12 May (cf. Appendix item 22). For the scholarly controversy, and the distinction between the inauguration of the Forum (when the temple was not yet complete) and the dedication of the temple (when it was finally ready), see Hannah (1998: 431–2) and note 103 below. To Hannah's discussion add Herz (1996: 278), defending the date of 12 May for the dedication of the temple of Mars Ultor on the grounds that 1 August could be the date on which the Forum Augusti was opened to the public in the previous year (3BC).

98 Dio specifies the venues: a *uenatio* in which 260 lions were dispatched took place in the Circus Maximus (55.10.7), which was also presumably the location of the *ludi circenses* and the *Lusus Troiae*; water was let into the Circus Flaminius for a *uenatio* in which 36 crocodiles were despatched (55.10.8); the *munus* was held in the Saepta Iulia, and the *naumachia* in the Stagnum Augusti (55.10.7).

99 Augustus gave the *naumachia* in his own name (*RG* 23), and the *circenses* (perhaps including the *uenationes*) in the name of Gaius and Lucius (Dio 55.10.6). Ville (1981: 104) deduces that the *munus* was also in the name of Gaius and Lucius: cf. Appendix item 19.

100 Suetonius ascribes sponsorship to Germanicus and Claudius, Pliny to Germanicus alone. Either this event was sponsored by Augustus in the name of Germanicus and Claudius, or it was financed by him but formally sponsored by Germanicus and Claudius: see Ville (1981: 105–6).

101 Pliny and Aelian mention only animals performing tricks, not animals being hunted; if this display included a *uenatio*, it would be the first time a *munus* and *uenatio* are known to have been combined: see Ville (1981: 112).

102 In choosing between the date of 12 May and 1 August for the Ludi Martiales, Ville (1981: 114–15) notes that – at least in the modern era – the Tiber is very unlikely to flood in August.

103 The displacement of the *ludi* as a result of this chain of natural disasters was a grim portent (Crook 1996a: 110), hence – no doubt – the anxiety to complete them in the proper venue (Dio 56.27.4–5): τά τε Ἄρεια τότε μέν, ἐπειδὴ ὁ Τίβερις τὸν ἱππόδρομον προκατέσχεν, ἐν τῇ τοῦ Αὐγούστου ἀγορᾷ καὶ ἵππων δρόμῳ τρόπον τινὰ καὶ θηρίων σφαγῇ ἐτιμήθη, αὖθις δὲ ὥσπερ εἴθιστο ἐγένετο, καὶ λέοντάς γε ἐς αὐτὰ ἐν τῷ ἱπποδρόμῳ διακοσίους ὁ Γερμανικὸς ἀπέκτεινεν ('Because the Tiber had overflowed the Circus, this time the Ludi Martiales were held in the Forum of Augustus and celebrated after a fashion by a

horse race and the slaughter of wild beasts. They were repeated in accordance with custom, and on this occasion Germanicus had two hundred lions slaughtered in the Circus'). Although Dio appears to distinguish between a *uenatio* in the Forum Augusti and another in the Circus Maximus involving 200 lions, it is perhaps more likely that the *uenatio* was suspended altogether until the games could be returned to the Circus, which was far more suitably equipped for *uenationes* than the Forum Augusti. Since the Forum Augusti is a restricting venue for *circenses*, Hannah (1997: 528) notes that there must have been a special link between this Forum and the Ludi Martiales that would qualify it to be used as an alternative venue. He adduces astronomical evidence to support the view that the Forum and the Ludi were inaugurated together on 12 May 2BC on the eve of Gaius' campaign in the East to commemorate the recovery of the standards from the Parthians on 12 May 20BC. One might note also the appropriateness of staging Ludi Martiales in front of the Temple of Mars Ultor, where the god could effectively preside over games in his own honour.

104 Since these *ludi* were the joint responsibility of the consuls (*CIL* vi.37836 = *ILS* 9349, *RG* 22.2), Germanicus may have co-sponsored them with his consular colleague, C. Capito; but in the second celebration the *uenatio* was held by Germanicus alone (Dio 56.27.5, quoted in the previous note). Ville (1981: 114) suggests that Augustus might have funded him.

105 The scale of this event (420 *Africanae* slaughtered) suggests that it took place in the Circus Maximus: cf. Appendix item 20.

References

Alföldy, G. (1995) 'Eine Bauinschrift aus dem Colosseum', *ZPE* 109: 195–226.

Benoist, S. (1999) *La Fête à Rome au premier siècle de l'Empire. Recherches sur l'univers festif sous les règnes d'Auguste et des Julio-Claudiens*, Brussels: Latomus.

Beyer, K. (1994) *Die aramäischen Texte vom Toten Meer samt den Inschriften aus Palästina, dem Testament Levis aus der Kairoer Genisa, der Fastenrolle und den alten talmudischen Zitaten*, Göttingen: Vandenhoeck & Ruprecht.

Bourne, F. C. (1946) *The Public Works of the Julio-Claudians and Flavians*, Princeton: Princeton University Press.

Brunt, P.A. and Moore, J.M. (eds) (1967) *Res Gestae Divi Augusti. The Achievements of the Divine Augustus*, Oxford: Oxford University Press.

Caldelli, M.L. (1993) *L'Agon Capitolinus. Storia e protagonisti dall'istituzione Domizianea al IV secolo*, Rome: Istituto Italiano per la Storia Antica.

Carettoni, G.F. (1956–8) 'Le gallerie ipogee del Foro Romano e i ludi gladiatori forensi', *BullCom* 76: 23–44.

Cavallaro, M.A. (1984) *Spese e spettacoli. Aspetti economici-strutturali degli spettacoli nella Roma giulio-claudia*, Bonn: Dr. Rudolf Habelt GmbH.

Churchill, J.B. (1999) '*Ex ea quod vellent facerent*: Roman magistrates' authority over *praeda* and *manubiae*', *TAPhA* 129: 85–116.

Coarelli, F. (2001) 'Gli anfiteatri a Roma prima del Colosseo'. In A. La Regina (ed.), *Sangue e Arena*, Rome: Ministero per i Beni e le Attività Culturali.

Coleman, K.M. (1990) 'Fatal charades: Roman executions staged as mythological enactments', *JRS* 80: 44–73.

Coleman, K.M. (1993) 'Launching into history: aquatic displays in the early Empire', *JRS* 83: 48–74.

Coleman, K. (2000) 'Entertaining Rome'. In J. Coulston and H. Dodge (eds), *Ancient Rome: The Archaeology of the Eternal City*, Oxford: Oxford University School of Archaeology.

Cozzo, G. (1928) *Ingegneria Romana*, Rome: Libreria Editrice Mantegazza di Paolo Cremonese.

Crook, J.A. (1996a) 'Political history, 30BC to AD14', *CAH*[2] 10: 70–112.

Crook, J.A. (1996b) 'Augustus: power, authority, achievement', *CAH*[2] 10: 113–46.

DeLaine, J. (1997) *The Baths of Caracalla: A Study in the Design, Construction, and Economics of Large-scale Building Projects in Imperial Rome*, Portsmouth, RI: Journal of Roman Archaeology (= suppl. series, 25).

Drexel, F. (1921) 'Gebäude für die öffentlichen Schauspiele in Italien und den Provinzen'. Appendix XVI in L. Friedländer (ed.), *Darstellung aus der Sittengeschichte Roms in der Zeit von August bis zum Ausgang der Antonine*, [9/10] Vol. 4, Leipzig: Verlag von S. Hirzel.

Duncan-Jones, R. (1990) *Structure and Scale in the Roman Economy*, Cambridge: Cambridge University Press.

Eck. W. (1984) 'Senatorial self-representation: developments in the Augustan period'. In F. Millar and E. Segal (eds), *Caesar Augustus: Seven Aspects*, Oxford: Clarendon Press.

Edmondson, J.C. (1996) 'Dynamic arenas: gladiatorial presentations in the city of Rome and the construction of Roman society during the early Empire'. In W.J. Slater (ed.), *Roman Theater and Society*, E. Togo Salmon Papers I, Ann Arbor: University of Michigan Press.

Étienne, R. (1965) 'La naissance de l'amphithéâtre: le mot et la chose', *REL* 43: 213–20.

Favro, D. (1996) *The Urban Image of Augustan Rome*, New York: Cambridge University Press.

Giuliani, C.F. and Verduchi, P. (1987) *L'area centrale del Foro Romano*, Florence: Leo S. Olschki Editore.

Golvin, J.-C. (1988) *L'Amphithéâtre romain*, Paris: Diffusion de Boccard.

Gros, P. (1996) *L'Architecture romaine du début du IIIe siècle av. J.-C. à la fin du Haut-Empire.* Vol. 1 *Les monuments publics*, Paris: Picard.

Gurval, R.A. (1998) *Actium and Augustus. The Politics and Emotions of Civil War*, Ann Arbor: University of Michigan Press.

Hannah, R. (1997) 'The Temple of Mars Ultor and 12 May', *MDAI(R)* 104: 527–35.

Hannah, R. (1998) 'Games for Mars and the Temples of Mars Ultor', *Klio* 80: 422–33.

Herz, P. (1996) 'Zum Tempel des Mars Ultor'. In J. Ganzert (ed.), *Der Mars-Ultor-Tempel auf dem Augustusforum in Rom*, Mainz am Rhein: Verlag Philipp von Zabern.

König, I. (1972) 'Der doppelte Geburtstag des Augustus', *Epigraphica* 34: 3–15.

Korres, M. (1995) *From Pentelicon to the Parthenon. The ancient quarries and the story of a half-worked column capital of the first marble Parthenon*, trans. D. Turner and W. Phelps, Athens: Melissa.

Kuttner, A.L. (1999) 'Culture and history at Pompey's museum', *TAPhA* 129: 343–73.

Le Glay, M. (1990) 'Les amphithéâtres: *loci religiosi*?'. In C. Domergue, C. Landes and J.-M. Pailler (eds), *Spectacula – I. Gladiateurs et amphithéâtres. Actes du colloque tenu à Toulouse et à Lattes les 26, 27, 28 et 29 mai 1987*, Lattes: Editions Imago.

Levick, B. (1999) *Vespasian*, London and New York: Routledge.

Millar, F. (1984) 'Condemnation to hard labour in the Roman empire, from the Julio-Claudians to Constantine', *PBSR* 51: 124–47.

Mocchegiani Carpano, C. (1977) 'Nuovi dati sulle fondazioni dell'Anfiteatro Flavio', *Antiqua* 7: 10–16.

Paparatti, E. (1988) 'Osservazioni sugli stucchi'. In A.M. Reggiani (ed.), *Anfiteatro Flavio. Immagine Testimonianze Spettacoli*, Rome: Edizioni Quasar.

Pensabene, P. (1988) 'Elementi architettonici in marmo'. In A.M. Reggiani (ed.), *Anfiteatro Flavio. Immagine Testimonianze Spettacoli*, Rome: Edizioni Quasar.

Petersen, H. (1986) 'Wörter zusammengesetzt mit ΑΜΦΙ', *Glotta* 64: 193–213.

Rea, R. (2001) 'L'anfiteatro di Roma: note strutturali e di funzionamento'. In A. La Regina (ed.), *Sangue e Arena*, Rome: Ministero per i Beni e le Attività Culturali.

Rich, J.W. (1980) 'Agrippa and the nobles: a note on Dio 54.29.6', *LCM* 5: 217–21.

Rich, J.W. (ed.) (1990) *Cassius Dio: The Augustan Settlement* (*Roman History 53–55.9*), Warminster: Aris & Phillips Ltd.

Shatzman, I. (1975) *Senatorial Wealth and Roman Politics*, Brussels: Latomus.

Stegemann, H. (1994) *Die Essener, Qumran, Johannes der Täufer und Jesus*[4], Freiburg–Basel–Vienna: Herder.

Suerbaum, W. (1980) 'Merkwürdige Geburtstage. Der nichtexistierende Geburtstag des M. Antonius, der doppelte Geburtstag des Augustus, der neue Geburtstag der Livia und der vorzeitige Geburtstag des älteren Drusus', *Chiron* 10: 327–55.

Tassaux, F. (1984) 'L'implantation territoriale des grandes familles d'Istrie sous le Haut-Empire romain', *Problemi storici ed archeologici dell'Italia nordorientale e delle regioni limitrofe dalla preistoria al medioevo, Incontro di studio, Trieste 28–30 ottobre 1982 = Quaderni dei Civici Musei Storia ed Arte di Trieste* 13(2): 193–229. Trieste: Civici Musei Storia ed Arte.

Taylor, R. (1997) 'Torrent or trickle? The Aqua Alsietina, the Naumachia Augusti, and the Transtiberim', *AJA* 101: 465–92.

Tucci, P.L. (1994) 'Il tempio dei Castori in Circo Flaminio: la lastra di Via Anicia'. In L. Nista (ed.), *Castores. L'immagine dei Dioscuri a Roma*, Rome: De Luca.

Tucci, P.L. (1996) 'L'entrata di un magazzino romano sotto la chiesa di San Tommaso ai Cenci', *MEFRA* 108: 747–70.

Ulrich, R.B. (1986) 'The Appiades fountain of the Forum Iulium', *MDAI(R)* 93: 405–23.

Verzár-Bass, M. (1995) 'A proposito della posizione extraurbana dei teatri romani: il caso cisalpino'. In G. Cavalieri Manasse and E. Roffia (eds), *Splendida Civitas Nostra. Studi archeologici in onore di Antonio Frova*, Rome: Quasar.

Ville, G. (1981) *La Gladiature en Occident des origines à la mort de Domitien*, Rome: École Française de Rome.

Walker, S. (2000) 'The moral museum: Augustus and the city of Rome'. In J. Coulston and H. Dodge (eds), *Ancient Rome: The Archaeology of the Eternal City*, Oxford: Oxford University School of Archaeology.

Welch, K. (1994) 'The Roman arena in late-Republican Italy: a new interpretation', *JRA* 5: 59–80.

Welch, K. (1998) 'The stadium at Aphrodisias', *AJA* 102: 547–69.

Wiedemann, T. (1992) *Emperors and Gladiators*, London: Routledge.

Zanker, P. (1988) *The Power of Images in the Age of Augustus*, trans. A. Shapiro, Ann Arbor: University of Michigan Press.

5

THE EMPEROR AND THE CITIES OF ITALY

John R. Patterson

Providing 'bread and circuses' (Juv. *Sat.* 10.77–81) for the inhabitants of Rome was a major concern of Roman emperors. 'The emperor did not neglect even actors and the other performers … knowing as he did that the Roman people are principally held fast by two things, the corn distributions and the shows …' (Fronto, *Princip. Hist.* 17). Imperial generosity was not limited to the city of Rome, though, as Veyne notes in passing in the book which borrows Juvenal's phrase as its title:

> I hardly need to list the Imperial buildings erected in Italy and the provinces. It is enough to have shown that Augustus' patronage was the origin of a public service and that it caused the Imperial government to abandon the narrow outlook of the City, which was that of the Republican censors, in favour of that of a great state.
>
> (Veyne 1990: 362)

This chapter, however, seeks to distinguish Italy from the provinces; it examines the phenomenon of imperial generosity towards the cities of Italy, in particular imperial building projects, road-building schemes, and grants of privileges to Italy more generally in the first two centuries AD, and explores possible motivations for such initiatives. In the case of 'bread and circuses' in the city of Rome the explanations seem fairly clear; in particular the need for the emperor to keep the favour of the *plebs urbana* and to maintain peace and order in the city, and his desire to demonstrate his own magnificence. In the case of imperial benefactions in the towns of Italy the motivation is much less obvious, since Italy was now of marginal importance in terms of the day-to-day politics of imperial rule (Millar 1986: 295; see also Dyson 1992: 89–121, Lomas 1996: 111–19 for general discussions); ideological considerations seem to have been of major importance. The subject is a large one and the evidence and bibliography cited necessarily selective.

Building

As always, the starting point is with Augustus himself, whose long reign takes us from the civil war years through to an established monarchy. For Octavian, the provision of public buildings was part of his strategy of establishing influence over communities during the years of his rivalry with Antony after the battle of Philippi, which culminated in the oath of allegiance sworn to him by the towns of Italy in 32BC (*RG* 25). Dio reports that Octavian

> added to his support all those who had been settled in colonies by Antony, partly by frightening them, since they were few in number, and partly by acts of generosity; for example, he personally re-founded the colony of those who had settled in Bononia
>
> (Dio 50.6.3)

and this seems to be confirmed by an inscription which records the building of a bath-house there by Augustus (*CIL* XI.720 = *ILS* 5764, with Fagan 1999: 233). Subsequently his concern must have been to cement loyalty during the first years of the Principate, which perhaps appear in retrospect more placid than they may have seemed at the time.

Octavian was in fact formally designated *patronus* of several individual cities (e.g. Saticula (*CIL* IX.2142 = *ILS* 76), Luna (*CIL* XI.1330 = *ILS* 78), and Capua (*CIL* X 3826 = *ILS* 79), as were other members of the imperial family, such as L. Caesar at Pisa (*CIL* XI.1420 = *ILS* 139); this model of individual attachment was however abandoned in the later Principate, when the prevailing ideology was presumably that the emperor was in effect the patron of *all* communities; the patronate of an individual community was more suitable for a private citizen (Harmand 1957: 155–82; Veyne 1990: 457, n. 251). Similarly, several of the colonies established by Augustus are known to have received generous benefactions from the princeps, who 'populated Italy by himself establishing twenty-eight colonies, and in many places provided public buildings and revenues' (Suet. *Aug.* 46; see also Keppie 1983: 114–15): Venafrum (*CIL* X.4842 = *ILS* 5743) and Brixia (*CIL* V.4307 = *ILS* 114) received aqueducts, while Hispellum (*CIL* XI.6266) and Fanum (*CIL* XI.6218 = *ILS* 104) received city walls. Other members of the imperial family were involved too; Tiberius and Drusus were responsible for building the wall circuit at Saepinum (*CIL* IX.2443 = *ILS* 147) which although it was not formally designated a colony, seems to have been the scene of veteran settlement (Keppie 1983: 9); and C. Caesar built roads at Ariminum (*CIL* XI.366 = *ILS* 133). The scale of resources required to construct a wall circuit (or especially an aqueduct) must have been very substantial and may well have been beyond the means of most communities, so the assistance of the emperors must have been essential in the realisation of some of these projects; and from the emperor's point of view, their purpose, to supply a community with water, or protect it from enemy attack (however unlikely in practice such an attack might have been) would have had a suitably high moral tone.

Jouffroy's book on public building in Roman Italy and Africa (1986) provides a valuable collection of data on the initiatives of the emperors in the cities of Italy. Judging from this archaeological and epigraphic evidence, the interventions of the Julio-Claudians and indeed the Flavians seem to have been limited in scope (Jouffroy 1986: 105–6), although Claudius improved the harbour facilities at Ostia and undertook a grand project to drain the Fucine Lake in the territory of the Marsi (Venturi 1985; Letta 1972: 132–9). Vespasian is attested as having built the Capitolium at Brixia (*CIL* V.4312), and a temple at Vicovaro near Tivoli (*CIL* XIV.3485), while Domitian built a temple of Isis at Beneventum, complete with obelisks and Egyptian statuary (Müller 1971: 27–30).

In the late first and early second centuries AD, though, more imperial building activity seems to be taking place in the towns of Italy, especially under Trajan, Hadrian and Antoninus Pius. Trajan undertakes extensive harbour works at Ostia, Ancona and elsewhere, road construction (for which see below), and other public building projects (Pliny, *Pan.* 28–9; Dio 68.7). Hadrian and Antoninus Pius build a series of temples in several towns; Hadrian embellishes the amphitheatre at Capua with columns (*CIL* X.3832, with Boatwright 2000: 126); Antoninus completes the construction of the the Baths of Neptune at Ostia, initiated by his predecessor (*CIL* XIV.98 = *ILS* 334; SHA *Antoninus Pius* 8, with Boatwright 2000: 126–7), another bath complex at Tarquinii (*CIL*.XI 3363: see DeLaine 1999: 72) and an aqueduct at Scolacium (*CIL* X.103 = *ILS* 5750), and there are other examples too (see Jouffroy 1986: 137–8; Boatwright 1989; 2000 for the reign of Hadrian). Thereafter there seems to be a further decline in imperial involvement in civic building, and with the exception of work on some bath-houses, attention is instead transferred primarily to the building of roads and bridges, although there are several instances of restoration of public monuments in the fourth century AD (Ward-Perkins 1984: 30; Jouffroy 1986: 152; Fagan 1999: 139).

How should we explain this sequence of imperial interventions? The central difficulty is that the emperor's prime motivation on any particular occasion lies for us in the realm of the unknowable. So it is essential to consider both the ways in which a given benefaction might have related to the needs of a particular community (so far as we can identify them) on the one hand, and how on the other it may have been tied in to the emperor's own priorities and contributed to the presentation of his image. We also need to allow for the ideological and literary perspectives of the literary authors attesting imperial activity; building programmes present particular problems in this respect since attitudes to them in the ancient sources tend to be ambiguous and relate to the view taken by posterity (or by the immediate successor) of an individual emperor (Elsner 1994: 115). Further complications include the implications for the pattern observed of variations in the 'epigraphic habit', as well as the fragmentary nature of the epigraphic and archaeological records.

In some cases, the motivation for imperial generosity is fairly straightforward. For example, emperors often gave assistance to communities in the aftermath of natural disasters, both within Italy and more generally around the Empire (Millar 1977: 423): Augustus helped the city of Naples following a fire in 2BC, and his generosity was ostensibly honoured with the institution of new games (Dio 55.10.9); while Vespasian and Titus contributed to reconstruction in the area around the Bay of Naples following the earthquake of AD62 and the eruption of Vesuvius in AD79 (Dio 66.24; Suet. *Titus* 8.3; *AE* 1902, 40; *CIL* X.1406 = *ILS* 250). Imperial concern for the peoples of the Empire could be demonstrated by a swift reaction to crisis.

Many of the imperial building schemes in Italy can be shown to have been motivated primarily by political concerns emanating from conditions in the city of Rome itself and the importance of maintaining stability there – a major priority of the emperors. Thus the work carried out at Ostia by Claudius and Trajan can be linked to the importance of maintaining a reliable corn supply for the *plebs urbana* (Meiggs 1973: 54–60; Rickman 1996), while Claudius' scheme to drain the Fucine Lake may have been motivated in part by a concern to increase the cultivable land in the vicinity of the capital (Dio 60.11). Nero's plan to build a canal from Puteoli to Ostia, traces of which have recently been identified north of Cumae (Johannowsky 1990: 1–8), can best be explained in this context, as despite its apparent megalomania it seems to have been intended as a serious proposal to improve the corn supply of the city (Stat. *Silv.* 4.3.8; Tac. *Ann.* 15.42; Pliny *NH* 14.61; Suet. *Nero* 31.3; Meiggs 1973, 57–8). Further harbour works were carried out at Puteoli under Hadrian and Antoninus (*CIL* X.1640= *ILS* 336). Campania also seems to have been a favoured setting for some of the more idiosyncratic imperial building projects, such as Caligula's bridge of boats across the bay of Baiae; perhaps this was a consequence of the area's traditional role as a place of cultured leisure and scenic pleasures. Both politically and culturally the Bay of Naples can be seen as an extension of the city of Rome itself (D'Arms 1970; Frederiksen 1984: 335–6; Amalfitano *et al.* 1990).

In most other cases of imperial building in Italian towns, the motivating factors are less clear, though it is reasonable to imagine that the model of petition and response (Millar 1977; Eck 1994: 340–5; Fagan 1999: 141) must also have been of major importance in encouraging acts of generosity and building projects. For example, we hear that the draining of the Fucine Lake had in fact been requested by the Marsi long before Claudius actually put the work in hand (Suet. *Claud.* 20). In many other cases we can only surmise the mechanisms involved in encouraging a particular imperial initiative or act of generosity. It is interesting to speculate, for instance, on the circumstances which led to the erection of statues and monumental inscriptions honouring emperors in the various Italian cities, although we are restricted by the partial recovery of these and our inability to make negative deductions from the absence of honours for a particular emperor. Sometimes it appears that the dedication of honorary statues to the emperor was related to specific episodes in the emperor's life (Cogitore 1992: 829–34); but it may also be that the setting up of a statue to a particular emperor may have represented an expression of thanks on the part of a community for a gift; or perhaps an expression of hope for future assistance, as the news of the dedication was presumably conveyed to the emperor himself by a communication or embassy from the city. If so, the latter did not always work; we have to feel sorry for the citizens of Capena, who dedicated a monument to Pertinax on 20 March AD 193, only for him to be assassinated six days later (*CIL* XI.3873 = *ILS* 409).

In other cases, we can detect that a particular attachment an emperor may have had for a particular town may have been significant; an emperor might show particular concern for the place of his birth, or a town with specific family associations. Nero established a colony at Antium, his birthplace, and built a harbour there; while Vespasian sent colonists to *his* home town, Reate (Keppie 1984: 86, 93–5). In the same way, Hadrian took on the office of *duumvir quinquennalis* at Italica in Spain, the town of his ancestors, to which he also made many generous gifts (Dio 69.10.1; SHA *Hadrian* 19.1; see Syme 1964, Boatwright 2000: 68, 162–7). Nerva was senatorial patron of Sentinum and restored a monument there before he became emperor (*CIL* XI.5743 = *ILS* 273), and it is possible that his concern for the community may have continued after his elevation to the imperial throne. Distinguished residents of a community might often have been well placed to encourage an imperial benefaction for a particular town, and we may imagine that informal acts of individual patronage may have been more successful in securing imperial support than formal embassies, but we would hardly expect such behind-the-scenes activity to be reflected in the public domain. Otherwise, an emperor might have a personal enthusiasm for a particular location, perhaps because there was an imperial palace there. Hadrian is known to have had a particular interest in ancient religious cults, and we can relate this to his acts of generosity at shrines which included those of Diana at Nemi and Juno at Gabii (Boatwright 1989: 252–4; 2000: 130).

The visit of an emperor to a particular town might be the occasion for an act of generosity. Veyne rightly emphasises that euergetism travelled with the emperor, and indeed the more emperors travelled – Hadrian being a prime example – the more scope there was for individual acts of generosity of this kind (Halfmann 1986; Boatwright 1989: 251–2). Indeed whim alone might induce the emperor to help a particular community. After all, the power to do completely as one wanted was a major element in the definition of the emperor's authority.

This combination of petition, patronage, and personal whim may serve to explain many of the imperial benefactions in Italy. But there are some more general trends which need further explanation. Why the apparent increase in imperial benefaction for the towns of Italy in the reigns of Trajan, Hadrian and Antoninus? These reigns seem to be highly significant in the Italian context in a number of different ways, which deserve further investigation.

Roads

One of Augustus' major concerns was the improvement of the road network in Italy; this was undertaken either by him personally (in the case of the Via Flaminia: Dio 53.22; *RG* 20.5), or with his encouragement through the agency of the *viri triumphales* (Suet. *Aug.* 30). For example, there seems to have been a major improvement of the roads of Samnium in 2BC (Donati 1974), and milestones also attest work on the Salaria and Appia during his principate. These road-building activities are commemorated on Augustus' coinage: coins of 17–16BC bear the legend 'quod viae mun(itae) sunt' (*RIC* I[2] (Augustus) 140–5), and depict a series of arches with triumphal chariots which (if actual rather than symbolic) must themselves have commemorated the road-building programmes. The arch set up at Ariminum to commemorate the building of the Via Flaminia and of other *celeberrimae Italiae viae* still survives (*CIL* XI.365 = *ILS* 84; De Maria 1988: 260–2; Laurence 1999: 42–5). The improvement of the road-system can be seen as yet another element in the increasingly formalised unification of Italy which we can see taking place under Augustus, together with the creation of new *municipia* in under-urbanised areas, the subdivision of the landscape into *pagi* and *fundi* (Frederiksen 1976) and the administrative organisation of the peninsula in the form of eleven *regiones* (Nicolet 1991: 202–4).

The pattern of road building in Italy after Augustus is strikingly similar to that of imperial building more generally, although a distinction has to be made between localised repair work and the construction of major new roads. Claudius built two major roads in the central Appennines: the Via Claudia Nova from Foruli just off the Salaria to the confluence of the Aternus and Tirinus at Popoli (Gardner 1920), and the Via Claudia Valeria, which connected Cerfennia at the eastern end of the Fucine plain with the mouth of the Aternus, where Pescara now is (Gardner 1913). Presumably these projects were in part associated with the work on the nearby Fucine Lake. Vespasian built a tunnel on the Flaminia at Furlo (O'Connor 1993: 13), and Titus' activities are known from a milestone in Picenum (*CIL* IX.5936); while Domitian constructed a new road which connected Puteoli with the Via Appia at Sinuessa and took his own name (*AE* 1973, 137; Matthews 1966; Johannowsky 1990; Dio 67.14.1; Statius *Silv.* 4.3; Coleman 1988: 102–35; Laurence 1999: 47). A further substantial sequence of road-building schemes was however undertaken by Nerva and Trajan (Dio 68.15). The centrepiece was the new Via Traiana, which considerably shortened the journey between Beneventum and Brundisium (Ashby and Gardner 1916), while the Via Nova Traiana, connecting Volsinii and Clusium in Etruria, was also constructed in Trajan's reign (*CIL* XI.8104; Bennett 1997: 138–9). Building activity by these two emperors is attested also on the Flaminia, Appia, Latina, Puteolana, Salaria, Valeria and Via Sublacensis (Donati 1974; Uggeri 1990; Di Vita-Evrard 1990; Laurence 1999: 47). Hadrian, too, undertook restoration work on the Appia, Flaminia and Cassia (*CIL* XI.6619 = *ILS* 5857; 6620; 6668; Boatwright 2000: 120).

Why did these emperors devote such expense and effort to the building of roads in Italy? Literary texts give us some idea of the prevailing ideological associations of road-building under the Empire. Plutarch stresses the 'utility', 'grace' and 'beauty' of the roads built by Gaius Gracchus, and observes that 'he measured out every road by miles and set up stone pillars in the ground as markers of the distances' (Plut. *C. Gracch.* 7, with discussion in Laurence 1999: 51). The emphasis on the milestones is interesting here; the construction of roads in the imperial period was usually accompanied by the erection of milestones, bearing the emperor's name and titles; not only did these often show the distance from Rome and so emphasise the unity of the peninsula under Roman rule, they also may have been seen as a means of publicising the emperor's initiative wherever the new roads were built. Road building was also seen as kingly and impressive because of its scale and the victory over the forces of nature that it entailed, manifested for example by the famous cutting for the Appia at Tarracina (Pliny *Pan.* 29.2; Purcell 1987). Pliny the Elder related *vias per montes excisas* to other man-made marvels, including aqueducts, the harbour at Ostia and the draining of the Fucine Lake (*NH* 36.124–5). Although Statius, in his encomium on Domitian's new road, pours scorn on Nero's ambitious canal project, he nevertheless compares the construction of the Via Domitiana with Xerxes' bridge of boats and his canal through Mount Athos (*Silv.* 4. 3.7–8 or 56–8 with Coleman 1988 *ad loc*). Galen, in a striking passage, compares his personal achievement in clarifying the work of Hippocrates with that of Trajan in improving the roads of Italy (Galen 10.632–3 Kühn; see Nutton 1978: 218–9). Milestones recording Roman republican road building in the Po valley often allude to rivers (rather than towns) as the starting or finishing points of new roads, thus stressing the impact on the natural landscape of road-building operations (Purcell 1990: 13). The milestones of the Via Claudia Nova likewise use the confluence of the rivers Aternus and Tirinus as a defining point (*CIL* IX.5959).

An important additional point is that close associations were perceived between road building and warfare. Coarelli has emphasised the links between conquest, colonisation and road building in the Republican period (Coarelli 1988; see also Curti *et al.* 1996: 186; Laurence 1999: 11–26), and these may be identified under the Empire too. Road building was an important element both during campaigns – allowing speedy access to the front – and afterwards, in the laying out of conquered territory. This may be true even of schemes which are apparently taking place far from the frontiers. Claudius' road-building activities in central Italy may well be related to the campaigns and road building being undertaken across the Adriatic in Dalmatia (Levick 1990: 156–7), just as his construction of roads in the Alps represented the completion of Augustus' conquest of that area (Levick 1990: 156–7, 173–5); and Laurence plausibly suggests that they may also have been intended to reflect the achievement of his distant ancestor, Appius Claudius Caecus, in constructing the Via Appia between Rome and Campania (Laurence 1999: 46–7).

A further attraction for military-minded emperors of road building was that even if their new roads were situated in apparently peaceful areas of Italy and constructed by convicts or civilians, they could nevertheless return along them in triumph after winning glorious victories. The Via Flaminia is a case in point: we are told that Augustus planned to lead an army out along this route (Dio 53.22.1–2), and the Ara Pacis, celebrating his safe return from victories in Gaul and Spain, was built next to it. Often the construction of a new road was marked by the erection of an honorary arch – in the case of Augustus' work on the Flaminia, in addition to the one at Rimini, another was built at the Pons Mulvius as the road approached Rome (Patterson 1999: 136). In view of the circumstances of his accession, it was particularly important for Claudius to gain prestige and military glory, and his victory over the Britons was duly marked at Rome by an honorary arch on the Via Flaminia (Barrett 1991; Rodriguez Almeida 1993). There seem to have been no fewer than three arches on the Via Domitiana, the Arco Felice near Cumae and others at Sinuessa and Puteoli (Coleman 1988: 128). Statius makes substantial use of military language in his description of Domitian as road builder: he draws special attention to the 'belligeris ducis tropaeis' ('leader's trophies of war') on the arch at Sinuessa (Statius *Silv.* 4.3.97); the river Volturno addresses Domitian as 'victor perpetuus' for building a bridge over him (Statius *Silv.* 4.3.84), and later Domitian is 'timendus armis' (Statius *Silv.* 4.3.134) The overall effect is to stress his military achievement (De Maria 1988: 123).

However, perhaps the most celebrated example of such an honorary arch in Italy is that at Beneventum where the Arch of Trajan, dedicated 'fortissimo principi' (*CIL* IX.1558 = *ILS* 296) marked the starting point of the new Via Traiana and commemorated (among Trajan's other achievements) his victories over the Dacians (Hannestad 1988: 177–86, with bibliography in n. 123). By the time of the high empire, arches were no longer exclusively symbols of victory, but their traditional association with military success gives additional strength to the case for seeing a link between road-building and military reputation. The construction of the road may also have been seen as a preliminary to Trajan's campaigns in Parthia; Brundisium, the destination of the new road, was the traditional starting point for expeditions to the East (De Maria 1988: 132), and an arch had been erected there (together with another in the Forum Romanum) to celebrate Augustus' victory at Actium (Dio 51. 19). If it was intended that Trajan should march through the arch at the head of his victorious army on his way back to Rome after a successful conquest of Parthia, this was not to be; in the event, his ashes were returned to Rome by ship (Lepper 1969: 252; SHA, *Hadrian* 5. 10).

Privileges

On the administrative side too, Augustus granted special legal and institutional privileges to Italy, and he was followed in this by other emperors, in a way which complements other manifestations of generosity towards the inhabitants and communities of the peninsula. Octavian had risen to power with the formal support of Italy, and as princeps, according to Suetonius, he 'gave Italy, at least to a certain extent, equal rights and dignity with the city of Rome'. In particular, the *decuriones* of colonies were entitled to cast their votes in their own town (rather than coming to Rome), and these were then taken to Rome in special ballot boxes; members of local aristocracies were admitted to the *militia equestris* 'by public commendation'; and Augustus distributed sums of money to individuals when travelling through Italy, at a rate of 1,000 sesterces per child (Suet. *Aug.* 46; see Nicolet 1991: 200–2).

In general, Italy tended to be treated by the emperors as something of an extension of the city of Rome (Lo Cascio 1991: 125). It is striking, though, that many of the specific new initiatives involving the legal status and privileges of Italy occur in the reigns of precisely those emperors who also expressed their concern for the cities of Italy in the form of building projects and the construction of roads. For example, initiatives were taken under Claudius, and quite probably at his own instigation, which seem to have been intended to maintain the quality of life in Italian cities: by the S.C. Hosidianum of AD45 demolition of buildings in Italian towns was forbidden unless these were to be immediately replaced – this was explained in terms of a concern for *totius Italiae aeternitas* (*CIL* X.1401 = *ILS* 6043 = *FIRA* I, 45; Phillips 1973; Garnsey 1976: 133–6); travel through them was prohibited other by means other than on foot, or in a chair or litter (Suet. *Claud.* 25: Friedländer 1928: vol 4, 30), though whether this was practical in aim – to counter problems of noise and traffic congestion – or symbolic – to stop people riding through Italian towns as though they were conquered or provincial centres – is unclear.

Again, though, it is with the emperors of the late first and early second century AD that the grant of privileges to Italy is most apparent and systematic. Nerva removed the obligation of *vehiculatio*, that is, the financial burden of maintaining the imperial postal service, which must have weighed excessively on the towns of Italy, as the peninsula was the nucleus of the imperial road system (Mitchell 1976; Lo Cascio 1991: 134), and he also instituted a land distribution scheme for the urban poor which seems to look back to the model of the Gracchan colony rather than those of the triumvirate (Dio 68.2.1; Pliny *Epist.* 7.31.4). Most important, though, was the introduction of the *alimenta* perhaps first by Nerva and then (on a larger scale) by Trajan. Identifying the motivation or motivations behind these schemes is of course problematic: views differ as to whether they should be seen as a response to agricultural crisis (e.g. Rostovtzeff 1957: 199; others in Duncan-Jones 1982: 295, n. 5), as a mechanism for improving the corn supply of Rome (Lo Cascio 1978), or as an initiative aimed at increasing the free population of Italy and increasing military recruitment (Garnsey 1968; Duncan-Jones 1982; Patterson 1987). Whichever view is taken about the economic and social background of the Italian alimentary schemes, it is clear that the *alimenta* were also regarded as an act of imperial generosity, and the emperor is duly thanked by the children who benefitted from the schemes (Woolf 1990). The imperial *alimenta* seem to have been almost entirely confined to Italy, with the exception of a scheme at Antinoopolis set up by Hadrian (Duncan-Jones 1982: 288; Boatwright 2000: 195); so they can be seen both as an imperial benefaction and as an initiative giving precedence to Italy. An inscription honouring the senator who set up the local alimentary scheme at Ferentinum commends the emperor because he 'aeternitati Italiae prospexit' (*CIL* VI.1492 = *ILS* 6106) – the same phrase as used in the S.C. Hosidianum under Claudius.

The special position of Italy under these emperors also emerges from the imperial coinage. The extent to which the legends and images depicted on coins reflected imperial policies – or alternatively the concerns of the young aristocrats who were directly responsible for the minting of the coins – is a subject of debate, but it seems unlikely that the coins would have expressed themes or sentiments with which the emperors would have disagreed (Crawford 1983, Howgego 1995: 70–3). After Augustus (whose road-building activities are commemorated on his coinage), with the exception of some rather doubtful allegorical figures under Vespasian and Domitian, there is very little sign of specific allusions to Italy appearing on the imperial coinage at all, until the reigns of Nerva and Trajan, when types relating to Italy become very common (Laurence 1999: 48). In addition to 'vehiculatione Italiae remissa S.C.' (*RIC* II (Nerva) 93, 104) and 'tutela Italiae S.C.' (*RIC* II (Nerva) 92) of Nerva, and 'Via Traiana' of Trajan (*RIC* II (Trajan) 266, 636–41), numerous types commemorate the *alimenta*, such as ALIM. ITAL. (i.e. *alimenta Italiae*: *RIC* II (Trajan) 93, 230, 243, 459–62, 604–6) ; REST. ITAL. (*RIC* II (Trajan) 105–6, 472–3) and ITAL. REST. (i.e. *Italia restituta: RIC* II (Trajan) 470). Coins of Antoninus Pius commemorate the *puellae Faustinianae*, beneficiaries of the alimentary schemes he set up in memory of Faustina (*RIC* III (Antoninus Pius) 397–9). Under Hadrian and Antonius Pius, Italy continues to appear regularly, but now often in the context of types referring to the provinces of the empire: ITALIA (*RIC* II (Hadrian) 307). A series of coins showing the *adventus* of Hadrian, includes one with the legend 'Adventui Aug(usti) Italiae' (*RIC* II (Hadrian) 320, 888–9), while Antoninus similarly issues a series of coins depicting both Italy and provinces (ITALIA: *RIC* III (Antoninus Pius) 73, 594, 746–7, 789). Hadrian is described on a coin as 'restitutor Italiae' (*RIC* II (Hadrian) 328, 956–7), but again in a series of coins depicting the emperor as the restorer of various provinces, and a coin of Marcus Aurelius of AD172–3 (*RIC* III Marcus Aurelius 1077–82) gives him the same epithet.

Discussion

As we have seen, many of Augustus' acts of generosity in Italy can be interpreted primarily in terms of considerations that would have been easily understandable by a Republican politician; support for colonies he had created; gifts to ward off potential sources of opposition, and reward loyalty; initiatives to bring the disparate parts of Italy together behind his principate. The situation thereafter is more problematic, since only occasionally – for example after natural disasters, where there was provision of structures on a scale beyond the capacity of local resources, or arguably in the case of the *alimenta* – did the benefaction seem to be determined primarily in terms of local need; rather we should look at other factors which motivated the emperors in terms of image and prestige. Emperors were fabulously wealthy, and were expected to be generous, but even they had many calls on their resources; they had to be selective in their benefactions. What they chose to do with their wealth was thus a significant element in defining their image. In this context it is striking that despite its apparent lack of political importance, Italy continued to occupy a privileged position under the empire, and several individual emperors in particular seem to have been especially concerned to manifest their generosity to Italy – in terms of buildings, road-construction, and more general privileges. Why?

I would argue that acts of generosity to Italy formed an element in the definition of the 'good emperor' within what we might call the 'ideology of the traditionalist senators'. This has been transmitted to us largely through the medium of the historical writings of authors such as those of Tacitus and Dio, senators themselves though ironically both originating outside Italy; in Pliny's *Panegyric*; and through the compilation of imperial biographies known as the Historia Augusta. In their eyes, the success or otherwise of a reign was assessed on how far the emperor succeeded in conforming to a series of stereotypes. The good emperor was distinguished by his respect for the Senate, his military achievements and his adherence to the traditional morality of the Roman elite; the bad emperor by his maltreatment of the senate, his excessive concern for the *plebs*, his devotion to undignified pursuits – for example acting and gladiatorial combat – and his rejection of traditional norms of conduct.

Woolf (1990: 220–2) has already drawn attention to the importance of the alimentary schemes in this context – good emperors supported the *alimenta*, bad emperors neglected them – and this approach can be applied more generally to other aspects of imperial treatment of Italy (Boatwright 2000: 11). Dio observes that Trajan's *alimenta* 'did much to please the better citizens' (Dio 68.5.4); the same emperor required provincial senators to hold a third of their *patrimonium* in Italy (Pliny *Epist.* 6.19), and in this he was followed by another 'good' emperor, Marcus Aurelius, though this time the proportion required was a quarter (SHA *Marcus Aurelius* 11.8). The repetition of the edicts need not necessarily indicate that the original edict was ineffective; it can perhaps also be explained in terms of respect shown to an admired imperial predecessor. In the same way, the idea of *aeternitas Italiae* can be traced from Claudius' measures for the upkeep of the urban fabric of Italian towns through to the *alimenta* of Trajan.

The extent to which an apparent concern for Italy on the part of individual emperors is a phenomenon partly generated by subsequent attitudes to an individual emperor's career remains problematic; it might be argued that Domitian's road building activities in Campania and his concern to improve Rome's corn supply by means of the vine edict (Suet. *Dom.* 7.2) give him credentials of concern for Italy which have been obscured by the hostile literary traditions. In the case of three emperors in particular, though, Claudius, Nerva and Trajan, the combination of benefaction, road building and coin-issuing programmes does however seem to combine key elements of the traditional ideology: zeal for military glory and respect for the traditions and pre-eminence of Italy went well together. Parallels can also be drawn between these three reigns in terms of the circumstances of the emperors' accession. Claudius, the reclusive scholar, discovered behind a curtain, was acclaimed emperor even as the Senate was discussing the restoration of the Republic (Josephus *AJ* 19.162–84; Dio 60.1; Suet. *Claud.* 10; Levick 1990: 29–34); Nerva, an elderly senator, was likewise acclaimed emperor after the assassination of his predecessor (Dio 68.1; Belloni 1974: 1069–71; Shotter 1983; Jones 1992: 193–6); Trajan, described by Dio as the first 'non-Italian' emperor, was adopted by his predecessor Nerva in preference to Nerva's own relatives (Dio 68.4.1; see Syme 1958: vol 2, 785–6). These emperors had everything to prove, and assiduous attention to the traditional imperial virtues was a prudent course for them.

Traditionally the Senate has been seen as the key focus of imperial attention here, but it would, I suspect, be wrong to forget the equestrians – who occupied key positions in the imperial service, and were in the Julio-Claudian period overwhelmingly Italian in origin (Demougin 1988: 520) – and the Praetorians. In the imperial period, the proportion of legionaries of Italian origin declined drastically (Forni 1953: 65–75; Forni 1974: 362–85); service in the praetorian guard, with its prestigious status, higher pay, and service primarily in the city of Rome was however still attractive to Italians, who formed a major proportion of that body (Passerini 1939: 144–69; Šašel 1972; Keppie 1996: 117–8). When Septimius Severus abolished the practice of recruiting the Praetorians only from Italy, Spain, Macedonia and Noricum, he was criticised for 'destroying the youth of Italy', who, according to Dio, 'turned to banditry and gladiatorial combat (75.2.4–6). The emperor had a special relationship with the praetorians, whose principal role was as his bodyguard (Campbell 1984: 110–11) and he needed their support especially in case of rebellion by legions on the frontiers. Although Campbell has argued that they were swayed largely by the prospect of cash donatives rather than any other factor, and that in practice their scope as kingmakers was limited (1984: 117–20), it would clearly have been prudent for a new emperor to conciliate them with favours and bonuses. Claudius owed his elevation to the throne in part to the praetorians (no doubt concerned for their own future should the Republic have been restored) and Nerva suffered a rebellion by them shortly after his accession to power (Dio 68.3.3).

Conversely the close contact the praetorians had with the emperor might well have allowed them to make representations on behalf of their communities. An inscription from Tuficum in Umbria demonstrates how influential a favoured soldier could be on behalf of his home community: Sextus Aetrius Ferox, a soldier of the Second Legion Traiana, who was promoted to the rank of centurion for his military ability, persuaded Antoninus Pius to delay exaction of a road tax from the town and was honoured with a statue as a result (*CIL* XI.5963–4 = *ILS* 2666, 2666a; see Campbell 1984: 272–3). This is no doubt an exceptional case, and commemorated as such, but if a legionary centurion was able to be this successful, then we might imagine that given the right circumstances the praetorians, who potentially had much more regular access to the emperor, must have had even more potential influence on behalf of their home towns.

Two groups within Roman society which we might imagine to have been especially impressed by a 'pro-Italian' policy, then, were the traditionalist senators and the praetorian guards, and these were the two key groups which an emperor would seek to conciliate on taking office. The ideology of military conquest and the primacy of Italy fitted well with the Italian origin of the praetorians and the traditionalist views of the Senate. It is striking that Tacitus places the most ringing condemnation of Nero as 'bad emperor' in the aftermath of the failed conspiracy of Piso in the mouth of Subrius Flavus, described as being 'tribune of a praetorian cohort' (*Ann.*15.49; 15.69; see Woodman 1993: 123–5).

But just as influential Italian senators, praetorians and others were able to exert influence over the emperors on behalf of their communities, backed up by the ideology of Italian pre-eminence, the position began to change. The senatorial (Hammond 1957; Panciera 1982) and equestrian (Demougin 1988: 501–52) orders became in the second century AD increasingly populated by landowners from outside Italy, and emperors – sometimes also themselves originating from outside Italy – became increasingly interested in the provinces, not just as the setting for military conquest or outlandish behaviour, but for the kind of intimate relationships of patronage, influence and prestige which had previously characterised their dealings with Italy and Italians. As the empire reached its maximum extent, the triumphalist ideology of military conquest gave way to a concern for the well-being of the empire as a whole, and this was reflected in the declining numbers of honorary arches erected in Italy after Trajan (De Maria 1988: 133). Hadrian travelled widely and carried out numerous building projects around the empire; he also built widely in Italy, and issued a series of coins which honoured Italy – but Italy was now honoured together with the provinces, rather than having a special, superior status. New offices were created for the administration of Italy – *iuridici*, consular *legati*, *curatores rei publicae* (Eck 1979; Eck 1994: 331–8) – which have been seen as blurring the distinction between Italy and the provinces; and the *alimenta* themselves can in some sense be seen as a form of taxation on the previously exempt peninsula (Lo Cascio 1978: 328). The Antonine emperors were happy to continue supporting the *alimenta* and to promote themselves as 'Restorers of Italy', but they were also looking forwards in a process which was to lead to the designation of Italy as one province among many.

References

Amalfitano, P., Camodeca, G. and Medri, M. (1990) *I Campi Flegrei: un itinerario archeologico*, Venice: Marsilio.

Ashby, T. and Gardner, R. (1916) 'The Via Traiana', *PBSR* 8: 104–71.

Barrett, A.A. (1991) 'Claudius' British victory arch in Rome', *Britannia* 22: 1–19.

Belloni, G.G. (1974) 'Significati storico-politici delle figurazioni e delle scritte delle monete da Augusto a Traiano, in *ANRW* II(1): 997–1144.

Bennett, J. (1997) *Trajan: optimus princeps*, London: Routledge.

Boatwright, M.T. (1989) 'Hadrian and Italian cities', *Chiron* 19: 235–71.

Boatwright, M.T. (2000) *Hadrian and the Cities of the Roman Empire*, Princeton: Princeton University Press.

Campbell, J.B. (1984) *The Emperor and the Roman Army, 31BC–AD235*, Oxford: Clarendon Press.

Coarelli, F. (1988) 'Colonizzazione romana e viabilità', *Dialoghi di Archeologia* 3(6): 35–48.

Cogitore, I. (1992) 'Séries de dédicaces italiennes à la dynastie julio-claudienne', *MEFRA* 104: 817–70.

Coleman, K.M. (1988) *Statius Silvae IV* (edited with an English translation and commentary), Oxford: Clarendon Press.

Crawford, M.H. (1983) 'Roman imperial coin types and the formation of public opinion'. In C.N.L. Brooke, B.H.I.H. Stewart. J.G. Pollard and T.R. Volk (eds), *Studies in Numismatic Method Presented to Philip Grierson*: 47–64, Cambridge and New York: Cambridge University Press.

Curti, E., Dench, E. and Patterson, J.R. (1996) ' The archaeology of central and southern Roman Italy: recent trends and approaches', *JRS* 86: 170–89.

D'Arms, J.H. (1970) *Romans on the Bay of Naples*, Cambridge, MA: Harvard University Press.

DeLaine, J. (1999) 'Benefactions and urban renewal: bath buildings in Roman Italy'. In J. DeLaine and D.E. Johnston (eds), *Roman Baths and Bathing. Proceedings of the first International Conference on Roman Baths*, held at Bath, England, 30 March–4 April 1992: 67–74, Portsmouth, RI: Journal of Roman Archaeology.

De Maria, S. (1988) *Gli archi onorari di Roma e dell'Italia romana*, Rome: 'L'Erma' di Bretschneider.

Demougin, S. (1988) *L'ordre équestre sous les julio-claudiens* (*Collection de l'École française de Rome* 108), Rome: École Française de Rome.

Di Vita-Evrard, G. (1990) 'Inscriptions routières de Nerva et de Trajan sur l'Appia pontine', *Archeologia Laziale* 10(1): 73–93.

Donati, A. (1974) 'I milliari delle regioni IV e V dell'Italia', *Epigraphica* 36: 155–222.

Duncan-Jones, R.P. (1982) *The Economy of the Roman Empire: Quantitative Studies* (2nd edn), Cambridge: Cambridge University Press.

Dyson, S. (1992) *Community and Society in Roman Italy*, Baltimore: Johns Hopkins University Press.

Eck, W. (1979) *Die staatliche Organisation Italiens in der hohen Kaiserzeit*, Munich: Beck.

Eck, W. (1994) 'Kaiserliches handeln in italienischen Städten'. In *l'Italie d'Auguste à Dioclétien* (Collection de l'École Française de Rome 198), 329–51, Rome: École Française de Rome.

Elsner, J. (1994) 'Constructing decadence: the representation of Nero as imperial builder'. In J. Elsner and J. Masters (eds), *Reflections of Nero*: 112–27, London: Duckworth.

Fagan, G.G. (1999) *Bathing in Public in the Roman World*, Ann Arbor: University of Michigan Press.

Forni, G. (1953) *Il reclutamento delle legioni da Augusto a Diocleziano*, Rome: Bocca.

Forni, G. (1974) 'Estrazione etnica e sociale dei soldati delle legioni nei primi tre secoli dell'impero', in *ANRW* 2(1): 339–91.

Friedländer, L. (1913) *Roman life and manners under the early Empire*, 4 vols. New York: Barnes and Noble.

Frederiksen, M.W. (1976) 'Changes in the pattern of settlement'. In P. Zanker (ed.), *Hellenismus in Mittelitalien* vol 2: 341–54, Göttingen: Vandenhoeck and Ruprecht.

Frederiksen, M.W. (1984) *Campania*, London: British School at Rome.

Gardner, R. (1913) 'The Via Claudia Nova', *JRS* 3: 205–32.

Gardner, R. (1920) 'The Via Claudia Valeria', *PBSR* 9: 75–106.

Garnsey, P. (1968) 'Trajan's *alimenta*: some problems', *Historia* 17: 367–81.

Garnsey, P. (1976) 'Urban property investment'. In M.I. Finley (ed.), *Studies in Roman Property*, 123–36, Cambridge: Cambridge University Press.

Halfmann, H. (1986) *Itinera principum*, Stuttgart: Steiner Verlag.

Hammond, M. (1957) 'Composition of the Senate, AD 68–235', *JRS* 47: 74–81.

Hannestad, N. (1988) *Roman Art and Imperial Policy*, Aarhus: Aarhus University Press.

Harmand, L. (1957) *Le patronat sur les collectivités publiques des origines au bas-empire*, Paris: Presses Universitaires de France.

Howgego, C. (1995) *Ancient History from coins*, London: Routledge.

Johannowsky, W. (1990) 'Appunti su alcune infrastrutture dell'annona romana tra Nerone e Adriano', *Bollettino di Archeologia* 4: 1–14.

Jones, B.W. (1992) *The Emperor Domitian*, London: Routledge.

Jouffroy, H. (1986) *La construction publique en Italie et dans l'Afrique romaine*, Strasbourg: AECR.

Keppie, L. (1983) *Colonisation and Veteran Settlement in Italy*. London: British School at Rome.

Keppie, L. (1984) 'Colonisation and veteran settlement in Italy in the first century AD', *PBSR* 52: 77–114.

Keppie, L. (1996) 'The praetorian guard before Sejanus', *Athenaeum* 84: 101–24.

Laurence, R.M. (1999) *The Roads of Roman Italy: Mobility and Cultural Change*, London: Routledge.

Lepper, F.A. (1969) Review of F.J. Hassel, 'Der Trajansbogen in Benevent: ein Bauwerk des römischen Senates', *JRS* 59: 250–61.

Letta, C. (1972) *I Marsi e il Fucino nell'antichità*, Milan: Cisalpino-Goliardica.

Levick, B.M. (1990) *Claudius*, London: Routledge.

Lo Cascio, E. (1978) 'Gli alimenta, l'agricoltura italica e l'approvigionamento di Roma', *Rendiconti della Accademia Nazionale dei Lincei: classe di scienze morali, storiche e filologiche* 33: 311–51.

Lo Cascio, E. (1991) 'Le tecniche dell'amministrazione'. In A. Schiavone (ed.), *Storia di Roma* 2.1: *i principi e il mondo*: 119–91, Turin: Einaudi.

Lomas, K. (1996) *Roman Italy, 338BC–AD200: A Sourcebook*, London: UCL Press.

Matthews, K.D. (1966) 'Domitian: the lost divinity', *Expedition* 8: 33–6.

Meiggs, R. (1973) *Roman Ostia*, 2nd edn, Oxford: Clarendon Press.

Millar, F. (1977) *The Emperor in the Roman World*, London: Duckworth.

Millar, F. (1986) 'Italy and the Roman Empire: Augustus to Constantine', *Phoenix* 40: 295–318.

Mitchell, S. (1976) 'Requisitioned transport in the Roman empire: a new inscription from Pisidia', *JRS* 66: 106–31.

Müller, H.W. (1971) *Il culto di Iside nell'antica Benevento* (translation of *Der Isiskult im antiken Benevent und Katalog der Sculpturen aus den ägyptischen Heiligtümern im Museo del Sannio zu Benevent*: 1969), Benevento: Saggi e studi del museo Sannio Biblioteca e Archivio Starico Provinciali di Benevento.

Nicolet, C. (1991) *Space, Geography and Politics in the Early Roman Empire*, Ann Arbor: University of Michigan Press.

Nutton, V. (1978) 'The beneficial ideology'. In P.D.A. Garnsey and C.R. Whittaker (eds), *Imperialism in the Ancient World*: 209–21, Cambridge: Cambridge University Press.

O'Connor, C. (1993) *Roman Bridges*, Cambridge: Cambridge University Press.

Panciera, S. (1982) *Epigrafia e ordine senatorio*, Rome: Edizioni di storia e letteratura.

Passerini, A. (1939) *Le coorte pretorie*, Rome: A. Signorelli.

Patterson, J.R. (1987) 'Crisis: what crisis? Rural change and urban development in imperial Appenine Italy', *PBSR* 55: 115–46.

Patterson, J.R. (1999) 'Via Flaminia'. In E.M. Steinby (ed.), *Lexicon Topographicum Urbis Romae* 5: 135–7, Rome: Quasar.

Phillips, E.J. (1973) 'The Roman law on the destruction of buildings', *Latomus* 32: 86–95.

Purcell, N. (1987) 'Town in country and country in town'. In E. MacDougall (ed.), *Ancient Roman Villa Gardens*: 185–204, Washington, DC: Dumbarton Oaks Research Library and Collection.

Purcell, N. (1990) 'The creation of provincial landscape in the Roman empire: the Roman impact on Cisalpine Gaul'. In T. Blagg and M. Millett (eds), *The Early Roman Empire in the West*: 7–29, Oxford: Oxbow Books.

Rickman, G. (1996) 'Portus in perspective'. In A. Gallina Zevi, A. Claridge (eds), *'Roman Ostia' Revisited*: 281–91, London: British School at Rome.

Rodriguez Almeida, E. (1993) 'Arcus Claudii'. In E.M. Steinby (ed.), *Lexicon Topographicum Urbis Romae* 1: 85–6, Rome: Quasar.

Rostovtzeff, M. (1957) *The Social and Economic History of the Roman Empire*, Oxford: Clarendon Press.

Šašel , J. (1972) 'Zur Rekrutierung der Praetorianer', *Historia* 21: 474–80.

Shotter, D.C.A. (1983) 'The principate of Nerva: some observations on the coin evidence', *Historia* 32: 215–26.

Syme, R. (1958) *Tacitus*, 2 volumes, Oxford: Oxford University Press.

Syme, R. (1964) 'Hadrian and Italica', *JRS* 54: 142–9.

Uggeri, S. (1990) 'La via Appia nella politica espansionistica di Roma', *Archeologia Laziale* 10(1): 29–39.

Venturi, E. (1985) 'La politica edilizia e urbanistica di Claudio a Roma e in Italia', *Rivista Storica dell' Antichità* 15: 257–83.

Veyne, P. (1990) (with an introduction by O. Murray) *Bread and Circuses* (abridged translation of *Le pain et le cirque* (1976) Paris: Seuil), London: Penguin.

Ward-Perkins, B. (1984) *From Classical Antiquity to the Middle Ages: Urban Public Building in Northern and Central Italy, AD300–850*, Oxford: Clarendon Press.

Woodman, A.J. (1993) 'Amateur dramatics at the court of Nero: *Annals* 15. 48–74'. In T.J. Luce and A.J. Woodman (eds), *Tacitus and the Tacitean Tradition*: 104–28, Princeton, Princeton University Press.

Woolf, G. (1990) 'Food, poverty and patronage: the significance of the epigraphy of the Roman alimentary schemes in early imperial Italy', *PBSR* 58: 197–228.

6

IMPERIAL BUILDING AT ROME

The role of Constantine

E.D. Hunt

I

After his forces had routed Maxentius at the Milvian Bridge on 28 October 312, Constantine entered Rome the following day to be greeted by the familiar protocol of imperial victory.[1] The traditional imagery of panegyric depicts senators and people thronging to hail their new-found liberator, who responded with the expected displays of triumphal generosity. Days of shows and games provided the opportunity for the populace to feast their eyes upon their benefactor, and bask in his liberality; while the Senate listened with appropriate gratification to imperial speeches denouncing the fallen régime, and restoring lost fortunes and ancient dignity (see principally *Pan. Lat.* 12(9).19–20, 4(10), 33–4). In the name of the whole of Italy, Constantine was accorded a golden shield and crown to honour his victory (*Pan. Lat.* 12(9).25.4). This official mood stands prominently reflected to this day in the surviving arch dedicated by a grateful *SPQR* to the *liberator urbis* who, in true Augustan fashion, had avenged the state on the tyrant and all his faction, and where scenes of traditional military success are complemented by reliefs which depict the emperor greeting, and bestowing largesse upon, his new Roman subjects arrayed before him.[2]

The overthrow of Maxentius appears thus as the prelude to a classic parade of imperial *beneficia* enacted at the heart of the empire. Yet the political realities of Constantine's arrival in Rome were far less benign than these rhetorical images of conventional generosity. The scenes of celebration and largesse were pointedly accompanied by the grisly display of the severed head of Maxentius, detached from the mutilated body fished out of the Tiber and stuck on a spear (*Pan. Lat.* 12(9).18.3, 4(10).31–2; *Origo Const. Imp.* 12; Zos. 2.17.1). For Constantine's panegyrists this was a spectacle to arouse joy and ridicule in a populace freed from tyranny; but more realistically in the immediate aftermath of civil war it sent a grim message to erstwhile adherents of his defeated adversary. It is important not to under-estimate the extent of the Roman support which Maxentius' six-year régime had enjoyed, difficult though it is to penetrate the damning distortions of the Constantinian version of history, and despite the reputation for acts of savagery and financial exorbitance which clung to his government: the fact remains that he was the last of Rome's rulers to make his residence in the capital, and, by reviving the continuous association of emperor and *urbs*, to make the most of its traditional opportunities for boosting the imperial power-base. The reported excessive demands for revenue, for example, where not simply the stuff of denunciation, are surely not unrelated to the task of financing the conspicuous programme of Roman public building which he instigated, with the aim of advertising the would-be stability of his rule, and its place in imperial history.[3] Although Maxentius' contribution to one major scheme of public works in the capital, the reconstruction and strengthening of the Aurelian Walls, now seems less extensive than was once commonly suggested,[4] there is no doubt of the impressive scale and grandeur of his redevelopment of the central zone between the Forum area and the Colosseum, which briefly saw a concentration of building work to rival previous imperial additions to the monumental heart of Rome: the 'forum of Maxentius', as one Italian scholar has labelled it (Fiore, cited by Cullhed 1994: 49). The colossal new basilica which dominated this Maxentian programme, probably intended as the focus of the judicial powers of the city prefect, was to be on a scale more akin to the tradition of huge imperial baths (like those of Diocletian only recently completed).[5] Between this and the Colosseum lay Hadrian's Temple of Venus and Rome, one of the largest and grandest of the capital's religious buildings. The accident of a disastrous fire in 306, presumably the impetus for the concentration of Maxentius' building plans in this area, provided him with a fortuitous opportunity to diversify his Roman munificence by setting about the rebuilding of this premier *templum Romae*.[6] On the other side of the basilica stands yet a third building belonging to Maxentius' programme of reconstruction, the circular structure which now forms the vestibule to the church of SS Cosmas and Damian. Traditionally known as the 'temple of Romulus' (*templum divi Romuli*), it was supposedly erected to honour the memory of Maxentius' son and fellow-consul Valerius Romulus (who died in 309), and whose very name alone was a potent symbol of the traditional Roman continuities being proclaimed by the régime. The building's connection with the imperial heir Romulus (which depends upon inconclusive coin evidence) has been the source of much recent controversy, and several alternative interpretations of its function have been proposed; but its architectural integration with the rest of the Maxentian complex embracing basilica and *templum Romae* is not in doubt.[7] If the dynastic significance of this edifice in the heart of the city remains unproven, we are on surer ground with the circular mausoleum built for Romulus amid burial grounds a short distance outside the walls on the Appian Way. This is the centre-piece of the other principal set of buildings deriving from the short period of Maxentius' rule, a suburban 'palace' and its associated circus capable of accommodating some 10,000 spectators; a dedication to the memory of '*divus Romulus*, son of Maxentius and grandson of Maximian', was discovered at the site.[8] The range of public works associated with Maxentius' short-lived government, both in the Forum area and on the Appian Way, in sum represented most of the principal concerns which traditionally claimed an emperor's attention in the capital, especially one aiming to reassert the presence of the ruler in his city: security and stability (the strengthening of the walls), orderly government (the audience-hall and judicial functions of the basilica), respect for Rome's gods (*templum Romae*), the patronage of the people (the new circus), and dynastic ceremonial (the honouring of Romulus). Maxentius may also have kept up with imperial precedents in providing yet another grandiose set of bath buildings, if, as now appears, the so-called 'Baths of Constantine' on the Quirinal had in fact already been under construction before Constantine's arrival in the city (Steinby 1986: 142). No chance was missed, we may conclude, to adorn the city of Rome with buildings which carried political and ideological significance for Maxentius' fragile régime.

Despite its 'incredible intensity' (Steinby 1986: 142) this extensive Roman building programme was only partially complete by the time that Maxentius fell victim to the victorious armies of Constantine. Rome's new master had no need to devise a monumental agenda of his own, since after October 312 it was open to him simply to hijack Maxentius' unfinished building legacy, and usurp for himself the political credit to which his rival had aspired. The whole complex between Forum and Colosseum became Constantine's. Maxentius' great basilica was completed to the glory of the victor and dedicated in his name, the *basilica Constantiniana*; pride of place in its western apse would go to a colossal statue – perhaps one originally depicting Maxentius, but reworked to represent a heroic Constantine – of which the famous head and other fragments are still to be seen on the Campidoglio.[9] Similarly the rebuilding of the temple of Venus and Rome alongside the new basilica was taken over as a Constantinian project – and the finished result would be prominent among the array of magnificent sights in the city which attracted the admiration of fourth-century visitors, not least of Constantine's son, Constantius II, making a celebrated appearance in the capital in 357.[10] The third Maxentian structure, the so-called 'temple of Romulus', was also a victim of Constantine's appropriations, to judge from an inscription in his honour recorded there in the sixteenth century (*CIL* VI.1147, with Curran 2000: 82–3). Whatever the original purpose of this building, it is evident that the strongly Roman imagery and dynastic potency symbolised by Maxentius in naming his son Romulus were now seized upon by Constantine, who was to be hailed as the 'true Romulus' displacing the false title of Maxentius; with such claims went the discrediting of his (and his offspring's) rights to the heritage of the Tetrarchy, as contemporary pronouncements began to affirm that Maxentius was no real son of Maximian, and to revive emphasis upon Constantine's own relationship with the late Augustus (his father-in-law).[11] By appropriating Maxentius' Roman buildings Constantine could thus be seen to be invalidating his imperial pedigree. The suppression of Maxentius as advertised by this Constantinian takeover of his building programme and the completed splendours of basilica and temple was also graphically proclaimed close at hand on the triumphal arch dedicated to Constantine in 315, where the drowning of Maxentius and his army in the flowing waters of the Tiber is depicted as the latest in the distinguished line of imperial successes from the past, through its juxtaposition with reused material from earlier

Roman victory monuments. By such means Maxentius' attempts, through an ambitious and hectic scheme of public building, to cast himself in the role of model emperor in his capital city were directly subverted by the advent of Constantine and his own carefully managed deployment of imperial munificence. Even Constantine's claim to fame as the last of Rome's emperors to contribute a substantial bath complex to the city ('not very different from the others'), the ruins of which have been located in the southern area of the Quirinal, is now seen to be yet another appropriation of a project instigated under Maxentius.[12]

Other traditional areas of imperial patronage in the capital also saw Constantine rivalling the building legacy of Maxentius. Where his ousted predecessor had built a new circus out along the Appian Way, Constantine addressed the demands of popular entertainment by the reconstruction of the Circus Maximus itself, which the orator Nazarius in 321 saw newly adorned with 'lofty porticos and columns glowing in gold': while lamenting Constantine's absence from Rome, Nazarius could still count among his *beneficia* to the city the provision of gleaming new buildings and the refurbishment of the old, enough to make his predecessors seem 'parsimonious' by comparison (*Pan. Lat.* 4(10), 35.4–5, with Aur. Vict. 40.27). Not yet to be seen was Constantine's most striking planned new addition to the Circus, the ancient obelisk which he ordered to be transported from Egyptian Thebes to match the one placed there centuries earlier by Augustus; the project took its time, and was brought to fruition only after the Roman visit of Constantius II in 357 (Amm. Marc. 16.10.17, 17.4.12ff., with Fowden 1987: 51–7; Nash 1968: 142–3). Constantine's obelisk stands in Rome to this day, the largest of such surviving imperial embellishments from the antiquities of Egypt, now the centrepiece of the piazza in front of St John Lateran.

The Roman building projects mentioned thus far to which Constantine gave his name serve to place him securely in a familiar tradition of imperial munificence lavished on the capital city.[13] Rome's victorious liberator could not but also be her material benefactor. From the start, I have argued, this was dictated by competition with the extensive building plans of his ousted rival: Constantine appropriated for himself, and added to, the largely uncompleted landscape of Maxentius' Rome.[14] But Constantine's contribution to the physical appearance of Rome's monumental centre went beyond any initial requirement to outdo or obliterate Maxentius. His building programme continued into later years when the civil war in Italy was a less immediate memory, and was sustained despite the imperial court's virtually permanent absence from the city: after his 'two-month' residence at the end of 312, Rome saw Constantine on only two further occasions, the *decennalia* ceremonies of July–September 315 and the even briefer visit for the culmination of the *vicennalia* in July 326.[15] None the less, his munificence to the city could be applauded still as a present reality in Nazarius' encomium of 321, despite the absence of the emperor and his young Caesars (whose *quinquennalia* was the occasion of the speech); and even in the last brief visit of 326 Constantine was harbouring extravagant plans in Rome to commemorate his *vicennalia* – if, as has been persuasively argued, an imperial emissary known to have travelled up the Nile to visit the Valley of the Kings in that year was actually there in search of the obelisk intended for the Circus Maximus (Fowden 1987). As late as 334, although not seen there in person for eight years, Constantine still presided over the centre of Rome, the year in which the urban prefect and consul Anicius Paulinus set up in the middle of the Forum an equestrian statue of the emperor, which would become one of the famous landmarks noticed by medieval visitors.[16]

Constantine's continued association with the ancient heart of the empire in the later years of his reign deserves emphasis when it has become a commonplace in much modern discussion to see the creation of Constantinople, after the defeat of Licinius in 324, as a definitive rejection of old Rome: despite the fact that the traditional bonds which united Rome and her emperors had thus far managed to survive the physical separation of court and imperial city, Constantine, it is argued, decisively turned his back on *urbs Roma*, alienated by its supposedly pagan-dominated establishment and the monopoly of the old gods.[17] It is a view which has its origins in the religious polemic of fourth-century sources, where from the pagan vantage-point the foundation of Constantinople is presented as a riposte to Roman disaffection at the spurning of its traditional cults (so esp. Zos. 2.30.1 (deriving from Eunapius), with principally Paschoud, 1971: 334–53).[18] There is indeed evidence which hints that Constantine encountered popular hostility during the vicennial visit in 326, and that this may have sprung from a refusal on the emperor's part to participate in religious ceremonies on the Capitol; but it is only the hostile thrust of pagan sources which exaggerates this ill-documented episode into the definitive abandonment of the ancient capital.[19] No such conclusion, however, need be drawn from Constantine's subsequent failure to return to Rome, in an age when the residence of emperors there was the (very) occasional exception to the rule. Nor was Constantine in any sense unique in having to endure confrontation with a disorderly Roman population, whose outspokenness was an almost characteristic feature of its dealings with now rarely-seen emperors: he will have had earlier experience of it as a member of the imperial entourage on the occasion of Diocletian's vicennial visit to Rome in November 303, which had been similarly disrupted by the *libertas populi Romani*.[20] Whatever popular protest accompanied Constantine's brief, and last, Roman sojourn in the summer of 326, it needs to be put in perspective against the background of continuing public munificence to the city which has been illustrated above: Rome's monumental centre could boast an array of Constantinian building and reconstruction – basilica, temple, baths, circus – which testified to the traditional liberality of the emperor in his capital. Amid such reminders of imperial patronage, it is not so incongruous that the same Roman population which voiced its discontent in 326 should (as reported in both pagan and Christian sources) participate in the formalities of public mourning on the news of Constantine's death and burial in Constantinople eleven years later, nor that the Roman senate should enact the traditional procedures enrolling him among the gods.[21] The protocol which governed an emperor's special relationship with his Roman subjects, and which had been on display since Senate and people acclaimed Constantine as their liberator in October 312, still appears intact at his death.

II

Constantine's Roman munificence has thus far appeared – like the baths on the Quirinal – as 'not very different from the others' (Aur. Vict. *Caes.* 40.27): continuing the long and well-established habit of imperial *beneficia* in the home of empire. But for Constantine's Christian biographer the familiar symbols of victory and scenes of acclaim which greeted his arrival in Rome were of no account when compared with 'the help he had received from God', in recognition of which, and as 'a vow of thanksgiving to the author of his victory', the emperor set up a 'great trophy against his enemies' in the middle of the city (Eus. *V. Const.* 1.39–40, cf. *HE* 9.9.9–11). In these words Eusebius alludes to that part of the triumphal display after October 312 which Constantine reserved for his newly-professed allegiance to the God of the Christians; and specifically to the 'saving sign' represented in the hand of one of the emperor's statues in the most 'frequented' area of Rome (widely assumed to be the colossal statue in the new basilica), a sign proclaimed by its accompanying inscription to be the agent both of the liberation of city from 'the yoke of the tyrant' and of the restoration of dignity to senate and people. Whatever the precise nature of this sign (was it simply a cross, or the chi-rho symbol which would become the new Christian standard, the *labarum*?),[22] the implication of its imagery and central location is that Constantine's religious conversion has here imported a novel element into the received victory language of liberation and vengeance which was otherwise ringing out from monuments at the heart of Rome. Where the triumphal arch declared its message in well-used images from the imperial past, this statue spoke with a symbol unambiguously indicative of the emperor's new-found faith. This once seemed too provocative an intrusion into the orchestrated traditionalism surrounding the victory over Maxentius, or too obvious an offence against the capital's old gods, and it was dismissed as a piece of idealistic fantasy from a Christian author writing far from the scene who knew nothing of the reality of Rome after the Milvian Bridge.[23] But Eusebius' authenticity, and the reality of Christian sign and inscription, have long been vindicated; nor is it unreasonable to conclude that Constantine would somewhere in the aftermath of victory allude to the sign which had already made its appearance on the shields which had successfully confronted Maxentius.[24] It is important not to forget, though, that it was the sign alone which pointed in a new direction, and one perhaps understood only by those relatively few Romans who viewed it through Christian eyes; reading the statue's inscription, by contrast, many more would recognise the orthodox and predictable language of victory and restoration, differing very little from the official dedication prominently displayed on the arch.

If the juxtaposition of Christian symbol and the conventional themes of the moment might pass relatively unnoticed in the hand of one imperial statue, the same can hardly be said of Constantine's most distinctive and innovative contribution to the physical appearance of the city of Rome and its surroundings – the series of major church foundations which began in the wake of the defeat of

Maxentius. Rome's Christian community, which had been no more than tolerated by Maxentius' régime and had only recently (311) recovered possession of the property confiscated from it during the last period of persecution, now found itself receiving the lion's share of imperial patronage and the largesse of Constantine's victory.[25] For the first time, Christian churches basked in the emperor's munificence. In the south-east of the city, where the imperial patrimony embraced an area of aristocratic residences, there arose a second *basilica Constantiniana*, on a scale comparable to the vast edifice beside the Forum which Constantine had appropriated from Maxentius.[26] With this great church, better known as the Lateran basilica (predecessor of the present cathedral of St John Lateran), Constantine's builders transformed Christian architecture from a domestic model into the grand dimensions and publicity of the Roman basilica, and placed it on a par with the secular buildings which dominated Rome's monumental centre (Ward-Perkins 1954: 69–90; Krautheimer 1967: 117–40, and 1986: ch. 2; White 1991: esp. ch. 2). A baptistery was added alongside the basilica, and both buildings were adorned with lavish gold and silver fittings and liturgical objects provided by gift of the emperor. The extent of these donations emerges from the detailed list incorporated into the later compilation of the *Liber Pontificalis*, which also includes a catalogue of the imperial properties with which church and baptistery were endowed to furnish their revenues.[27] Despite the problems associated with this evidence (the disproportionately large sums of wealth assigned to the baptistery, for instance, seem to derive in part from post-Constantinian additions), it is at least possible to deduce an early date for the initial endowments of the Lateran from the commonly noted fact that the allocation of imperial lands is confined almost exclusively to estates in Italy and Africa (with the curious exception of property on the Adriatic island of Cephalonia),[28] which would have been recovered from the territory won from Maxentius in October 312. The foundation of the Lateran basilica followed hard upon the heels of Maxentius' defeat – perhaps even within days of Constantine's 'liberation' of Rome, if we are to accept the authority of a tradition preserved in medieval times which celebrated the annual feast of the dedication of the basilica on 9 November (a date which would appropriately have fallen on a Sunday in 312).[29] Even if this specific date is disregarded, there seems little doubt that the creation of this second *basilica Constantiniana* at the Lateran belongs integrally to the victory context of the rest of the imperial building programme in Rome in the years immediately following the Milvian Bridge. There is an ideological as much as an architectural connection with the other (secular) basilica in the heart of the city, and its message of victory over Maxentius. It was an association of ideas reinforced by the siting of the church, for in the midst of the wealthy housing which it supplanted had also lain the camp of the *equites singulares*, the cavalry arm of the praetorian guard: the praetorians had been the mainstay of Maxentius' resistance to the advance of Constantine on Rome, and with their defeat came disbandment and the destruction of their garrisons – including the camp at the Lateran, which now made way for the new basilica.[30] The theme of triumph over the tyrant which we have seen reflected in the formal language of public inscriptions and in the appropriation and reconstruction of Maxentius' buildings was thus also operative here in the Christian resurrection of a former enemy garrison, and in the redirection, for the benefit of the church, of revenues from former properties of his defeated foe now at the victor's disposal. Embellished and funded from the profits of the very victory which Constantine attributed to the Christian God, the Lateran basilica was (I would suggest) a more universally obvious expression of triumph over enemies than a little-known symbol placed in the hand of the statue in the Forum, and one which proclaimed the handsome benefits to be enjoyed by Rome's Christians, as by the rest of her citizens, after the liberation of their city.[31]

The remainder of Constantine's Christian building programme for Rome concentrated on the veneration of the martyr saints whose memory shaped the historical identity of Roman Christianity, and whose tombs stood guard in a kind of protective ring among the cemeteries which lay outside the city walls. Rome's Christian community was now to discover in Constantine a lavish patron of its principal cults. Pre-eminent were those of the founding fathers of the Roman church, the apostles Peter and Paul, whose traditional resting-places in the Vatican necropolis and in a cemetery a short distance beyond the city gate along the Ostian Way had been honoured at least since the end of the second century;[32] while in the mid-third century another venerated site united the cults of both of them among the catacombs of the Appian Way, the location of the earliest recorded commemoration in the Roman calendar of martyrs.[33] In the early decades of the fourth century this shrine of Peter and Paul at the third milestone on the Appian Way was enclosed within a new *basilica apostolorum* (the present church of S. Sebastiano) which would both accommodate the assemblies of worshippers and provide burial space for the faithful in the closest proximity to the apostles: it is an amalgam of functions which was to be especially characteristic of Constantine's new martyr-basilicas rising amid Rome's outskirts, and is thus suggestive of Constantinian inspiration for this church building, despite its absence from the list of donations in *Lib. Pont.* (On this church see Krautheimer *et al.* 1970: 99–147 (for chronology, 144–6); Pietri 1976: 40–6). It cannot escape notice that this site on the Appian Way lay opposite the place where Maxentius had lately constructed the mausoleum of his son and heir Valerius Romulus, and its surrounding complex of 'palace' and circus: and building similarities in the construction of mausoleum and *basilica apostolorum* have invited the suggestion that the latter too may have begun life in the time of Maxentius, as part of the same suburban development (Krautheimer *et al.* 1970: 144–5; cf. Curran 2000: 99). Whatever the truth of this, from the proximity of the location alone it is hard to resist the conclusion that among the tombs along the Appian Way SS Peter and Paul were being drawn into that same competition with (and appropriation of) the building legacy of Maxentius which characterised Constantine's secular edifices in the centre of the city: was the new monument to the apostolic forbears of the Roman church Constantine's own distinctive answer to the heritage of Romulus claimed by his ousted predecessor and advertised in the mausoleum across the road?

This new-found imperial patronage of Peter and Paul could naturally be expected also to embrace their separate shrines on the Vatican and beside the Ostian Way. Constantine's involvement at the latter site is shrouded in obscurity. The *basilica Pauli* which the *Lib. Pont.* attributes to him can only in fact have been a very modest foundation which was soon outgrown by the number of worshippers visiting the shrine – as is clear from the surviving imperial correspondence with the prefect of Rome relating to the rebuilding of the church in the 380s.[34] There is indeed so little archaeological trace of any Constantinian building that its existence has been denied; while the list of (disproportionately large) imperial endowments preserved in *Lib. Pont.* is an unreliable record interpolated from the era of the later basilica, which would vie with St Peter's for supremacy of status among the great martyr shrines of Rome.[35] Constantine's original benefaction for his foundation on the Ostian Way may have amounted to nothing more than an island estate in the neighbourhood of Tarsus in Cilicia (presumably lying at the mouth of the river Cydnus), which heads the surviving list of donations (*Lib. Pont.*, p. 178 and n. 73): it would surely have seemed a pointedly appropriate gesture of imperial largesse that the Roman shrine where Christians venerated Paul's martyrdom should benefit from proceeds emanating from the apostle's eastern homeland. This Tarsus donation must have postdated the defeat of Licinius in September 324, which first gave Constantine possession of imperial lands east of the Bosphorus; and it provides further confirmation that, as was the case with his 'secular' building-progamme, Constantine's attentions to the city of Rome and its environs were actively pursued into the later part of his reign.

In keeping with the eastern origins of the mission which had brought the apostles to Rome, Constantine's basilica over St Peter's tomb on the Vatican was also endowed with income from the diocese of Oriens, including a number of small urban properties in the city of Antioch as well as suburban estates there and in Egypt, which were detailed to supply both revenue in cash and other goods in kind, including papyrus, oil, spices and linen (not all of these seem aimed at serving the immediate needs of the church, and may have been intended to raise cash on the commercial market).[36] As in the case of the *basilica Pauli*, Constantine's St Peter's can only have received this eastern patrimony at a date after the emperor had seized control of Licinius' former domain. The building work itself, on what was the largest of Constantine's Roman churches (122 m × 66 m, compared with the Lateran's 100 m × 55 m), probably did not see its finishing touches until the time of Constantius II's visit of 357; but it was already under way in the course of the 320s, during which period Constantine's mother, the Augusta Helena (who died *c.*328), was associated with the construction over St Peter's tomb.[37] More precision may be possible. The dedicatory text which medieval visitors to St Peter's read on the triumphal arch as they approached the shrine linked Constantine's foundation of the basilica specifically to victory achieved under Christ's leadership: in the contemporary context *Constantinus victor* must have alluded most immediately to the defeat of Licinius, who had embarked on a renewal of persecution and by whose defeat Constantine had finally won the world for Christianity – he himself had claimed no less in addressing his new subjects in the eastern empire.[38] Where the Lateran basilica had been an expression of victory after the Milvian Bridge, similarly the great church honouring Rome's founding apostle Peter may be seen to reflect the triumph against Licinius. Constantine's Christian edifices, and the veneration of Rome's apostles which they embodied, were now providing the religious symbols of victory which had once been the preserve of Jupiter on the Capitol.

The list of Constantinian basilicas adorning catacombs and martyr-sites around Rome extends to three other locations beyond the walls. To the north-east, along the *via Tiburtina*, among the tombs in the area known as the *ager Veranus* Roman Christians honoured the resting-place of the deacon Lawrence (a victim of the Valerianic persecution of 258). Here, alongside the shrine and attached to it by a new stairway, Constantine built and endowed a basilica of similar type to his foundations at other extra-mural martyr sites, a combination of covered cemetery and assembly hall for the faithful (*Lib. Pont.* 181–2, with Krautheimer *et al.* 1962: 1–146; Pietri 1976: 37–40; Curran 2000: 102–5). The same happened in the cemetery area further north along the *via Nomentana*, where a new basilica was provided adjacent to the tomb of the Roman martyr Agnes;[39] and to the south-east along the *via Labicana*, in a burial-ground which later tradition came to associate with the tombs of the little-known Diocletianic martyrs Marcellinus and Peter (whereas the earliest Roman martyrology names only an obscure 'Gorgonius' in connection with this area).[40] In this latter case, any martyr tombs were perhaps more incidental to the construction and endowment of a church building than the strong imperial connections which the area – close to the new Lateran basilica – already boasted. Surviving epitaphs indicate that the necropolis on the *via Labicana* had at one time also been the burial place for men of the *equites singulares*, whose nearby garrison had been razed to make way for the Lateran (Deichmann and Tschira 1957: 68–70; Guyon 1987: 30–3). Furthermore, an accumulation of evidence indicates that much of these south-eastern outskirts of Rome had recently come into the possession of Constantine's mother Helena. The principal imperial endowment of the new basilica, for example, comprised extensive suburban properties (including baths) described in the *Lib. Pont.* as the possession of Helena; while listed among the gifts presented to the church was a gold chalice inscribed with 'the imperial name', probably that of the Augusta.[41] Helena's association with this area of Rome is confirmed by inscriptions which link her closely with the imperial complex just inside the Aurelian Walls known as the 'Sessorian Palace', one of whose halls was converted by Constantine's builders into the church later to be known as S. Croce in Gerusalemme: when, in later generations, the name of Helena came to be synonymous with the discovery of relics of the cross, it was the obvious place for Roman Christians to house their fragments of the sacred wood.[42] On Helena's death her body was laid to rest in Rome in an imperial mausoleum constructed alongside the new basilica on the *via Labicana*, the Augusta in common with others of the faithful taking her place among the venerable company already buried there. In similar vein, Constantine's daughter Constantina would be laid to rest in a mausoleum built for her beside the shrine of Agnes and the new basilica on the *via Nomentana.*

The imposing scale of Helena's mausoleum (the 'Tor Pignattara'), as of the (still surviving) porphyry sarcophagus which it contained, has suggested to some that this building was originally the intended resting-place of Constantine himself – until the attractions of a tomb where he would be surrounded by memorials of no less than the twelve apostles in his eponymous new city outweighed the company of obscure Roman martyrs.[43] Yet the relocation of Constantine's burial to his new mausoleum in Constantinople, as indeed the whole issue of the foundation of 'new Rome', ought not to cloud the political and religious significance of the church building programme which was still continuing in the old capital: the attentions lavished on the creation of Constantinople did not, as we have seen, entail the abandonment of the emperor's Roman munificence in either its secular, or its increasingly Christian, expression. The material provision of new Christian basilicas embraced the same political arena as the building of baths or circuses, publicising the message of victory over enemies (Maxentius, Licinius) and of Constantine's assumption of the traditional imperial patronage of *urbs Roma*: the language differed, in that it was now the God of the Christians who received the recognition for success achieved, and it was the Christian heritage of Rome's apostles and martyrs which defined the sphere of imperial *beneficia*; but the context was still recognisably that of an emperor's special responsibility for the city and his Roman subjects.

III

In seeking to view the church foundations in much the same light as the rest of Constantine's public works in the capital, and seeing similar principles reflected in both, my discussion takes issue with long-running arguments which have emphasised the essential separateness and isolation of the Christian building programme from the emperor's otherwise 'mainstream' additions to the city's landscape. Despite their impressive size and rich splendour of decoration, and the claims to public standing implicit in the adoption of the architectural form of the basilica, the new churches have been regarded as a marginal divergence from the long-standing tradition of imperial building which had shaped Rome's urban centre, and which Constantine still sustained in his secular edifices. On this understanding, it was a matter of deliberate Constantinian policy to banish Christian building to the outskirts, in most instances beyond the walls, in order not to disturb the historic domain of the old gods amid the city's central monuments.[44] Hence Rome's entrenched pagan masters might turn a blind eye to the most obvious physical manifestation of the emperor's idiosyncratic religious allegiance: it was, in Krautheimer's words, 'a policy of sparing pagan sentiment' (Krautheimer 1983: 29). Whether in reality Constantine was obliged to proceed with such diplomatic delicacy in confronting the Roman establishment of his day is now a matter of question, in the light of a series of recent studies which have demonstrated more extensive Christian penetration of its ranks than was previously thought, and a public ethos which was increasingly reconciled to the service of a Christian ruler: it is less easy than it once was to be confident that old-fashioned paganism had a monopoly of the religious loyalties of the senatorial aristocracy in the early years of the fourth century (Novak 1979: 271–310; Champlin 1982: 71–6; Barnes and Westall 1991: 50–61; Barnes 1995: 135–47).[45] Moreover, even if it be accepted that the pagan gods had not yet relaxed their grip on Rome's leaders, Krautheimer's 'peripheral' view of Constantine's church foundations would still invite some reconsideration, in the context of my attempt to view them in the same terms as the rest of his building programme in the capital.

The argument that Rome's Constantinian churches were a deliberately distant and discreet expression of imperial munificence is based on two principal features of their foundation – their remote suburban location, and the supposedly 'non-public' nature of a legal transaction which transferred land and properties from one private owner to another, from the imperial *res privata* into the 'private' possession of Rome's Christian community. This latter aspect, it is argued, kept the church-building programme out of the public domain, avoiding the need for the involvement of Roman officials (the urban prefect and his subordinates) or the senate, and ensuring that the basilicas, however lavish and whatever their pretensions to public status, remained strictly a private donation to the Christians of Rome.[46] If this were the position, then this 'private and personal character' of Constantine's church benefactions in Rome would be in stark contrast not only with the centuries-old procedures of imperial building in the capital, (which had certainly not been confined to the 'private' sphere, depending – for example – upon the collaboration of a range of senatorial *curatores* and other officials (Kolb 1993: e.g. 53–8), but also with what can be discerned of the emperor's church building schemes elsewhere in the empire, where evidence points to the active co-operation of state functionaries in the process.[47] The fact is that we lack information about the formal procedures by which Constantine made arrangements for the building of the Roman churches, and for the transfer of land ownership and property; yet it seems improbable – given the whole history of imperial building in Rome and Constantine's own continuing contribution to that tradition – that the emperor could embark on this series of major projects purely as a matter of 'private' negotiation between himself and the Christian congregation. The boundaries between the emperor's public and private finances, always notoriously difficult to determine, by the fourth century have all but disappeared, with the terminology of *res privata* seemingly an anachronistic residue from earlier subdivisions of imperial wealth;[48] while from the era of Constantine a similar ambiguity surrounds the status of Christian communities, at this date less akin to private individuals than institutions emancipated and recognised by the state as owners of wealth and property (see Gaudemet 1958: 288–315; Jones 1964: 895; Millar 1992: 577–84). For the contemporary observer of the real world, these new Christian basilicas must have seemed eminently public buildings: their architectural style and affluent possessions made them grandiose, highly visible additions to the Roman horizon – and they were accessible to all who approached them (with the exception, perhaps, of the new 'palace-church' in the Sessorian grounds, which remained within the limits of Helena's imperial residence). Whatever the fine print of legal procedure and formal ownership, it is hard to see how they would be distinguished from the temples, baths and circuses which made up the traditional deposit of imperial *beneficia* to the city of Rome, and which placed Constantine in direct descent from the example of Augustus' lavish expenditure.[49]

A more significant obstacle to this line of argument (and a prominent feature of Krautheimer's discussion) is the undeniably peripheral location which set Constantine's Roman churches at a considerable distance from the usual arena of imperial building in the heart of the city. Yet is it really the case that these grand new edifices in the suburbs owed their siting to a deliberate intent on the emperor's part to marginalise his patronage of Christianity in the face of entrenched paganism, in deference to the established ascendancy of the old gods in Rome's traditional centre? To be sure, in the political aftermath of the overthrow of Maxentius, heralded by the familiar language of liberation and scenes of victory, it would have been unthinkable to shatter this ideological harmony by the destruction of ancient temples or other public buildings in the heart of Rome to make way for intrusive demonstrations of the emperor's newly-proclaimed Christianity: only in the East much later in his reign, and then only in especially significant settings like Jerusalem, would Constantine resort to such officially sanctioned demolition of temples.[50] With the centre of Rome crowded by its monumental heritage, it was no more than realistic that Constantine should look to the outskirts to site his Christian foundations. But it would be false to conclude that this was mere pragmatic necessity or political convenience, aided by the availability of suburban imperial estates (as, for example, in the area of the Lateran). That the chosen location for the Lateran basilica comprised properties apparently at the emperor's disposal is of less consequence than the juxtaposition which we have noted with the camp of Maxentius' defeated troops: its siting, I would suggest, was dictated more by the current ideology of triumph over a rival than by the convenience of using imperial land on the outskirts to avoid disturbing Rome's ancient heritage.[51]

Moreover, the historic focus of Rome's Christian identity (as in other cities with long-standing congregations) was precisely among the catacombs and cemeteries to be found outside the walls, where the faithful kept the memory of the saints and martyrs who had formed and shaped their community.[52] The heart of Christian Rome was nowhere in the Forum and its surroundings, but in the Vatican necropolis and along the Appian and Ostian Ways; and by making these and other extra-mural locations the object of imperial building and lavish patronage Constantine was the first to give visible endorsement to this inverted 'inside-out' profile of the city.[53] Not only would the new Christian basilicas, standing prominently beside some of the main approaches to Rome, often be the first great buildings to catch the visitor's eye; they would also give real substance to an emerging alternative topography which rivalled that of Rome's traditional landscape. The churches would likewise provide the setting for a new public network of religious ceremonial.[54] In contrast to the domestic privacy and disparately scattered nature of Christian worship as it had thus far existed in the capital, these grandly spacious new arenas would bring together bishop and congregation under one roof, and enable the evolution of a unitary cycle of annual festivals: before Constantine's death the Christian community in Rome was already observing a public calendar of commemorations of martyrs and past bishops, which involved a peripatetic circuit of ceremonies embracing various cemetery sites around the outskirts, in addition to marking both the ancient season of Easter, extending from Lent to Pentecost (a period deliberately left free of martyr observances), and the newly-introduced feast of Christmas.[55] The Constantinian basilicas provided the context and space for the communal celebration of these high points in the Christian calendar: Easter focused on the Lateran and its adjacent baptistery (it was the festival when baptisms were conducted), while the ceremonies of Christmas would come to concentrate on the Vatican basilica of St Peter – at least by the time of its completion in the 350s (Pietri 1976: 112–15). For Rome's Christians Constantine's church buildings were thus anything but marginal: they defined those places which Christians viewed as the focal points of their community, fostering a new unity for the public life and liturgy of the Roman church under the lead of its bishop, and beginning the process of transforming Rome into a Christian city.

As yet, of course, this Christian reordering of both space and time at Rome was far from displacing the traditional sacred cults and festivals of the city's year; and the twenty-five or so days in the year devoted to Christian martyr ceremonies in the suburbs hardly stand comparison with the two hundred or more days of celebrations and holidays which dominated Rome's official calendar in the middle of the fourth century. The fledgling observance of Christmas at the Vatican, for example, must have found it hard to compete with the popular festivities for the birthday of *Sol Invictus* on 25 December, which were accompanied by no less than thirty races in the circus.[56] But the significance of Constantine's contribution to the eventual creation of a Christian version of *urbs Roma* was not lost on the Roman church. In its official fourth-century calendar of dates for the observance of Easter in Rome, the list began with the year 312: Roman Christians evidently recognised the advent of Constantine in the capital as the definitive starting-point of a new era in the history of their community.[57] When Constantine died in May 337, a grieving Roman public (we are told), seeing another city favoured with his burial, took it ill that the emperor was not laid to rest in his rightful place in the Rome 'which he had all but renewed' ('*quasi novatam urbem Romam*', Aur. Vict. *Caes.* 41.17). It was a historic debt to Constantine's munificence in rebuilding their city which Rome's Christians had good cause to remember.

Notes

1 Salzman 1990: 135. On Constantine's *adventus*, MacCormack 1981: 33ff.; McCormick 1986: 84–91. For general victory context see Grünewald 1990: ch. II. On the vexed question of whether it was on this occasion, or later, that tradition was broken to the extent of refusal to sacrifice on the Capitol, see Fraschetti 1986: 59–98, and now Curran 2000: 71–5. Cf. below, note 19.

2 For the dedicatory inscription, see *ILS* 694; with MacCormack 1981: 35–7, and Peirce 1989: 387–418, for discussion of iconography.

3 Cullhed 1994, esp. ch. 3; on his Roman building programme, Curran 2000: 54–63; Coarelli 1986: 1–35, and summary by Krautheimer 1980: 7–8. For examples of the 'bad press', see Eus. *HE* 8.14.2–6; Aur. Vict. *Caes.* 40.24; *Chron. Min.* I, 148.

4 Following Richmond 1930: 251–6 (cf. Todd 1978: 46–59); but see now Cullhed 1994: 56.

5 On the basilica of Maxentius, see *LTUR* I.170–3, with Nash 1968: 180–2; Richardson 1992: 51–2. Still useful is Minoprio 1932: 1–18.

6 *Chron. Min.* I, 148. For Hadrian's temple, Boatwright 1987: 119–33, with Nash 1968: 496–9; Richardson 1992: 409–11.

7 For summary, see Cullhed 1994: 53–5, with Nash 1968: 268–71; Richardson 1992: 333–4. The dynastic connections were defended by Coarelli 1986: 10–22 (on the basis of the traditional associations of earlier buildings on the site, e.g. temple of Jupiter Stator, with the mythical Romulus), but have been disputed by Krautheimer, *loc. cit.* (arguing for office of city prefect, following A. Frazer).

8 *ILS* 673. For the building of the circus 'in catecumbas', see *Chron. Min.* I, 148; on its size, as the location of public games (not a 'private' venue), Humphrey 1986: 586, 601–2. On the Via Appia site, see Cullhed 1994: 57–60, with Pisani Sartorio and Calza 1976, esp. 146 ff.

9 Aur. Vict. *Caes.* 40.26. On this, and other Constantinian secular buildings in Rome, see Krautheimer 1983: 25–6; Curran 2000: 76–90. The traditional view that the reconstruction and north–south realignment of the basilica (with a second apse on the north side) are Constantinian alterations (e.g. Minoprio 1932: n. 5) was questioned by Coarelli 1986: 32–4 (cf. *LTUR* I.170–3), who saw them as later fourth-century changes, but now Curran 2000: 81, affirms that 'the changes … may be assigned with some confidence to Constantine' (it is Coarelli too who argued that the statue is a reworking of Maxentius).

10 Amm. Marc. 16.10.14 ('urbis templum'). For Constantine's completion of the project, Aur. Vict. *l.c.* ('urbis fanum').

11 Barnes 1981: 47; for Maxentius as illegitimate, see *Pan. Lat.* 12(9).3.4, 4.3, with *Origo Const. Imp.* 12, *Epit. de Caes.* 40.13. Constantine as Romulus: *Pan. Lat.* 12(9).18.1.

12 Aur. Vict. *Caes.* 40.27; with Nash 1986: 442–7, Richardson 1992: 390–1. Cf. above, p. 107.

13 On the role of buildings as part of imperial beneficence, see (in general) Veyne 1990: 361–6.

14 'Constantine's military victory cost Maxentius his monumental legacy as well as his life' (Curran 2000: 90).

15 For summary documentation on Constantine's stays in Rome, see Barnes 1982: 71, 72, 77. The 'two-month' stay after the Milvian Bridge derives from *Pan. Lat.* 4(10).33.6, where it is explicitly contrasted with the 'six years' of Maxentius' domination.

16 *ILS* 698; cf. Walser 1987: 91–2. For the statue, see Nash 1968: 388; Richardson 1992: 144; *LTUR* II: 226–7.

17 The thesis of Alföldi 1948, esp. ch. vii, and Macmullen 1970: 141ff. The rejection of Rome is accorded less prominence by Jones 1948: 232–8, and Barnes 1981: 212, 222–3.

19 For the case to link Zosimus' notorious account of the abandonment of sacrifice on the Capitol (2.29.5) with Libanius' allusions to popular discontent with Constantine in Rome

(*Or.* 19.19, 20.24), and dating the episode to the 326 visit, see Fraschetti 1986: 87–98, and Wiemer 1994: 469–94.

20 As recounted by Lactantius, *De Mort. Persec.* 17.2. For the long-standing tradition of confrontation between emperor and Roman people, see (e.g.) Cameron 1976: ch. 7; Millar 1992: 368–75.

21 For the deification (and the accompanying appearance of a comet), see Eutrop. 10.8.2. Public mourning in Rome: Eus. *V. Const.* 4.69, Aur. Vict. *Caes.* 41.17.

22 Eusebius' language supports the cross as the symbol (N.B. *V. Const.* 1.40.2 'a lofty spear in the shape of a cross'), but Barnes 1981: 46 (following Alföldi) asserts the *labarum*; cf. Lane Fox 1986: 616–7.

23 Eusebius was notoriously accused of falsification by Grégoire 1932: 135–43.

24 Lact. *De mort. persec.* 44.5, cf. Eus. *V. Const.* 1.29–30 (on the military context of the sign, see now Curran 2000: 78–9). For the case against Grégoire, see Chadwick 1972.

25 For precise summary of Maxentius' handling of Christian matters, see Barnes 1981: 38–9, with Corcoran 1996: 144–5. On Constantine's Roman church foundations, see principally Pietri 1976, ch. 1; Krautheimer 1983: ch. 1; Davis 1989: introd. xix–xxvi; Curran 2000: 90–114.

26 For the name, see *Liber Pontificalis* (Duchesne 1886: 172). Other sources use the term 'Lateran': e.g. *Coll. Avell.* 1.6, Jer. *Ep.* 77.4, Prudent. *C. Symm.* 1.585. For full literary and archaeological documentation on the basilica, see Krautheimer *et al.* 1977: 1–92; on the site before the fourth century, Santa Maria Scrinari 1991.

27 *Lib. Pont.* 172–5 (Davis 1989: 16–18). For discussion of the lists of donations in *LP* see Duchesne's introduction, (1886: cxl–cliv), and Pietri 1978: 317–37.

28 Constantine gained possession of Greece at the end of the first conflict with Licinius in 317.

29 Krautheimer 1983: 127 n.6; cf. Curran 2000: 94–5. Pietri (1976: 8) commits himself only to 'vraisemblablement avant 324' for commencement of the work.

30 On Constantine's suppression of Roman units which had supported Maxentius, see Aur. Vict. *Caes.* 40.25 ('praetorians and their allies'), and Zos.2.17.2 ('wiping out the praetorian troops and destroying the camps which they occupied'). On *equites singulares* and the praetorian guard, see Durry 1938: 29–34; von Domaszewski 1967: 50–3. Camp at the Lateran: *LTUR* I.246–8.

31 To go further, with Krautheimer 1983: 12, and interpret the building of the Lateran basilica as a personal thank-offering of Constantine to his new God, depends on Eusebius' language of 'thanksgiving and prayer to the author of his victory' (*V. Const.* 1.39.3); but in the context this is better associated with the statue and its Christian sign: see above, pp. 110.

32 Eus. *HE* 2.25.7 (citing a Roman source, Gaius) 'if you go to the Vatican or to the Ostian Way you will find the trophies of those who founded this church'.

33 On the complex early tradition of the Roman commemoration of Peter and Paul, see (e.g.) Chadwick, 1957: 31–52; Pietri 1976: 366ff.

34 *Coll. Avell.* (= *CSEL* 35) 3.1: the emperors' intention, among other things, was to 'enlarge the basilica *pro quantitate conventus*'.

35 So Davis 1989: xxii. For full documentation on the 'Constantinian' building, see Krautheimer *et al.* 1977: 93–164; Curran 2000: 105–9, is sceptical on Constantine's involvement.

36 *Lib. Pont.* 176–8, with introduction, and Millar 1992: 186–7.

37 For chronological considerations, Pietri 1976: 51–64; Krautheimer *et al.* 1977: 272–7; Krautheimer 1987: 317–20; Curran 2000: 110–12.

38 As cited by Eusebius, *V. Const.* 2.28; cf. Grünewald 1990: 134ff. St Peter's inscription: *ILCV* 1752 (Walser 1987: 67) 'quod duce te mundus surrexit in astra triumphans / hanc Constantinus victor tibi condidit aulam'; cf. Krautheimer *et al.* 1977: 273–4.

39 *Lib. Pont.* 180–1, with Krautheimer, 1937: 14ff.; Pietri 1976: 47–51. A dedicatory inscription preserved in a manuscript of Prudentius' *Peristephanon* (= *ILCV* 1768) attributes the foundation of the basilica specifically to Constantine's daughter Constantina, who would later be laid to rest in an adjoining mausoleum, the present S. Costanza.

40 For this site, see *Lib. Pont.* 182–3; Krautheimer *et al.*, 1937: 193–206; Pietri 1976: 29–33; Curran 2000: 99–102; with Deichmann and Tschira 1957: 44–110, and Guyon 1987. For Gorgonius, *Chron. Min.* I, 72.

41 See Drijvers 1992: 30–34; on the possible extent of Helena's estate (the so-called *fundus Laurentus*) see Coarelli 1986: 35–40, and Guyon 1987: 243–8. For the gold chalice, mss. readings of *Lib. Pont.* offer both 'nomen August*i*' and 'nomen August*ae*'.

42 *Lib. Pont.* 179–80, falsely claiming that relics of the cross were deposited there by Constantine; cf. Hunt 1982: 48. For Sessorian basilica (also called *basilica Heleniana*: *Lib. Pont.* p. 196, n. 75), Krautheimer, 1937: 165ff.; Pietri 1976: 14–17.

43 For Constantine's mausoleum in Constantinople, see Eus. *V. Const.* 4.58–60, with Mango 1990: 51–61; for the suggestion that *via Labicana* building was intended for the emperor, see Deichmann and Tschira 1957: 74; Pietri 1976: 32; Guyon 1987: 257–8.

44 MacMullen 1970: 115 '... he built nothing for Roman Christians within the city'; Pohlsander 1996: 37; (principally) Krautheimer 1983: esp. 26ff. Cf. the view of Alföldi 1948: 50–1 (citing H. von Schoenebeck).

46 Krautheimer (1983: 25) 'an inherent contradiction at the very basis of Constantine's church foundations in Rome.' The argument from supposed private ownership is central to Krautheimer's discussion.

47 Eus. *V. Const.* 2.46.3, 3.31.2 (emperor's instructions to eastern bishops on building churches, guaranteeing assistance from officials); Optatus (*CSEL* 26), App. 10 (transfer of imperial property for building church at Cirta in Numidia, to be authorised by *rationarius*). For imperial consultation of urban prefect and senate over rebuilding of St Paul's in 380s, see *Coll. Avell.* (*CSEL* 35) 3.

48 On this immensely complex issue, I take my cue from Millar 1992: 189–201; see further, Delmaire 1989: 675–78.

49 Millar 1992: 201: 'something much more than a mere similarity links the temples which Augustus built in Rome, and the *dona* worth 100,000,000 *sesterces* which he dedicated in those of Divus Julius, Apollo, Vesta and Mars Ultor, to the churches which Constantine built there, and the ornaments in gold and silver which he placed within them'.

50 Barnes 1981: 247–9; for destruction of temple of Venus to be replaced by church of Holy Sepulchre in Jerusalem, see Eus. *V. Const.* 3.25ff.

51 Krautheimer's (misplaced?) emphasis on the 'private' nature of Constantine's church foundations relies heavily on the point that he made use of 'property under his uncontested control' (1983: 30).

52 For the significance of martyr cult in the Christian redefinition of urban topography, see (e.g.) Brown 1981: 3–8; Markus 1990: esp. 145ff.

53 I cannot resist drawing attention to a celebrated, but much later (early fifth cent.), depiction of Rome's Christians forsaking the city centre for their extra-mural shrines: Jer. *Ep.* 107.1 ('movetur urbs sedibus suis et inundans populus ante delubra semiruta currit ad martyrum tumulos').

54 For the significance of Constantine's churches to the evolution of Rome's Christian liturgy, see Baldovin 1987: ch. 3.

55 The basic evidence is the *Depositio Martyrum* preserved by the Roman *Calendar of 354*: text in *Chron. Min.* I, 71–2, with Salzman 1990: 42–7; Pietri 1976: 126–9.

56 For festivals listed in *Calendar of 354*, see Salzman 1990: 119–30; on *Sol Invictus*, 150.

57 Salzman 1990: 39; she is mistaken in explaining the 312 starting-point by reference to Constantine's 'famous edict of religious toleration' (if by this is meant the so-called 'edict of Milan', it was in fact agreed with Licinius early in 313).

References

Alföldi, A. (1948) *The Conversion of Constantine and Pagan Rome* (repr. 1969), Oxford: Clarendon Press.

Baldovin, J.F. (1987) *The Urban Character of Christian Worship*, Rome: Pontificum Institutum Studiorum Orientalium.

Barnes, T.D. (1981) *Constantine and Eusebius*, Cambridge, MA: Harvard University Press.

Barnes, T.D. (1982) *The New Empire of Diocletian and Constantine*, Cambridge, MA: Harvard University Press.

Barnes, T.D. (1995) 'Statistics and the conversion of the Roman aristocracy', *JRS* 85: 135–47.

Barnes, T.D. and Westall, R.W. (1991) 'The conversion of the Roman aristocracy in Prudentius' *Contra Symmachum*', *Phoenix* 45: 50–61.

Boatwright, M.T. (1987) *Hadrian and the City of Rome*, Princeton: Princeton University Press.

Brown, P. (1981) *The Cult of the Saints*, Chicago: University of Chicago Press.

Cameron, A. (1976) *Circus Factions*, Oxford: Clarendon Press.

Chadwick H. (1972) 'Preface'. In N.H. Baynes, *Constantine the Great and the Christian Church*, 2nd edn, London: British Academy.

Chadwick, H. (1957) 'St. Peter and St. Paul in Rome', *JTS* n.s.8: 31–52.

Champlin, E. (1982) 'Saint Gallicanus (consul 317)', *Phoenix* 36: 71–6.

Coarelli, F. (1986) In A. Giardina (ed.), *Società romana e impero tardoantico*, Vol. II: 1–35, Rome: Laterza.

Corcoran, S. (1996) *The Empire of the Tetrarchs*, Oxford: Clarendon Press.

Cullhed, M. (1994) *Conservator Urbis Suae: Studies in the Politics and Propaganda of the Emperor Maxentius*, Stockholm: Aström.

Curran, J.R. (2000) *Pagan City and Christian Capital: Rome in the Fourth Century*, Oxford: Oxford University Press.

Davis, R. (1989) *The Book of Pontiffs (Liber Pontificalis)*, Liverpool: Liverpool University Press.

Deichmann, F.W. and Tschira, A. (1957) 'Das Mausoleum der Kaiserin Helena und die Basilika der heiligen Marcellinus und Petrus', *JDAI* 72: 44–110.

Delmaire, R. (1989) *Largesses sacrées et res privata: l'aerarium impérial et son administration du ive au vi^{e} siècle*, Rome: Ecole Française de Rome.

Drijvers, J.W. (1992) *Helena Augusta*, Leiden: Brill.

Duchesne, L. (ed.) (1886) *Liber Pontificalis*, Paris.

Durry, M (1938) *Les Cohortes prétoriennes*, Paris: Boccard.

Fowden, G. (1987) 'Nicagoras of Athens and the Lateran Obelisk', *JHS* 107: 51–7.

Fraschetti, A. (1986) 'Costantino e l'abbandono del Campidoglio'. In A. Giardina (ed.), *Società romana e impero tardoantico*, Vol. II : 59–98, Rome: Laterza.

Giardina, A. (1986) *Società romana e impero tardoantico*, Rome: Laterza.

Gaudemet, J. (1958) *L'Église dans l'empire romain*, Paris: Sirey.

Grégoire, H. (1932) 'La statue de Constantin et le signe de la croix', *L'Antiquité Classique* 1: 135–43.

Grünewald, T. (1990) *Constantinus Maximus Augustus*, Stuttgart: Steiner.

Guyon, J. (1987) *Le Cimetière aux deux lauriers*, Rome: École Française de Rome.

Humphrey, J. (1986) *Roman Circuses: Arenas for Chariot Racing*, Berkeley: University of California Press.

Hunt, E.D. (1982) *Holy Land Pilgrimage in the Later Roman Empire AD312–460*. Oxford: Clarendon Press.

Jones, A.H.M. (1948) *Constantine and the Conversion of Europe*, Harmondsworth: Penguin.

Jones, A.H.M. (1964) *The Later Roman Empire*, Oxford: Blackwell.

Kolb, A. (1993) *Die kaiserliche Bauverwaltung in der Stadt Rom*, Stuttgart: Steiner.

Krautheimer, R. (1937) *Corpus Basilicarum Christianarum Romae*, Vol. 1, Vatican City: Potificio istituto di archeologia cristiana.

Krautheimer, R. (1967) 'The Constantinian Basilica', *DOP* 21: 117–40.

Krautheimer, R. (1980) *Rome: Profile of a City 312–1308*, Princeton: Princeton University Press

Krautheimer, R. (1983) *Three Christian Capitals: Topography and Politics*, Berkeley: University of California Press.

Krautheimer, R. (1986) *Early Christian and Byzantine Architecture* (4th edn), London: Penguin.

Krautheimer, R. (1987) 'A note on the inscription in the apse of Old St. Peter's', *DOP* 41: 317–20.

Krautheimer, R., Corbett, S. and Frankl, W. (1962) *Corpus Basilicarum Christianarum Romae*, Vol. 2, Vatican City: Pontificio istituto di archeologia cristiana.

Krautheimer, R., Corbett, S. and Frankl, W. (1970) *Corpus Basilicarum Christianarum Romae*, Vol. 4, Vatican City: Pontificio istituto di archeologia cristiana.

Krautheimer, R., Corbett, S. and Frankl, W. (1977) *Corpus Basilicarum Christianarum Romae*, Vol. 5, Vatican City: Pontificio istituto di archeologia cristiana.

Lane Fox, R. (1986) *Pagans and Christians*, Harmondsworth: Penguin.

MacCormack, S.G. (1981) *Art and Ceremony in Late Antiquity*, Berkeley: University of California Press.

McCormick, M. (1986) *Eternal Victory*, Cambridge: Cambridge University Press.

MacMullen, R. (1970) *Constantine*, London: Croom Helm.

Mango, C. (1990) 'Constantine's mausoleum and the translation of relics', *Byz. Zeit.* 83: 51–61.

Markus, R. (1990) *The End of Ancient Christianity*, Cambridge: Cambridge University Press.

Millar, F. (1992) *The Emperor in the Roman World*, 2nd edn, London: Duckworth.

Minoprio, A. (1932) 'A restoration of the Basilica of Constantine', *PBSR* 12: 1–18.

Nash, E. (1968) *Pictorial Dictionary of Ancient Rome*, Vol. I (rev. edn.), London: Zwemmer.

Novak, D.M. (1979) 'Constantine and the Senate: an early phase of the Christianisation of the Roman aristocracy', *Ancient Society* 10: 271–310.

Paschoud, F. (1971) 'Zosime 2, 29 et la version païenne de la conversion de Constantin', *Historia* 20: 334–53 (= *Cinq Etudes sur Zosime* (Paris, 1975): 24–62).

Peirce, P. (1989) 'The Arch of Constantine: propaganda and ideology in late Roman art', *Art History* 12: 387–418.

Pietri, Ch. (1976) *Roma Christiana*, Rome: École Française de Rome.

Pietri, Ch. (1978) 'Evergétisme et richesses ecclésiastiques dans l'Italie du ive à la fin du ve s.: l'exemple romain', *Ktema* 3: 317–37.

Pisani Sartorio, G. and Calza, R. (1976) *La villa di Massenzio sulla via Appia*, Rome: Istituto di studi romani.

Pohlsander, H.A. (1996) *The Emperor Constantine*, London: Routledge.

Richardson, L. (1992) *A New Topographical Dictionary of Ancient Rome*, Baltimore: Johns Hopkins University Press.

Richmond, I.A. (1930) *The City Wall of Imperial Rome*, Oxford: Clarendon Press.

Salzman, M.R. (1990) *On Roman Time*, Berkeley: University of California Press.

Santa Maria Scrinari, V. (1991) *Il Laterano Imperiale*, Vol. 1, Vatican City: Pontificio istituto di archeologia cristiana.

Steinby, E.M. (1986) In A. Giardina (ed.), *Società romana e impero tardoantico* Vol. II, Rome: Laterza.

Todd, M., 1978. *The Walls of Rome*, London: Elek.

Veyne, P. (1990) (O. Murray, trans. and ed.) *Bread and Circuses* (abridged translation of *Le pain et le cirque* (1976) Paris: Seuil), London: Penguin.

von Domaszewski, A. (1967) *Die Rangordnung des römischen Heeres*, 2nd edn, Cologne: Böhlau.

Walser, G. (1987) *Die Einsiedler Inschriftensammlung und die Pilgerführer durch Rom (Codex Einsidlensis 326)*, Stuttgart: Steiner.

Ward-Perkins, J.B. (1954) 'Constantine and the origins of the Christian basilica', *PBSR* 22: 69–90.

White, L.M. (1991) *Building God's House in the Roman World*, Baltimore: Johns Hopkins University Press.

Wiemer, H.-U. (1994) 'Libanios und Zosimos über den Rom-Besuch Konstantins I. im Jahre 326', *Historia* 43: 469–94.

7

FAVOR POPULI

Pagans, Christians and public entertainment in late Antique Italy

Jill Harries

In AD375, soon after an earthquake had devastated part of Campania, the rich pagan senator, Q. Aurelius Symmachus, visited Beneventum. There he found the local *optimates* 'working night and day' to restore their city (Symm. *Epist.* 1.3). The noble visitor was greeted by public plaudits, 'civium cultus' and 'honor', all of which he reported with pride, because they enhanced his status. However, such public honours were not altruistic. Symmachus was uneasily aware that he was expected to do something in return for these attentions, commenting that flattery without a return was a nuisance: 'sedulitas enim, quae non compensatur, onerosa est'. Fearful (he wrote), of being an encumbrance at a difficult time, he withdrew tactfully to Baiae, thus, apparently, evading the obligation to provide assistance to the hard-pressed Beneventines.

The incident encapsulates much of what is widely accepted of late Roman aristocratic behaviour. The noble potential patron arrives, is given public honours, and is offered the chance (which he is expected to take) of expanding his clientela. Power, prestige, patronage, ceremony, status and hierarchy are the keywords of late Roman life. So too was eloquence: Symmachus himself remarked on the cultural sophistication of the Beneventum *optimates*, whom he described as 'amantissimi litterarum morumque mirabiles'. Thus we move easily into a world dominated by authority, 'power and persuasion' (Brown 1992) and a history of late antiquity dominated by aristocratic sources and therefore written largely *de haut en bas*.

The 'crowd' was a necessary part of the backdrop to displays of power by the elites. As the source of acclamations (see Roueché: 1984) on matters concerning them, including for governors, on which Constantine required to receive full reports (*CTh* 1.16.6 (of 331) = *CJ* 1.40.3; *CTh.* 8.5.32); as the ceremonial backdrop to public events, such as the *adventus* of an emperor; and, in Rome, as the demanding audience for public entertainments, which could riot if food or other privileges were denied them, the less fortunate have an established place in modern accounts of late Roman life. But crowds did not, apparently, have the means to take initiatives, nor, apart from acclamations, was the role of the 'people' (*populus* or *demos*) in decision-making given general constitutional recognition. The popular assemblies, wrote Ammianus, were silent, as Rome had delegated her government to the Caesars, as to her children.

While we see groups of the less privileged in late Antiquity largely as the aristocratic sources themselves wished to see them, as clients, audiences and, on occasion, threats, the realities of social interaction were more complex. Most communities in the Empire would have numbered no more than a few thousand people and conformed to the dynamics common to small communities. These communities welcomed – and needed – patrons, and could resort to actively unconventional methods to get them: the rich senator Paulinus was forcibly ordinated at Barcelona in 394 (Paul. Nol. *Epist.* 1.10) but escaped to Nola, and Augustine, in the early fifth century, had severe problems in wresting an unwilling patron from the clutches of his congregation at Hippo (Aug. *Epist.* 125–6). The best documented source of patronage in Antiquity, Christian bishops, had to resort to a variety of devices to keep their congregations in order, precisely because their acquiescence could not be taken for granted. The *populus Dei* could not have displayed an appetite for active involvement in church services on Sundays, and holy days, only to relapse into deferential passivity for the rest of the week.

The *populus* as legitimator

The institutions of the later Roman Empire were not formally 'democratic', although, as we shall see, there was still scope for popular participation with some form of constitutional framework. However, popular participation and pressures could take many forms, which were recognised by custom and use, whether or not they were formally institutionalised. Much has been made in recent scholarship on the Roman Republic of suggestions that second and first century BCE Rome was a 'democracy' or had 'democratic' elements (see especially Millar 1998). The debate has been conducted in terms both of the institutions of government, such as the popular assemblies, and of the operation of politics and the importance attached by real politicians to popular opinion, as manifested in public meetings (*contiones*) or political trials. What was at stake in encounters between the elites and the masses was not always simply getting elected. Ex-consuls had life membership of the Senate and guaranteed *dignitas* but they still kept talking. What they sought was continuing popular endorsement of their personal influence and, where applicable, their political programme.

In considering, then, the question of 'popular' legitimacy, we have to be aware of both institutional and other factors. 'Popular' power under the Republic had recognised forms of expression, as also did the 'people' or 'everyone' under the Empire. The labelling of a system as democratic, republican or imperial-autocratic is no guide as to the real operation of power relationships between rulers and ruled. What is clear is that, under Republic and Empire alike, the elites required legitimation through at least the appearance of popular consent. So as we move in this survey from the constitutional expression of popular sovereignty in a small Italian town to Symmachus' response to popular demands for novel entertainments at Rome, and to Paulinus of Nola's garnering of popular support for his saint, Felix, we see intricate patterns forming of co-operation, interdependence and exploitation between the rich and poor, the patron and the client.

Populus and patron in the *colonia Paestanorum*

We begin in small-town Italy, in the reign of the Augusti Constans and Constantius II. On 1 August AD347, the *cives* of the *colonia Paestanorum* assembled together, conducted a debate and formulated a resolution acknowledging the *beneficia* of one Aquilius Nestorius, who had generously endowed the town with many buildings. The *cives* also formally agreed to confer the *patronatus* of Paestum on Nestorius' son, Aquilius Aper, and voted that this should be done and recorded their decision on a bronze tablet (*AE* 1990, 211, 65–7).

This brief epigraphical snapshot of the constitutional operations of a small town, which still prided itself on a colonial status dating back to 273BC, runs counter to the generally accepted picture of late Roman city life, in which the *populus* were denied even a semblance of a constitutional role. So prevalent is this assumption that the editors of *L'Année Épigraphique* seek to explain away this inconvenient outbreak of popular participation in constitutional decision-making at Paestum: 'C'est en fonction d'un vote du peuple – en fait *probablement* une décision de l'ordo decurionum confirmée par une acclamation du peuple – que le patronat a été accordé ...' (*AE* 1990, 211, 66). This alleged 'probability', however, is clearly contradicted by the phraseology of the inscription, which refers specifically to a formal assembly of the *cives* ('cum cibes frequentes ... in uno adfuissent'), a debate and the drafting of a resolution. The decision is presented in terms of the *cives*' response to the edifices, which meet their gaze wherever they look, and it was the *cives* and *populus* as a whole who expected to 'gain more honour than they had offered' by honouring the two Aquilii (see Appendix to this chapter).

The *curia*, on the other hand, is conspicuously absent from these proceedings. There is no indication in this very formal and correct document that a motion was put by the *duoviri* or other leading decurions and no hint that the *populus* was expected to acclaim a decision taken on its behalf by others. The focus of the inscription recording the proceedings of the *cibes* [sic] is consistently and completely on the formal activities of the *populus*, whose vote is taken, after discussion, and represented, in a formulaic phrase ('quod fieri placet de ea re ita censuerunt') as constitutionally binding. As another inscription from the same day reveals (*CIL* X.477), the decurions also passed their own resolution, but this was at a separate meeting, at which it was agreed that a bronze *tabula patronatus* should be forwarded to the new honorand (Nicols 1980; Corell 1994). This resolution must have been passed subsequently to the popular vote and represents the final stage of the process. From the wording of both inscriptions, it is clear that the *cives* of the *colonia Paestanorum* clung jealously to the form – and some therefore of the substance – of popular sovereignty (for the physical backdrop, see Greco and Theodorescu 1980, 1983, 1987; Pedley 1990).

The formal presence of the *populus* and its relationship procedurally to the *curia* in Italian towns can be further defined from other epigraphical evidence from the same period, also relating to the awarding of *tabulae patronatus*. In AD337, the *duoviri* of the *colonia Paestanorum* addressed the 'frequentes decuriones' in the council chamber, the Curia Caesarea, requesting ratification of an earlier decree honouring one Aurelius Gentianus (*ILS* 6112). These, being curial proceedings, excluded the *populus*, and, if this inscription were an isolated survivor, we would not know that the *populus* had any part to play. Indeed, the impression of a curial monopoly of such decisions would have been reinforced by the reuse of the Gentianus bronze tablet ten years later to record the curial decree honouring the Aquilii. It is the separate survival of both the curial and the popular resolutions which establishes that, in 347 and doubtless earlier, constitutional proceedings at Paestum entailed at least two separate meetings of separate assemblies, both of which made permanent records of their deliberations. This is reinforced, for Paestum, with a further commemoration of honours, this time a statue, awarded by the 'cibes frequentes coloniae Paestanorum', whose 'berba' (verba) formally honouring Helpidius were recorded on a statue base (*ILS* 6114 of AD344). Nor was the constitutional setup at Paestum unique in Italy. At the small *emporion* of Nardo (Neretum) in Calabria, one inscription drew together reference to the work of both assemblies (*ILS* 6113, of AD341). The recorded decree is that of the *curia*, honouring one Valerius, but its wording reveals that, as at Paestum, the popular resolution came first. While the phrase 'succlamante populo … secundum voces eiusdem et voluntatem' could refer to informal acclamations, the inscription includes as well the formulaic q.d.e.r.f.p.d.e.r.i.c. (*quod de ea re fieri placet, de ea re ita censuerunt*), which was also the term used for recording votes for *senatusconsulta* at Rome (Talbert 1984: 303–4). Moreover, the two offers are mentioned as distinct: Valerius had served not only the *municipes* but also 'ourselves'. Thus the offer of the status of patron could be made by the whole community, as the two assemblies, popular and curial, are fused as the *universus populus*.

Although a few inscriptions do not establish a trend, they encourage reassessment of the place of the *populus* in late Roman society, at least in Italy, and of the attitude of patrons to *populus*. The Aquilii of Paestum could have been reasonably confident in advance that honours would be voted to them, because it was in the interests of the *cives* to conciliate their patrons, in the hope of further favours to come. However, the Aquilii also depended on the *cives* to act in ways that would both legitimate and enhance their own status as patrons. It was important for their standing that they should be seen to be honoured by the whole *populus* in assembly and by formal vote, not merely by a small elite group. Public acknowledgement of patronage by the *populus* was not merely an optional ego-boost to patrons but an essential part of the confirmation of status in the highly pressurised environment of aristocratic competition for honours and office. Patronage, then, was, as it always had been, a two-way process and the 'favor populi' was of far more than symbolic importance.

Popular favour and the Roman games

This was also true at Rome, where the traditional rights of the people were entrenched and the obligations of their senatorial masters to provide a regular supply of 'bread and circuses' were taken for granted by all parties. However, the continued willingness of senators at Rome to lavish vast sums and enormous effort on entertaining the plebs cannot be accounted for only in terms of the *mos maiorum*. Fear of rivals and the unremitting pressure on ambitious men to assert and maintain their position in the hierarchy underlay the compulsion on senators not to be outdone by others or to suffer the shame of being caught spending less than a competitor. The relationship of the 'senatorial Romans of Rome' with their public may have been less intimate than that of the Aquilii with the people of Paestum but the need to conciliate popular favour was no less imperative.

The experience of Q. Aurelius Symmachus, regarded by the historian Olympiodorus (fr.44) as a senator of 'moderate' means, may be taken as representative of his class. His writings reveal an ambiguity on the part of the Senate as a collective over the problems caused to the less affluent of their number by the enormous expense entailed (see Matthews 1989: 418–9). As the Senate's official spokesman in 384, he welcomed attempts by the emperor to limit the expenses of the games and to determine who was obliged to give them (*Relatio* 8). In the course of his speech, he deplored the 'foeda iactatio', the ugly tendency to ostentation, which could beggar poorer senators, who were 'ashamed' to be seen to spend less than others. He was also vigorous in his denials of any desire on his part to pander to popular tastes. Symmachus' rhetoric, however, is contradicted by his actions. In the last years of his life, from 391, when he was consul, to 401, when he presented praetorian games for his son, Memmius, Symmachus presented gladiatorial games, wild-beast hunts (*venationes*) and chariot races no less than three times. When preparing for the games of 401, Symmachus' main concern was that they should surpass the 'magnificentia' of the earlier celebrations of his consulship in 391 and Memmius' quaestorship in 393 and that he should not produce anything that was merely 'average' (*Epist.* 4.59 and 60; 5.82). Stinginess, he observed, with a reference to Cicero, should not characterise the magistrates of 'the great city' (Symm. *Epist* 4.60); the 'plebis favor' must be won for his son's quaestorship (*Epist.* 2.77) and that must be done through the supply of high-quality performers (*Epist.* 5.59). Variety and novelty were essential as 'our city' became bored with looking at the same thing all the time. New animals, including new breeds of horse for the races, were in constant demand; Nicomachus Flavianus was to be praised as a 'novarum repertor' for acquiring for his friend seven very fierce Irish (wolf-?) hounds (*Epist.* 2.77). Symmachus' sensitivity to popular tastes and, as we shall see, the enormous effort and expense he devoted to Memmius' games belie his assertions of indifference to the 'plebis favorem'.

Witnesses of the end product in the circus or amphitheatre would have had little idea of the complexity of the operation behind the scenes. Symmachus' letters about his son's games provide a limited but nonetheless highly revealing insight into the administrative burden entailed by one aspect of the operation, the searching out, purchase, transport, housing and financing of horses for the races and other animals for the *venationes*. They portray his manipulation of connections on his own behalf and that of his agents; his worries that preparations may not be completed in time; problems of transport, feeding and accommodation in the winter months; and a determination to save money where possible by getting exemption from customs dues. They also provide a stark reminder of how all the effort and expenditure could go for nothing. Twenty-nine Saxon prisoners killed themselves, sooner than make their deaths a source of entertainment for the rabble (*Epist.* 2.46); a number of horses in a troupe from Spain died before reaching Rome and the team was depleted by further fatalities after arrival (*Epist.* 5.66); and a consignment of crocodiles, by which Symmachus had set great store (*Epist.* 9.141 and 151), went on hunger-strike, 'perseverante inedia', for fifty days (*Epist.* 6.43) and all but two perished. Given the slowness of transport and the disruptive effect on the animals of being dislodged from their natural habitat, some wastage was perhaps inevitable, but Symmachus' losses underlined the importance of making suitable arrangements for the conveyance of the animals, to minimise the risks both to them and to Symmachus' over-stretched resources.

Symmachus' main concerns in the *Letters* were with bears and Spanish horses. His recruiting ground for bears in 399–400 seems to have been Dalmatia, to which he despatched agents in 400 (*Epist.* 9.137). Their search for 'as many as possible' (*Epist.* 7.121) proved profitable and Symmachus' friends were brought in to requisition carts for transport (*Epist.* 9.142), for which they were to pay out of Symmachus' personal resources – if necessary. Danger, however, confronted the bears in the shape of the hazardous winter crossing of the Adriatic, the risk of loss was too great and lodging and fodder for the creatures during the winter months had to be found – and paid for (*Epist.* 9.132). Nor was weather the only threat. 'Avaricious cheating' *en route* might disrupt the safe conveyance of the bears (*Epist.* 7.121) and it was a stroke of luck for Symmachus that an *amicus* was in post as governor of Apulia and in a position to safeguard the animals on their arrival in Italy (*Epist.* 9.135). Thus Symmachus' management of his bears reveals a curious combination of munificence and parsimony. No expense was to be spared in finding as many bears as he could. At the same time, he was naturally unwilling to lose any by fraud and he was eager to exploit publicly financed systems of transport, where possible.

While he would use his private means for the bears, if necessary, he went to great lengths to ensure that horses from Spain were conveyed to Italy at public expense and with the permission of two successive governors, the second of which was nervously requested by the senator to confirm in writing the 'equorum tractoriae', free passes for horses, conceded by his predecessor (*Epist.* 9.25). Equally revealing of Symmachus' determination to control what might be termed invisible expenditure – as the Roman plebs would never see the results – was his line on exemptions from *portoria* (customs dues) levied on the importing of wild animals for the games. In two separate letters on behalf of friends addressed to the chief minister for taxation, the *comes sacrarum largitionum* (*Epist.* 5.62 and 65),

Symmachus urged that the *mos maiorum* forbade senators carrying out public functions from being burdened with 'immoderate expense.' Moreover, he argued, games were for the good of the *populus* and the granting of exemptions from customs dues for the importing of animals for the shows benefited the people, because it granted immunity from the charge to their entertainments. Whatever the real merits of this argument, Symmachus presumably meant it to have more than a merely rhetorical effect; the claims of the *populus* were to be taken seriously.

Horses for the chariot races, however, were perhaps even more important than bears (Humphrey 1986: 579–638). In 399–400, Symmachus used every possible connection to search out, select, purchase and transport 'pedigree' bloodstock from the stud farms of Hispania. One horse breeder, Euphrasius, was repeatedly begged by the anxious senator to come up with suitable horses, despite an earlier fiasco, when Euphrasius produced a team suitable for neither riders nor the yoke (*Epist.* 4.58). Symmachus had mixed fortunes too in his dealings with one Sallustius, whose generous offering of several teams of horses from Spain, which were in fact surplus to requirements, was rendered less impressive by the deaths of several horses on the journey and more after their arrival at Rome (*Epist.* 5.66). Perhaps he had better luck with Pompeia, one of the few women with whom Symmachus did business, who owned a stud farm and who was urged to select her best horses, which Symmachus' agents would buy at a fair price (*Epist.* 9.18). Help was requested for the agents at every stage of their journey. The brothers Patruinus and Petronius were required to speed the agents' passage to Spain (*Epist.* 7.105 and 106), other friends, including two praetorian prefects (Italy and Spain being in different prefectures), and the vicar of Spain, were to help the agents on arrival (*Epist.* 9.12) or supply them with letters of introduction to yet more useful people (*Epist.* 7.82 and 97; 9.21, 23 and 25) – and even the great Stilicho, the emperor's chief minister, was approached (*Epist.* 4.7). The return journey would have been made cheaper and easier by the letters confirming the 'equorum tractoriae' so painstakingly acquired by Symmachus, but, like the bears, some horses were held up by the onset of the winter. Bassus, owner of estates near Arles, was now brought in to supply stabling and provisions for the precious animals during the three or four months of winter (*Epist.* 9.20 and 24). Never a man to miss an opportunity, Symmachus added a supplementary request: his agents would welcome the chance to buy outstandingly swift, pedigree horses from the Arles area, as local dealing reduced the risk of accidents.

As Symmachus' letters and agents made their way across the Mediterranean area in one direction and bears, crocodiles, horses and other animals were transported back in the other, in varying degrees of distress and discomfort, the senator's dealings over his games acquire a wider significance for the economies of the regions affected by him and others like him. The Roman games would have been a major source of revenue for hunters, horse breeders, shippers, warehousemen, manufacturers of cages and owners of animal accommodation, not to mention workers in, among other things, ivory or silk. In particular, the Spanish suppliers of horses to Symmachus did not confine their operations to the western

Mediterranean. Symmachus' friend, Euphrasius, supplied bloodstock to Antioch for cross-breeding (*Epist.* 4.62) and was requested by Symmachus (who ended up in 401 with a surplus of horses) to provide a team of 'Laodicean' horses to satisfy the 'city's' fondness for a change (*Epist.* 4.63.2). The connection between Spain and the East is attested also in the mosiac decorations of Spanish villas. Among a number of opulent dwellings featuring illustrations of horses is that of Aguilafuente near Segovia, where a damaged mosiac gives the names of two horses as 'Tagus' and 'Euphrata', confirming the mixed geographical origins of the Spanish herds (Lucas and Viñas 1977; Argente Oliver 1977; de Palol 1977; Humphrey 1986: 337–87). But the Spanish horse breeders and traders would not have engaged in such long-distance and potentially risky enterprises had there not been a market for their wares. The strength of the Spanish villa economy of the late fourth century depended in part on established local links between town and country; but it rested also on the links by sea and land with Italy and the continuing popularity with the plebs of chariot racing at Rome.

Christians against the games

Competition, then, between aristocrats for status and the self-interest of local Mediterranean economies combined to underpin the Roman games and smaller-scale public entertainments elsewhere. Too many interest groups had too much to lose by their abolition. We should therefore not overestimate the significance of the contempt voiced by some members of the elite for the amusements of the mob and their corrupting effect upon onlookers – even though that disdain appears to have been shared by pagans and Christians alike. The Christian astrological writer, Firmicus Maternus, proclaimed that an astrologer was a kind of priest who should live a modest, upright and abstemious life (*Mathesis* 2.30.2) and keep away from the allurements of the shows 'in case anyone takes you for a patron of that kind of thing' (*ibid.* 12). Similarly, the emperor Julian, admittedly not a typical pagan, imposed a rule banning pagan priests from attending *venationes* or theatrical performances and even sacred *ludi* were out of bounds if women were present (Julian, *Epist.* 304B–D). Such religiously inspired concerns would have reinforced the general aristocratic tendency to distance themselves publicly from the popular culture they affected to despise but in practice made every effort to support. The Roman senatorial elite were no strangers to double standards and this divergence of rhetoric from populist reality came naturally to senators who loudly advertised their yearning for *otium*, while strenuously competing for the offices and honours essential for their positions in the hierarchy.

A condition of success, then, in both catering for and changing popular tastes was to understand when – and when not – to take this rhetoric at face value. Conversely, failure to appreciate the underlying realities which supported the continuance of public games may explain why general Christian attacks on the cruelty, immorality and corrupting effects of the circus, the arena and the theatre had limited practical effect (Tert. *Adv. Marcianum* 1.27.5; Jer. *Ep.* 43.3; Aug.

Serm. 199.3; 19.51; *De Civ. Dei* 1.32f). Ambrose revealed his close knowledge of what he attacked when he complained of aristocratic obsessions with 'pedigree horses', an observation which could have applied directly to Symmachus' dealings in Spain (Amb. *De Nabuthe* 13); and he conceded tacitly, when complaining of the extravagance that won 'popular favour' for a mere hour, that such munificence did have the desired effect. The fact was that the bishops in their churches and aristocratic entertainers of the populace both competed for what they affected to despise. This became explicit in the rhetoric of the aristocrat-turned-ascetic, Paulinus of Nola who accepted that approval and applause were worth having, but then claimed that it was the source of the approval who really counted: people who spent money on beasts and gladiators should be thinking about their own salvation; they should fear Christ, not the hissing of the mob and look for God's approval, not that of the 'common herd'; works of Christian charity, not the purchase of gladiators or animals won acclamation in the 'theatre of Christ' (*Epist.* 13). Paulinus had had no hesitation in jettisoning his aristocratic lifestyle; the same could not be said of the values which had accompanied it — yet he too, as we shall see, sought and indeed needed popular endorsement for the causes dear to his heart.

Outside the world created by Christian rhetoric, Christian leaders found it hard in practice to compete directly with the traditional amusements of the people. On days when public games coincided with a Christian festival, bishops were liable to find themselves denouncing the 'many different shameful acts of the theatres, the madness of the circus, the cruelty of the amphitheatre' (Aug. *Serm.* 199.3) to an empty church. The success of these rival attractions was in itself unacceptable to bishops who were in the entertainment business themselves as preachers and liturgical showmen. It was therefore a notable victory for ecclesiastical lobbyists at the imperial court, when theatrical shows, chariot-races and wild-beast hunt were banned on Sundays and holy days by Theodosius I and his sons in the 390s (*CTh* 2.2.8; 23–5), but the need for such a ban was also an admission of weakness: the Church could not sideline the circus unaided.

Although 'keeping Sunday special' was one notable victory, the Church had little overall success in limiting the popularity and content of the shows. One victory claimed by the Church but more plausibly due to wider cultural changes, fashion and problems of supply was the decline in contests between gladiators (Ville 1960). Both the Theodosian and the Justinianic Codes record a law of Constantine in 325 as the definitive enactment abolishing gladiatorial contests (*CTh* 15.12.1 = *CJ* 11.44) but Constantine's own intention may have been a restricted measure of some kind, the details of which were left out by the Theodosian compilers working in the mid-430s; certainly gladiatorial displays continued through the fourth century, not only in Rome, where Symmachus staged gladiatorial combats as late as the 390s, but also probably elsewhere in Italy and beyond; near Tergeste in Northern Italy a *munerarius*, Constantius, entombed a pair of 'his' gladiators, with an inscription recording their achievements and ultimate fates (*CIL* 5.563), while a late mosaic in a villa on the Via Appia records the acclamations given to a *munerarius* called Symmachius at a contest between two *secutores*, Habilis, the victor, and Maternus, whose doom is signified by the 'black theta' (Oliver 1957). By the late fourth century, however, gladiators were losing popularity with the Roman plebs, who, according to Ammianus, were uniquely preoccupied with horses and chariot racing (14.6.26) and they fade out of the evidence altogether in the fifth century. Too much, therefore, should not be made of the attack by the Spanish poet Prudentius on gladiators in his second book *Against Symmachus* in 402/3. The poet may have been either anticipating an otherwise unknown measure of Honorius against gladiators, or reacting against Symmachus' presentation of his son's praetorian games in 401; either way, the vehemence of Prudentius' attack is no indication of the strength of his adversary, as Symmachus himself, the main object of the polemic, was dead.

Apart from the manipulation of public opinion from the pulpit and through the written word, Christian opponents of public games had two further potential lines of attack: the emperor; and the faltering economy and growing insecurity of the fourth and fifth century West. It is striking testimony to the aristocratic obsession with courting popularity by traditional munificence that neither of these had the desired effect. Christian emperors, who honoured the symbolic capital of Empire more often with their generosity than with their presence, took great pains to safeguard their supply of horses to the Roman games (*CTh* 15.7.6) and went to the length of pensioning off horses of special breeds at their own expense (*CTh* 15.10.1). Emperors also took steps to counteract Christian inroads into the supply of actresses, whose conversion to Christianity could enable them to esape from their 'degraded profession', provided they did not relapse thereafter into their previous immoral habits. That the Roman city authorities shared the emperor's determination to guarantee the supply of entertainers at any cost is shown in their response to an outbreak of famine in 383, when immigrants were expelled but 3000 dancing girls, with their trainers, were allowed to remain (Ammianus 14.6.19). Their assessment of the plebs' priorities continued to hold good in the more disturbed conditions of the fifth century; when Pope Leo organised a festival of thanksgiving for those who had survived the Sack of Rome by the Vandals in 455, the attendance was sorely depleted thanks to the simultaneous holding of public games; regrettably, 'the lunacy of the games produced a higher turn-out than the blessed shrines of the martyrs' (Leo, *Serm.* 84.2).

Relative aristocratic poverty also failed to provide any obvious check to the provision and popularity of games in the capital. As we have seen, senators at Rome were uneasily aware of the effects of unrestricted competition on the poorest of their number and formally welcomed imperial attempts to restrict expenditure on shows, providing regulations on, for example, the types of prizes and gifts to be dispensed (*CTh* 15.9.1); giving less than the permitted maximum was allowed to be 'not only a permitted but also an honorable action'. Such legislation, however, was not without precedent and it foundered, as previous attempts had done, on the aristocratic value system which, as Symmachus' writings reveal, obliged a patron to surpass competitors' previous efforts – and his own. One Probus, son of Olypius, or Olybrius, spent 1,200 pounds of gold on his son's praetorian games in 424–5; Symmachus, regarded as a 'middle-ranking' senator in terms of wealth, spent 2,000 pounds of gold in 401 for Memmius' praetorian games, while twice that amount was lavished on a similar occasion by the greatest of early fifth-century Christian senators, Petronius Maximus (Olymp. fr.44). Despite assertions to the contrary by the Christian clergy, the entertainment agenda was dictated by traditional expectations, not by religious dogma; pagan and Christian lay patrons alike could not concede ground to their rivals by failing to do what was expected of them, or by alienating the favour of the mob.

Paulinus of Nola and the Christian alternative

The plebs in the circus, to whom so much attention was paid, were but one construction of a 'people' whose support confirmed the dignity of the aristocrat. Acclamations, the *plebs Dei* in church or at festival, the crowds that greeted the imperial *adventus*, the public assembly that voted the status of patron to a benefactor, all were constructions of a *populus*, whose role was to legitimate their imperial, curial or episcopal leaders. What all have in common is that the *populus*, *demos* or 'people' is defined in terms that serve the ends of their rulers but which are also acceptable to society at large. In other words, there is a tacit negotiation between the elite in search of legitimacy and the 'people' who alone have the right to confer it, and part of that negotiation consists of attempts to define what the 'people' is at any given time and how its will is made manifest. That constitutional mechanisms were only one of the methods involved would not have worried thoughtful Romans at all; notions both of ancestral custom, the *mos maiorum*, and more broadly of the customary law which does not have to be written down because everyone agrees it, ensured that non-constitutional 'understandings' could also underpin recognised demonstrations of public opinion.

It follows from this that there was also a necessary connection between the various recognised expressions of the 'favor populi' and the legitimacy or social acceptability of saints, bishops or any other community leaders. Moreover, as we have seen, the importance of the *populus* bears no relation to the constitutional construct that was the Roman Empire. Instead, the establishing of legitimacy by, or on behalf of, elites is the outcome of several processes, which are themselves in a constant state of flux and liable to challenge: one is the construction of the *demos/populus*; the second is the evolution of a tacit consensus between ruler and ruled about how the power of the ruler can be accepted and expressed. The third, which was necessary for the elite's efficient operation of the first two criteria, was their manipulation of the agreed conventions to produce the desired result, confirmation of their positions as leaders.

Like all leaders, Christian saints required the 'favor populi' as a demonstration of success. His, her or their, promotion was delegated to Christian devotees, who naturally had a stake in the success of the chosen saint. Felix of Nola and his sponsor, Paulinus, illustrate the processes required to establish the position of a minor confessor saint, whose qualifications appear, at first sight, unimpressive. Priest at Nola from 395 and bishop from about 410, Paulinus publicised Felix to the world at large in a series of annual poetic bulletins on Felix's 'birthday', that is the day of his death, in January. These poems were suitably entitled *Natalicia*, birthday poems, they were of varying length and they covered Felix's career both on earth and in the hereafter. There is a logic to their arrangement which suggests that Paulinus did plan his poems as a series. Two shorter poems on Felix's kindnesses to Paulinus personally begin the cycle; then an account of his life is spread over two years; more is then offered on his miracles, the celebration of his cult and special events, such as the building of his churches (Goldschmidt 1940), controversy over 'his' water-supply and a distinguished senatorial visitation in 407. Nor were the 'masses' and the impact on the local economy of religious tourism forgotten; 'for although her whole area is crowded with her own inhabitants, she has room for all, so that you might imagine that the walls themselves were being stretched to accommodate the countless guests' (*Carm.* 14.79–80).

Paulinus' early career had not been ecclesiastical. A native of Aquitaine and a prosperous landowner, Paulinus' skills as an eloquent Latin linguist had been developed by his teacher, Ausonius of Bordeaux, and his early career path was that of an imperial governor. As *consularis*, governor, of Campania in the early 380s, Paulinus knew and patronised the towns of Nola, Fundi, where Paulinus built a hospice, and Beneventum, where Symmachus had visited in 375 and which was later a base for opposition to Augustine's doctrines of grace and predestination. But Paulinus' promising career fell victim to the political uncertainties in Gaul and, late in the 380s, he renounced public life for a vocation of private religiosity, basing himself in northern Spain. After being forcibly ordained at Barcelona in 394, he removed to Italy and thenceforth dedicated himself to Felix and the promotion of his cult.

In Paulinus, then, we have the aristocratic promoter (and manipulator) of the product, Felix. Part of his task was to prove not only Felix's efficacy as a saint, through a recounting of his life and miracles, but also to establish and verify his base of popular support. The main marketing tool with which we are concerned is the *Natalicia*. In one crucial respect, these poems are problematic; their audience is uncertain. In a recent, sensitive study of Paulinus, Catherine Conybeare includes the *Natalicia* among expository works 'directed to a faithful but not particularly educated audience' (Conybeare 2000: 53). In other words, the poems were aimed directly at the local *populus*, whose allegiance was a prerequisite for Felix's success. But there are also indications that the texts, as we have them, were designed for a more select readership. Some of the poems are long and would take some time to recite; experienced givers of sermons, like Augustine, knew very well that one should not try the *patientia* of the faithful. Moreover, an elite audience is also suggested by the care taken over literary presentation. Even direct liturgical references do not establish the case for direct recitation, as the hymn was a recognised literary form and Paulinus' contemporary, Prudentius, had included references to live performance in poems which were probably not designed for public presentation (Palmer 1989: 75–86).

However, while the form of the *Natalicia* leaves the question of the immediate audience open, it may safely be assumed that the contents connect with what Paulinus communicated to his local public, in whatever form suited him and them best. The narrative of the *Natalicia* featured two main characters, Paulinus and Felix, and an assortment of other individuals, groups and animals. Some of the last were actors, others audience but all were deployed to enhance the credibility of Felix as a saint in the eyes of the Nolan agricultural community. Paulinus' place in the narrative is central, but in social terms subordinate to Felix; he is the servant or adjunct (*famulus*), not the friend (*amicus*) of his saint. The intention of this was to convey respect, rather than distance; the terrestrial noble had put off the trappings of this world to serve the saint whose churches he financed, whose festivals he celebrated and whose house he shared.

Whatever the readership of the *Natalicia*, Paulinus' 'people', whom he had to convince of Felix's merits, were the inhabitants of Nola and the surrounding areas. To them he offered stories containing humour, suspense — and the terror of the divine. Paulinus' audience of agricultural workers would have appreciated the story of the overweight but enthusiastic pig, who walked all the way to Nola from the other side of Beneventum to be eaten at the feast of Felix (*Carm.* 20.312–87). The tale of a devout heifer, who agreed to pull a cart to Nola, once she understood the purpose of her journey (*Carm.* 20.388–436), would have reinforced the unspoken message behind these improving tales – that Felix both expected and relied on contributions from the farming communities of which he was patron. Nor did Felix rely only on the goodwill of his fellow-citizens; fear was also an element in his cult. The saint could not be cheated of what was due to him, as a half-hearted benefactor from Abella discovered, when he brought a pig to Felix, but then tried to make off with the best parts of the carcases for himself, only to find himself inflicted with a temporary paralysis, which disappeared once the pig had been stewed and served up to the hungry poor (*Carm.* 20.62–300). Popular support for the cult of saints was necessary for practical, as well as for symbolic, reasons. In small towns, where the resources held by the local church might be few, the effectiveness of the entertainment and assistance offered by the local saint would be dependent on the willingness of the local farmers to provide from their perhaps meagre surplusses the pigs and other livestock served up to the poor in the name of the saint.

Felix's power to punish the wrongdoer was conveyed also in the tale of the thief who abused the saint's right of sanctuary by pretending to seek refuge from military service in order to steal the cross of Nola; he was detained by Felix in the neighbourhood, until apprehended (*Carm.* 19.378–715). In any conflict of interest, even with the poor, whom he was alleged to serve, Felix' rights were paramount, at least in the eyes of his servant Paulinus, who gave short shrift to the unhappy *colonus* who refused to surrender his two small cottages, which happened to be cluttering up the facade of Felix's beautiful new basilica: when one of the huts was burned down and the peasant was forced to demolish the other, Paulinus' comment was that the *colonus* had only himself to blame 'for losing the goodwill [*gratia*] earned by obedience to us, while gaining for himself instead the disgrace of his punishment' (*Carm.* 28.165–6). Such *exempla* are a reminder of the fear which could also prompt the formalities of popular acclamation. The *populus* could be coerced, as well as cajoled.

But Paulinus and Felix could also be coerced by the *populus*. However arrogant the rhetoric of his promoters, and however confidently the saint might assert his rights, his popularity was unlikely to survive suspicions among the local people that patronage based on their contributions was being used for the saint's sole benefit, rather than that of the community as a whole. By the early 400s, Paulinus, who had settled at Nola in 395, had become impatient with the inadequacies of the water supply at Felix's shrine at Cimitile, which depended on the collection of rainwater in cisterns (*Carm.* 27.463–79). He therefore offered to repair a local aqueduct bringing water from the neighbourhood of the hill town of Abella, provided that a part of the supply could be diverted for Felix's use at Cimitile, roughly one kilometre outside the town. The response to the anticipated reduction in their water supply by the Nolani was a riot, which much upset Paulinus: 'forgetful of Felix, you thought that your gift would be extended to my own needs' (*Carm.* 21.76), a not unnatural assumption, given that Paulinus was living in 'Felix's' house and making use of it to entertain guests, as if it was indeed his own. Despite his brave words, Paulinus could not ignore the outburst of popular feeling against him and his plans were modified to create a two-stage programme of renovation of the local water supply as a whole. By 407, he had completed his restoration of one aqueduct from Abella, bringing new water to both Nola and Cimitile and had also put in hand the repair of a second channel, which would bring water directly to Nola itself. The episode illustrates the interdependency of people and patron: the people of Nola profited from the pilgrim trade and the prestige accruing to their small community from the increasing fame of Felix but they were no mere passive clients of the saint, while Paulinus, for his part, while insisting in his rhetoric on his unique dependence on Felix and aristocratically contemptuous of the rights of the individual poor who sought to frustrate his designs, was nevertheless obliged to respond to public manifestations of discontent.

Conclusion: the power of the *populus*

The two senators who have been the main subjects of this chapter had, superficially, little in common. Q. Aurelius Symmachus, pagan champion, citizen of the Eternal City, Prefect of Rome and consul, and munificent entertainer of the Roman mob, lived a life far removed from that of the provincial Aquitanian noble, Meropius Pontius Paulinus, who abandoned a modest career in government for a religious life as Christian priest and servant of the small-town confessor, Felix of Nola. In fact, however, both embody examples of the double standards adopted by the elite in the unremitting competition between aristocrats for status, and in their dealings with the *populus*. Symmachus, while conforming to the convention that he was indifferent to applause, nonetheless combed the Mediterranean for new and top-quality attractions, enlisted friends and friends of friends, and spared no unnecessary expense to appeal to the popular thirst for quantity, quality and variety; Paulinus, while appearing to share the contempt voiced by some Christian ecclesiastical spokesmen for all forms of public show, promoted the cult of Felix as a form of public entertainment and revealed in his rhetoric and, when confronted by serious opposition, in his actions, his understanding that popular support was essential for his saint's legitimacy and success.

While it was true that the *populus* could be exploited as pawns in elite status-games, the elite needed popular support to support their status and could be themselves forced into concessions. The inscription at Paestum, with which we began, the sensitivity to popular tastes exhibited by Symmachus in his search for ever more exotic delights for the Roman plebs, Paulinus' sensitivity to the tastes of his notional audience and the successful self-assertion of the people of Nola concerning their water supply, confirm not only that that popular power was a living reality, but that there were a number of ways in which it could make itself felt. That power could be expressed, still, in what we would recognise as constitutional terms, through a formal vote, as at Paestum; more often it is evidenced, in ways also recognisable from the Republic, through demonstrations recognised by tradition and unwritten custom. It may be doubted that the nobility could have hoped to alter or undermine long-established popular rights, at least at Rome, to traditional amusements, even had they so wished. Popular taste combined with elite self-interest to protect the continuance of public games against all that influential Christian opinion-formers could urge. When the desires of their popular clientela conflicted with rhetoric from the pulpit, patrons at Rome, Christian and non-Christian, from the emperor downwards, responded to the former. As under the Republic, control of the 'favor populi' represented for the elite as a whole, the all-important middle ground, and in the dialogue between patrons and *populus*, which lasted throughout Roman history, the *populus*, even in late Antiquity, could have the last word.

Appendix: Paestum inscription, AD347

Bronze tablet of imprecise local provenance, 57.5 × 38 × 5cm, inscription 38.5 × 38 cm. Published by P. Sabbatini Tumolesi (1990), *Miscellanea greca e romana* 15, 235–56 and *AE* 1990, 65–7 (No. 211).

Vulcacio Rufino et Fl. Eusebio cons. Kalendis
Augustis
Cum **cibes frequentes** coloniae Paestanorum in uno
adfuissent, **consilioque habito**, berba fecerunt: cum
tot tantaque beneficia sblendentia de domo Aquilini Nes-
torii, probi adulescentis, descendant, quibus colonia nos-

tra exornata unicuique nobis **cibibus** in oculis adque animis sint praecipuae cum unusquisque **civium** se con verterit opera ab his extructa oculis eorum occurrant sic faciem cibitatis honestam reddent, utinam qui tantus populus esset status ut tantis muneribus domus eorum aliis quoque gloriosis muneribus remunerandus esset; fateri beneficia eius, munera populi, intebimque contentos esse; hoc munere flaminis gratulit (populus) quod, **publica voce**, et offerendum etiam **cibes cupierant.** Cum Aquilius Nestorius contemplatione mutui honoris, nos municipies sua dignatione unice diligat, sitque similem nobis adfectionem etiam Aquilius Aper, filius efus, praebiturus, **placere cibibus** patronatus cibitatis eidem offerre, ut fulti patrocinio eorum, **populus noster** plus honori consecutus quam optulissent videatur.
Quod fieri placere de ea re ita censuerunt.
Feliciter.

Translation

The citizens of the *colonia* of Paestum convened in a fully attended assembly, held a debate and passed the following resolution.

Because there have accrued to us from the house of Aquilius Nestorius, this upright gentleman, such numerous, great and splendid benefactions, with which our *colonia* has been adorned and which are visible to the eyes and minds of our citizens, especially when each citizen looks about him and buildings raised by them meet their gaze, and thus they have made glorious the appearance of our city, wherefore the full(?) citizen body (*populus*) has resolved that a return should be made to them for the great services rendered by their house, and their other outstanding services too; that they acknowledge his benefactions as public services to the *populus* and are pleased with them. (The citizen body) gratefully offers him the position of *flamen*, because, by public acclamation, the citizens desire that he should be given that additional honour.

Since Aquilius Nestorius, in consideration of honours given and received, loves us, his fellow-citizens, with an unparalleled affection, and his son, Aquilius Aper, will offer us the same affection, the citizens formally resolve to confer on him the patronage of the city, so that, by relying on the protection of both, our people may be seen to receive greater honour than we have offered.

The resolution on this matter was passed by formal vote.

References

Argente Oliver, J.L. (1977) 'La villa tardoromana de Baños de Valdereados (Burgos)', in *Segovia. Symposium de Arqueologiá romana*: 61–76, Barcelona: Universidad de Barcelona, Instituto de Arqueologiá y Prehistoria.

Brown, P. (1992) *Power and Persuasion in Late Antiquity*, Madison: University of Wisconsin Press.

Conybeare, C. (2000) *Paulinus Noster: Self and Symbols in the Letters of Paulinus of Nola*, Oxford: Oxford University Press

Corell, J. (1994) 'Nueva *tabula patronatus* procedente de la Baetica', *Epigraphica* 56: 59–68.

Goldschmidt, R. (1940) *Paulinus' Churches at Nola*, Amsterdam: Noord-Hollandsche Uitg. Maatschappij.

Greco, E. and Theodorescu, D. (1980–87) *Poseidonia–Paestum* (*Coll. de l'École Française de Rome* 42), Rome and Paris: École Française de Rome.

Humphrey, J.H. (1986) *Roman Circuses. Arenas for Chariot-racing*, Berkeley and Los Angeles: California University Press.

Lucas, M.R. and Viñas, P. (1977) 'La villa romana de Aguilafuente (Segovia)'. in *Segovia: Symposium de Arqueologiá Romana*: 239–56, Barcelona: Universidad de Barcelona, Instituto de Arqueologiá y Prehistoria.

Matthews, J. (1989) *The Roman Empire of Ammianus*, London: Duckworth.

Millar, F. (1998) *The Crowd in Rome in the Late Republic*, Ann Arbor: University of Michigan Press.

Nicols, J. (1980) 'Tabulae patronatus: a study of agreement between patron and client-community', *ANRW* ii(13): 535–61.

Oliver, J.H. (1957) 'Symmachi, homo felix', *Memoirs of the American Academy in Rome* 25: 9–15.

de Palol, P. (1977) 'Romanos en la meseta; el bajo imperio y la aristocracia agricola' in *Segovia. Symposium de Arqueologiá romana*: 297–308, Barcelona: Universidad de Barcelona, Instituto de Arqueologiá y Prehistoria.

Pedley, J.G. (1990) *Paestum: Greeks and Romans in Southern Italy*, London: Thames and Hudson.

Palmer, A.M. (1989) *Prudentius on the Martyrs*, Oxford: Clarendon Press.

Roueché, C. (1984) 'Acclamations in the later Roman Empire: new evidence from Aphrodisias', *Journal of Roman Studies* 74: 181–99.

Talbert, R.J.A. (1984) *The Senate of Imperial Rome*, Princeton: Princeton University Press.

Ville, G. (1960) 'Les Jeux de gladiateurs dans l'Empire chrétien', *MEFRA* 71: 273–335.

8

'RESTORED UTILITY, ETERNAL CITY'

Patronal imagery at Rome in the fourth century AD

Rowland B.E. Smith

Late Roman patronage: terms of debate

Surveys of the later Roman Empire have commonly depicted it as a period in which the workings of an increasingly pervasive web of patronage were helping to undermine established patterns of political and economic activity in many spheres (e.g. Jones 1973: 775–8; Liebeschuetz 1972: 204–5; de Ste Croix 1954: 32–44; Brunt 1988: 420, 440). Provided that 'patronage' is broadly construed, it seems a fair depiction. But debate about patronage's role and importance in particular historical settings slips easily into arguments about terms: patronage wears many faces, and the issue rests in part on the range of social relationships we mean the word to convey in the late Roman setting. Are we focussing mainly on the personal patronage of individual dependants – and how firmly, if so, do we propose to distinguish them from 'mere' graft and corruption (Brown 1992: 16–17; Veyne 1981: 339–60; cf MacMullen 1988: 103, 150–3)? Or are we also including relationships holding between *patroni* and collective groups or communities? In any case, do we mean to refer just to the kind of reciprocal relationship which rested on formalised and hereditary obligations on each side, or are we thinking as much of a broader range of social display, of the tradition (say) of civic euergetism fuelled by local elites and their 'love of honour'; or of the largesse of the emperor himself, or that of his governors? A lot, too, may hang on what we make of certain emergent forms of support which in late antiquity seem to challenge the assumptions and interests of groups who had long been accustomed to view patronal benefits as theirs to dispense, or theirs to receive: do we classify provision for the destitute, say, as 'patronage', still, in some extended sense, or rather (as a powerful strand in recent scholarship would insist)[1] as a type of charity rooted in Christian conceptions and ideals that were quite distinct from the ideology of old-style civic benefaction?

If views of Roman patronage differ, however, what is in question is not just whether such and such a type of relationship is to be accommodated under the term. A working definition tends to be adopted with a purpose in mind, and the modern debate about Roman patronage, like many another in the study of anti-

quity, can reflect a tension in aims: there is a wish, on the one hand, to differentiate accurately in describing the kinds of relationships and behaviour at issue, and a wariness in trying to generalise from evidence which is mostly regionally localised;[2] but a wish, too, to conceptualise 'patronage' in a way that allows it explanatory force in a broader analysis of historical change. To that end, some follow a sociological lead and propose a 'systemic' significance for patronage, construing it as a pattern of influence and dependency that in some historical conditions may become normalised and play a prime role in the maintenance and reproduction of a state's power relations. In such a case, they argue, patronage is not to be conceived simply as an alternative, and a threat, to the 'normal' institutional workings of a state; rather, it effectively now constitutes the form taken by that state (Johnson and Dandeker 1988: 223; cf for a later period the debate in Kent and Simons 1987: 1–21).

On one view, the emergence of the princeps as effectively (if not in name) a super-'patron' whose very existence restricted the free play of patronage among the elite, together with a devaluation of plebeian support in elite eyes as the popular assemblies became sidelined as an active force in politics, diminished the 'systemic' significance of Roman patronage in a classic form epitomised by the image of the elite Republican *patronus* and his personal *clientela*.[3] It is a view open to question, even as it relates to personal patronal exchange within the Roman elite (Garnsey and Saller 1987: 149–54), and it certainly does not entail that patronage in one form or another was a less important phenomenon in the Empire than in Republican times: the picture of the emperor as the apex of a vast pyramid of influence by which individual careers were advanced could suggest just the opposite; and that is to leave out of account the growth in the period of collective, as opposed to personal, forms of patronage (patronage of cities, for instance, or of guilds). On the other hand, if we construe the patronage of collective groups to include the gifts and favours of *euergetai*, we must surely admit a degree of decline in the third century – *some* diminution, anyway, in *some* regional settings – in the willingness, or the capacity, of local elites to continue to spend generously on civic buildings and amenities.[4] A revival of sorts in the fourth century might arguably be granted, but not one that matched the scale and spread of local munificence attested for the Antonine age: in that sense, then, 'patronage' could be said to have declined by our period. But it is also plain that Constantine's buildings at Rome, in the Holy Land, and in his new capital, along with the many other endowments and immunities he showered on the Church, present us with the workings of imperial largesse on a scale matched by very few of his predecessors;[5] and plain, more generally, that a successful career in the fourth century empire depended as much as ever it had (perhaps, more than ever) on the manipulation of factions and networks of patronage – not least, within the enlarged Imperial Court.[6] An obvious symptom of the times in this respect is the normalisation in this period of the sale of offices, and Veyne's discussion of the phenomenon could be said to anticipate the line of argument that we noted above – the argument focussing on patronage's 'systemic' force –, but (for the fourth century, at least) with a different twist: 'le patronage et la clientèle, pour le meilleur ou pour le pire, ne violaient pas le droit, mais collaboraient avec lui et se partageaient les tâches … l'État ne peut rien contre une administration corrompue – surtout lorsque cette corruption est aussi une condition indispensable du functionnement de l'État' (Veyne 1981: 344–5).

As for civic euergetism, if the habit of voluntary expenditure by local elites had indeed declined in the third century, that is not to say that the ethos of *philotimia* and love of the home-town had utterly collapsed; and other agents of benefaction and support were emerging at this level. Increasingly, cities now looked to the subventions of imperial governors and officials to finance public works, in pursuit of which, an eloquent or well-connected local bigwig could often still do useful civic service as a *euergetes* (Robert 1948: 35–114). In their varied localised settings, too, military officials and great landowners, and the bishops and aristocratic lay members of a vastly enriched Church[7] – and in time, some of the eastern Christian 'holy men'[8] – all came to offer support and protection on patterns that extended to groups whom the older style of patronage had largely or wholly ignored: to rural populations, say, or the destitute. If we admit these late forms within the count, patronage will be found not just thriving in late antiquity, but more widely spread than ever as a presupposed and guiding feature of social experience. But the point is doubtful: on another view, we have already noted, the inclusion of support for the destitute would be a mistake obscuring a key transition bound up with the Christianising process in the fourth and fifth centuries, and what it really heralds is rather the demise of a fundamental and distinctive principle of Veynian euergetism: the decay of public benefaction as something provided for a citizen collective on the strength of civic entitlement, and with some form of reciprocal benefit in prospect, and its replacement by charity dispensed on the basis of the giver's impulse to alleviate economic need in a party unable to offer any worthwhile favour or honour in return (Veyne 1990: 19, 24–34; Brown 1992: 78–103; Patlagean 1977). And it is likewise arguable that the sort of 'protection' that now came to be offered in the countryside by great landowners and imperial officials is a mark of crisis rather than continuity in patronage: inasmuch as it looks often to have involved the reduction of dependants' status from free peasants to *coloni*, and the transfer of land into the 'protector's' possession, it seems to many more like feudalism, and a precursor of medieval warlordism (Marcone 1998: 309–11).

If the lines of the modern debate seem slippery at times, there is perhaps some comfort in the fact that ambiguity in the representation of patronage is no new thing. The ancients' usage of words like 'patron' and 'client' could itself at times be ambiguous and imprecise; and among them, too, there was room for disagreement over what constituted patronage's proper forms, and what did not.[9] Not that anything requires us to frame our own definitions to accord with the Romans' prevailing prescriptions: antique discourse on the 'proper' working of patronage is, by and large, bounded by the self-interested mental horizons of the imperial authorities and urban elites, and moderns in search of a 'systemic' significance for

Roman patronage will not be inclined to let elite sectional presuppositions and concerns dictate the shape of their inquiry. But whatever the shortcomings of the discourse as testimony to the 'systemic' status of patronage in a given period, it clearly retains great interest and value – be it in the writings of patrons themselves, or in the commemorative inscriptions and contemporary judgements that their actions elicited – for the terms in which it represents the activities of such benefactors: the roles and styles it portrays and implicitly or explicitly commends, its conception of the 'normal' operation of patronage, its reaction to adaptive forms – in short, one might say, the idealised 'image' of patronage conveyed in the texts. For the study of the elite's self-definition, at least, the importance of such testimony is patent: in this connection, one need only recall the coyness often displayed in correspondence between upper-class patrons and clients, their preference for dressing up the seeking and granting of patronal favours in the language of 'friendship', *amicitia.*[10]

In the setting of the fourth century, the terms in which texts of the day represent patrons and their activities may be thought to hold an additional interest. It is partly the brute fact of the volume of relevant evidence: fourth-century inscriptions, Latin and Greek, offer an abundance of dedications to patrons and benefactors; a mass of personal correspondence survives from the period to illustrate the etiquette of patronal exchange and brokering from variously nuanced viewpoints within the western and eastern elites – the letters of a Roman senator, say, or of an Antiochene notable such as Libanius, or of Christian bishops such as Ambrose and Basil; and from Constantine's time onward, there is revealing evidence of governmental attitudes in the matter, in the shape of numerous regulating Titles in the Theodosian Code. But it is not merely the profusion of extant evidence that is at issue: the special interest of fourth-century patronage derives also from the distinctiveness of the period itself. The watchword here has been 'change and continuity'. Change on various fronts in government, society and culture is plain enough in the period, and one would certainly expect signs of the changes to show up in the discourse generated by patronage: on close analysis, a word such as *suffragium* is shown to alter in meaning, and current scholarship is much concerned with such topics as the shift 'between philanthropy and Christian charity' or the passage 'from patronage to *patrocinium*' (de Ste Croix 1954; Marcone 1998: 340–4, 361–3). But one would certainly also find countervailing signs of continuity in the discourse to weigh against them: the fourth century was not *all* change, and recent work on the period has tended to stress the degree of resilience in the imperial system, finding many elements of social and cultural continuity in the late Empire.

Patronage at Rome in the fourth century: context and style

In what follows I select from the rich body of fourth-century evidence to illustrate the texture of what I have called the elite 'image' of patronage as it impinged on the aristocracy at Rome itself – a particular and in some respects a special case, but not one without a wider interest. Given that my present concern lies more with the ancients' representations of patronage than with the question of its objective 'systemic' importance, and given the fluidity of the ancients' own usage in their discourse, 'patronage' can reasonably be granted its broader frame of reference. As I use the word here, its application is not restricted to personal relationships, nor to persons acting generously in a strictly private capacity: it will often relate to euergetistic services to groups and communities – services offered, moreover, by 'benefactors' who were frequently holding a magistracy or imperial office at the time.

Activities of this latter sort have figured prominently in modern studies of late Antique patronage, marking a tendency, perhaps, to attach greater significance to collective than to personal forms of patronage in the period (on one view, we have observed, the 'systemic' importance of personal patronage declined in imperial times). All the more point, then, to remark that the classic image of the *patronus* and his *cliens* nevertheless retained a forceful appeal in late Roman discourse; and that the image still had a sound basis in social reality. A letter of the celebrated fourth-century Roman senator Q. Aurelius Symmachus will serve for illustration:

> Dusarius, a most distinguished man [*vir clarissimus*], who has rightly achieved the highest rank among professors of medicine, desires that his kinsman and namesake be recommended to your patronage [*patrocinium*] at my request. I am glad to gratify a man very close to me so that, by one and the same means, I can pay my respects to you, by wishing you good health, and also do him a favour. Be kind enough, then, to take care of this man recommended to you, while bestowing on me a substitute for personal contact with you.
>
> (Symmachus *Epist.* 3.97, trans. Croke and Harries 1982. No. 94)

Hundreds of letters in a similar vein are preserved in Symmachus' extensive correspondence. Our letter was written *c.* AD390 to Ambrose, bishop of Milan, but in tone and substance it could almost have been written three centuries earlier: it hardly differs much from the many similar requests that one finds scattered throughout the correspondence, say, of the Younger Pliny. The resonance could have been consciously worked for, to be sure; to Symmachus, when he wrote his letters (and to his son, when he edited the collection in its final form), Pliny's correspondence could offer not simply a literary model, but a classic expression of elite Roman style in social relations and deportment.[11] It has been Symmachus' lot to be remembered above all else as the traditionalist defender of a 'doomed' pagan cause, and it might perhaps be suspected that the evocation of a Plinian patronal style marks a comparably 'backward-looking' tendency, a self-conscious attachment to an ideal of personal patronage that in reality had been marginalised, or degraded to the status of mere financial transaction.[12] But, if there is an element of self-consciousness in Symmachus' patronal discourse, it gives no reason to treat the picture that his letters offer of the workings of personal patronage as largely a literary mirage, as if the image of elite patronal style and influence evoked in his correspondence owed more to the nostalgia of a cultured senator for lost and more congenial days than to the social and political realities of late fourth-century Rome. On the contrary: in Ammianus' jaundiced portrait of the Roman elite of the time, it is implicit both that patronal activity remained central to their status and influence, and that their contacts with dependants still revolved around an elaborate traditional etiquette (Amm. Marc. 14.6.12–13). On this score, the very fact that over a quarter of all of Symmachus' extant letters relate to his efforts to secure for protégés the support of well-placed acquaintances is surely telling[13] – and so too, in its way, is the absence of any clear and simple correlation between his efforts in this connexion and his sympathies as a pagan. In a famous instance in AD384 – his recommendation, as Prefect of Rome, of Augustine for the chair of rhetoric at Milan – the fact that Augustine was a non-Catholic at the time was no doubt appealing (Brown 2000: 69–71); but elsewhere we can find him urging his brother, as Vicarius of Africa, to lend support to the Christian bishop of Mauretanean Caesarea.[14] So, too, the letter to Ambrose quoted above is only one in a sequence of such notes of recommendation that Symmachus sent to the most notable and influential Italian bishop of the day; taken as a group, they offer an interesting sidelight on the personal repercussions (or the lack of them) arising from the opposed stances of the two men in their famous 'debate' over the removal of the Altar of Victory from the Senate House at Rome in 384. That dispute, whatever else it may have signified or entailed, certainly did not prevent the pagan spokesman of 384 from continuing to write politely to Ambrose as an eminent acquaintance (and a relative by family, it is usually supposed) whose influence at Court as Bishop of Milan made him a most valuable contact in the workings of patronage.[15]

To dwell on such details is hardly to do more than to particularise from fine work done by a number of modern scholars on the social and political context of the activity of the aristocracy in late fourth-century Rome. John Matthews, to take a prime instance, has emphasised in various studies that the senatorial elite of Symmachus' day, although it might affect an ideology of preference for private *otium* over the demands of public office, and an indifference to popular acclaim, had in fact retained much of its ancient social and political prestige, and much practical significance as a governing class.[16] And in this connexion the continuance of patronage on a familiar pattern, both personal and collective, must be counted an important factor. At Rome, throughout Italy and in North Africa, Symmachus and his kind 'exercised a durable, tenacious influence in the traditional manner of their class; by multiple landholding, by munificence, and by complex ramifications of *clientela* of which only the most tenuous traces are still visible' (Matthews 1975: 30). Even when no inscription survives to prove a man's official status as patron in a given connexion, the fact can often be inferred indirectly: in Symmachus' case, for instance, from his representations on behalf of the people of Campanian Formiae, where his family is known to have possessed a villa (Symm., *Epist.* 9.58). In the nature of the evidence, it is often very hard to distinguish firmly in this connexion between patronal activity undertaken in a private capacity and actions performed in a public or official capacity: the inscriptions honouring such men as patrons frequently also disclose them as current office-holders. But the ambiguity is not unique to the late Imperial period, and the fundamental value of the distinction for our understanding of imperial Roman patronage is anyway open to question (Veyne 1990: 10–11; MacMullen 1988: 204–8). The ambiguity certainly does not entitle us to infer any general dilution of 'true' patronal practice in the fourth century: patronage had always reached into the public sphere (Pliny, say, as governor of Bithynia, had readily used his lines of contact with the Emperor to petition on behalf of protégés and clients: a better and a grander patron because a governor, then).[17] If one insisted that the ambiguity held a particular significance in the fourth-century inscriptions at issue, it could perhaps be said to mark a further extension of patronage's pre-existing reach within the public sphere, an aspect of what has been called 'privatisation in late Roman government'.[18] So Symmachus, for instance, congratulating an appointee to high office at Court, can find it quite fitting to tell him that 'your official position shines forth through the granting of *beneficia*; and since the estimate of your merit [that is, the appointment] makes you the intimate of the most eminent persons, may you seek the glory of fame and influence by your gracious acts'. That can be taken as a grandiloquent way of saying that 'the very purpose of one's official position is to increase one's fame as a great *private* patron'; but then again, 'what Symmachus takes for granted is no different from the ethic of power prevailing in Pliny's day'.[19] Just the same purpose, of course, was fundamental to the very habit of patronal letter-writing that Pliny and Symmachus exemplify: countless notes of recommendation, devoid of content beyond the name of a protégé adorned with a few conventional superlatives, in which the protég0233's interest counts for little beside the writer's overriding concern – the wish to advertise and enhance his own influence and reputation.

Against this background, it would not do to discount the 'Plinian' flavour in Symmachus' patronal discourse as nostalgic archaism; it is rather a witness to the persistence and importance of a long-familiar pattern of patronal activity. Its practice, and the customary etiquette bound up with it, could be viewed as a stabilising factor that canalised the competitiveness of the elite and helped maintain its social cohesiveness in a period of social and religious flux: like shared tastes in art or poetry, this was an aspect of elite style about which Roman aristocrats, pagan and Christian alike, could still readily agree (see Brown 1961: 1–11). Bishop Ambrose, in this respect, behaved in a way typical of the well-born senator's son that he was, promoting clients commended to him by correspondents such as Symmachus, commending individual protégés of his own by letter, and exercising patronage on a traditional model over influential groups of Milanese businessmen.[20] In the fourth-century inscriptions of Rome itself, a good many grandees are formally commemorated in similar time-honoured fashion as *patroni* of trade-guilds, often in connexion with their holding office as Urban Prefect or *praefectus annonae*.[21] Thus the guild of leatherworkers honours Anicius Paulinus (*praef. urbi a.* 334; *ILS* 1220), and the guild of swine-dealers and slaughterers Valerius Proculus (*praef. urbi a.* 337; *ILS* 1240), 'worthy patrons' both; and the bickering Ostian guilds of the river boatmen and corn measurers thank their 'outstanding patron' Ragonius Vincentius Celsus (*praef. annonae a.* 389; *ILS* 1272 with Meiggs 1973: 293) for resolving a labour dispute to their mutual satisfaction. So too, the inscriptions show such grandees hailed as *patroni* of Italian cities or administrative districts: Manilius Rusticus is '*curator* and patron of the most noble colony of Ostia', Clodius Celsinus a 'most worthy patron' of Beneventum, Betitius Perpetuus an 'outstanding patron' of the provincial district of Tuscia and Umbria (*CIL* XIV suppl. 4455; Meiggs 1973: 187; *ILS* 1239, 1251). Such titles were often offered on the strength of a visit made to a town by a grandee in the course of public duties, and in some cases (a fair number) they confirmed or renewed an hereditary patronal link between an elite family and a 'client' city: Anicius Bassus and Nicomachus Flavianus, for instance, are *patroni originales* of Naples, Postumius Lampadius *patrono longe a maioribus originali* at Capua (*ILS* 8983–4, 1278; other late Roman *patroni originales* in Harmand 1957: 188–9, 304). The same pattern extended to North Africa: Ceionius Italicus (while governor, one assumes) is honoured as patron by 'the council of the happy colony of Constantina [Cirta] and the Numidian province' (*ILS* 1235); and in Symmachus' own case, we have noted earlier, a connexion with Caesarea in Mauretania, where the family possessed estates, lay behind his commendation of the local bishop as a service to the city (Amm. Marc. 14.6.12–13).

The continuance of high-profile patronal activity by aristocrats witnessed at Rome itself for the mid- and late fourth century, it is true, could give a misleading impression of the broader pattern and scale of patronage in Italy and elsewhere at that time. It needs to be viewed both against the general background of a decline of local euergetism in the empire, and with an eye to more particular changes affecting Italy's towns and the Roman senatorial elite. After Diocletian's reforms, Italy was in effect provincialised – divided into administrative units assigned to governors, and rendered liable to taxation. On the archaeological evidence we have, its municipal elites were no longer willing, or could no longer afford, to fund public works. Where building works in Italian towns are attested for the fourth century, at least, the inscriptions almost always credit them to imperial officials rather than local magistrates;[22] as for secular buildings indisputably to be credited to a private individual's initiative, the record is a virtual blank, and the few fourth- and fifth-century cases that are known might be explained as special ones. They mostly belong to Campania and Samnium, areas where there was a particularly high density of Roman senatorial estates – and hence, perhaps, where a tradition of private munificence survived longer than elsewhere in Italy (Ward-Perkins 1984: 19–20). Even at Rome's doorstep, at Ostia, a long and proud tradition of generous spending and service as guild-patrons by leading local families such as the Egrilii and the Lucilii Gamalae had apparently now dissolved: 'the complete absence of surviving inscriptions recording public benefactions by local men is a sign that central control had dried up the springs of public-spirited generosity', and Ostian building works were now initiated by the *praefectus annonae* – which is to say, mainly by Roman senators of the kind we have met above.[23] The prominence of elite Romans as *patroni* in the Italian inscriptions of the time, then, is probably a mark of the evaporation of euergetism at the local level, and reflects the fact that Roman senators now were serving as governors in the peninsula itself: the Italian cities that hailed these Roman aristocrats as patrons often encountered them as governors of their districts, and they looked to them to give what local elites no longer gave. In this setting, 'patron' could serve as a flattering title with which to honour and oblige a man whose wealth or influence a city had profited from, or hoped to profit from; it did not neccesarily connote any close prior connexion between an individual family and the town, and the town was not obliged to attach itself exclusively to one such patron only.

As for the capacity and willingness of the Roman grandees to engage in patronage on this scale, two other factors intrude. First, despite the economic difficulties under which the later Empire laboured, the upper level in the propertied elite had continued to prosper, and more than prosper. The economic sign of the times in this connexion was not outright elite discomfiture, but a greatly widened gulf between rich and poor – and among the propertied senatorial class, between an elite minority and the rest: wealth had 'drained to the top' (or had been purposefully sucked up by it), fourth-century grandees at Rome, it seems, being several times richer on average than their first-century counterparts.[24] These were men who, if they were so minded, could afford generosity. Moreover, there was another sense in which they were freer to display themselves as public benefactors than their earlier counterparts had been. From the days of Augustus onwards, it is a commonplace, that the very presence at Rome of a Princeps – when not as a physical presence, at least as one for whom Rome was the acknowledged natural home – had restricted the field in which the aristocracy could indulge in high profile collective patronage: the Emperor was the *euergetes* of the Roman plebs, its patron in all but name (Veyne 1990: 386–92, 457 n.251), and not to be challenged in the part. By the mid-fourth century, though, Rome had ceased to be the privileged residence of Emperors, and seldom served even as a temporary one: when an Emperor sojourned in Italy he now usually resided at Milan, and imperial visits to Rome, if made at all, were brief and irregular. For practical purposes, the city was no longer the administrative capital of the Empire, but merely of a Diocletianic diocese. Not that imperial munificence at Rome ceased in the fourth century: by no means. Maxentius and Constantine both initiated major building programmes there,[25] and even after the foundation by Constantine of a new capital, his successors well recognised the symbolic force of the *Urbs aeterna* – a factor in imperial publicity nowhere more strikingly emphasised than in Ammianus' famous account of Constantius' public deportment on his visit in 356, and of his decision in the course of it 'to add to the ornaments of the city by the erection of an obelisk in the Circus Maximus'.[26] It was a consideration that helped to ensure the continuance at one remove of a routinised imperial largesse: the established imperial funds that provided the subsidised corn supply of Rome and the upkeep of its fabric continued to operate. Inscriptions of the 360s, 370s and 380s, some of which may represent extra *ad hoc* grants, credit the reigning Emperors with bridge- and arch-building and the beautification of fora at Rome, and with a restoration '*curante praefecto annonae*' of Ostia's Maritime Baths; and around 402, Arcadius and Honorius provided for a major renovation of Rome's city walls.[27] But still, the founding of Constantinople changed perceptions of what had been a special relationship between the Emperor and the people of the old capital. Rome no longer occupied the place it once had held in the Emperors' thoughts, and the withdrawal of the Emperor and Court from Rome gave its great senatorial families a renewed opportunity to indulge in civic self-display, and in doing so to evoke a senatorial style of times long gone. Just as Italy was now effectively provincialised, so Rome, it could be said, became 'municipalised'. The highest office, the Urban Prefecture, boasted an Augustan pedigree and was highly valued. The Prefect, typically an elite senator serving in tenure for a year or so, was now both the president of the Senate and the official in supreme charge of the city, responsible for the upkeep of its fabric and for the distribution of the food supply through the agency of a *praefectus annonae* (in principle, an office under the Prefect's dispensation).[28] Because of its high concentration of old public buildings, upkeep of the urban fabric was by this time an especially pressing need at Rome, and was felt as such. In this connexion, it is significant that the principal antique gazetteers of the architecture of the city still extant, the *Curiosum* and the *Notitia*, were compiled in the earlier fourth century (Nordh 1949: 60). Restoration works could plainly offer particular scope to elite Roman senators, if they wished, to spend munificently on their own account – or else at least to seem to play the part, winning a reputation on the cheap by manipulating monies from the imperial funds to which they could gain access as holders of public offices. The names of Prefects – sometimes specified baldly as 'restorers', sometimes as agents of an Emperor's initiative – figured on the public buildings and monuments whose repair they had undertaken, and the same Prefects, we have seen, were now often hailed as *patroni* in the inscriptions set up to commemorate their *beneficia*: 'for the first time, Rome had *patroni* like the other cities' (Veyne 1990: 469 n.321; Chastagnol 1960: 257–8, 353).

In an Italian municipality, a prominent man might be explicitly honoured as *patronus* of the local plebs,[29] and by the later fourth century, the title could sometimes serve to denote an imperially-sanctioned local office: the Praetorian Prefect of Illyricum in the late 360s was under orders to install honest and experienced men as 'patrons of the plebeians' in every municipality in his diocese.[30] At Rome itself it was different, because there the benefactor at issue had long been pre-eminently the Emperor himself, and his etiquette had shunned the explicit title of *patronus* as the mark of a mere *privatus* (Veyne 1990). None the less, in any picture of the self-display of the fourth-century Roman elite, the relations of the grandees with the Roman plebs must have a significant place. The make-up and condition of the plebs at this time is a relatively understudied topic, but it is clear that its relationship with the elite was far from distant, and highly volatile.[31] The plebs now looked more to the aristocrats who filled the city's high offices for some of the *beneficia* that had traditionally been provided and maintained by Emperors – the games, the baths, the assured availability of subsidised oil, and corn and wine. Aristocrats, for their part, might sometimes jib at the presumption, and the cost to their pockets, of the popular appetite: Avianius Symmachus, the father of our letter-writer, for instance, who as Urban Prefect of 364/5 had overseen the construction of a new bridge 'to the delight of the citizens', had his house set alight ten years later by a rioting crowd when he vowed he would divert wine from his estates to use for slaking lime rather than sell it at the reduced price demanded of him.[32] But grandees still viewed popular esteem in the eyes of the people of Rome as an important mark of their prestige. The Games remained an obvious means to that: a paradoxically 'involuntary' form of patronage, strictly speaking, in that quaestors and praetors were legally obliged to provide Games; but on this score, rich senators were prepared to spend far larger sums than the law required. Probably the best known of all Symmachus' letters are those which record the expense and trouble he took to provide games worthy of the family name to commemorate his own son's early magistracies – a business, it is telling, that required his getting around a law of 384 intended to limit expenditure in just that connexion (Jones 1973: 537–8, 561; *C Th* 15.9.1).

As for the expectations of the people, there are signs that in the fourth-century plebeian consciousness a distinction still held which modern study has taken to be fundamental to the working of ancient patronage, and a mark of its distance from the ideal of Christian charity: the assumption, that is, that patronal largesse should operate to the benefit of the citizen-body, not to the relief of the poor *qua* poor – with the consequence that in practice it tended to exclude the truly destitute (see e.g. Brown 1992: 83–4). A revealing episode in Ammianus tells how Rufius Volusianus Lampadius, as praetor, offended popular feeling in this regard. He began well enough, giving 'magnificent games and exuberant largesses'; but then, apparently 'unable to withstand the demands of the plebs that much should be given to unworthy persons' – favourites of the plebs at the theatre or Circus, we may suppose – he distributed largesse in such a way as to show his contempt for the crowd: 'he summoned some beggars from the Vatican, and enriched them with great gifts' (Amm. Marc. 27.3.5–6). Such paupers, it is implicit, might beg for charity at the doors of St Peter's or the papal cathedral at the Lateran, but in the eyes of the Roman plebs they were singularly inappropriate beneficiaries of patronal largesse: Volusianus' act was a calculated insult to plebeian self-esteem. His later behaviour in 365, when he was Urban Prefect, seems to bear a similar stamp: Ammianus notes that his tenure of office was marked by serious riots of 'the incensed poor' – which in context, it is clear, connotes plebeian tradesmen from whom he had requisitioned materials without payment for the restoration of public buildings (Amm. Marc. 27.3.10). In Volusianus' case, we may add, such cynical behaviour kept company with a vanity that was literally monumental: Ammianus criticised his practice of having his name inscribed on ancient buildings in the city repaired at his initiative *non instaurator, sed conditor* – 'not as their restorer, but as their founder': 'a small thing', Ammianus granted, 'but something to be avoided by high officials' (Amm. Marc. 27.3.7).

Turning on a point of style in public display, Ammianus' rebuke is likelier to mark his own sensitivities on this score than those of Volusianus's peers. An outsider at Rome, Ammianus drew mordant portraits of the Roman aristocracy of his day as a monument to vanity and philistine taste: men of the sort he depicted, one suspects, would tend to take a more indulgent view of Volusianus's claim to be a *conditor* – all the more so in his case, perhaps, for the fact that an imperial law of the previous year had forbidden the Prefect of the City to undertake any new construction, urging him instead 'to restore those buildings said to have fallen into unsightly ruins' (*C Th* 15.1.11, AD364). The law witnesses both a special problem posed at Rome, where the upkeep and restoration of the very large number of ageing public monuments had become an endless and expensive business, and the continuing wish of Prefects none the less to leave their mark not just as 'restorers' of existing structures, but as 'founders' of new amenities. In this setting, it is not surprising that in public honours the distinction between 'restoring' and 'founding' could be conveniently blurred, and by the end of the century, or early in the fifth, we find more than one Prefect commemorated as *fori conditor* (*ILS* 807/8, 1281, 5357), which was surely to stretch the phrase: in practice, it will hardly connote more than either the adornment or cleaning up of an existing public space, or else a private ornamental square (we know of several)[33] laid out at the front of an aristocrat's mansion.

The measure of the past

Perhaps most grandees at Rome were as a rule less provocative than Volusianus Lampadius in their dealings with the people, and a bit less hyperbolic in the commemorative honours they looked for: but they played on the same robust public stage (Symmachus himself was on one occasion forced by popular anger to leave the city, only to be recalled soon afterwards at the demand of a theatre crowd)[34] and their claims to popular gratitude as benefactors are pitched high in a language which – like Symmachus' style in the discourse of personal patronage – evoked and measured itself against a proud past. The wording of many of the dedications to patrons that we noted earlier bears clear witness on this count. The inscription honouring Anicius Paulinus as *patronus* of the leatherworkers, for instance, praises him for 'the providence and *civilitas* and *integritas reipublicae* that saw to the repair and the adornment to their pristine state of the *insulae* of the guild of leatherworkers, in accordance with the laws of previous *principes*, the Augusti Septimius Severus and Aurelius Antoninus' (*ILS* 1220). Vitrasius Orfitus, the Urban Prefect of 355, is hailed as 'famous at home and abroad for his self-control and justness and constancy and providence and all the virtues, on the model of former times', thanked by the 'most ancient guild of the contractors of Ostia and Portus [for] outstanding and salutary provision in most difficult times and for the restored utility of the city of Rome' (*ILS* 1243); or there is the patron we met earlier reconciling two Ostian guilds at loggerheads, who had 'exercised control (*rexit … potestatem*) over the corn supply of the Eternal City with such fairness … as to show himself more a parent than an official' (*ILS* 1272). It is the same with the Prefects' activities in other spheres, and other moods: there too we find commemorative texts evoking Roman tradition as the yardstick for present conduct, and the same paternalist overtones. Thanks from senators could be as fulsome as those from guildsmen, and no less insistent that the honorand measured up to a proud Roman past: a *curator statuarum* hails Ceionius Rufius, Prefect of 335–7, for acting to restore to the Senate some cosmetic emblem of *auctoritas* that it had not enjoyed 'since the times of [Julius] Caesar, that is to say, for 381 years'.[35] Sterner in context, but just as ready to appeal to the yardstick of the past, an edict of Tarracius Bassus, the Prefect of 375/6, witnesses a paternalist act of public shaming: it orders the publication on bronze tablets of a list of individually named plebeian shopkeepers (*tabernarii*) reprimanded for having laid somehow improper claims 'to money[-prizes] and places at the shows and to the bread of the People, contrary to the Roman custom [*disciplina*]' – entitlements, it is implied, whose proper regulation in the interest of 'the people' Bassus proposes to ensure by reasserting an established precondition of eligibility.[36] (And Bassus may also have meant to invoke a more particular memory of Rome's past; if a recently suggested restoration of a textual gap in the edict is correct, what went 'contrary to *disciplina romana*' in the actions of those denounced was their continuing to claim entitlements formerly due to them after they had ceased actually to reside in the city. The loaded phrase at issue, *derel[icta urbe Roma]*, could make antiquarian allusion to one of the best known and blackest tranches of Roman historical memory: the popular agitation *c.* 390BC to abandon the city and migrate to Veii – the occasion in Livy of Furius Camillus' famous appeal to patriotic steadfastness and piety – and the Gallic capture of a largely deserted Rome which followed soon afterwards.)[37] Even in the municipal praises of such senatorial bigwigs – the governors and their like hooked by a town as patron – one finds the measure of the past intruding: so the *corrector* Clodius Celsinus, for instance, noticed earlier as a 'most worthy patron' of Beneventum, is 'outstanding in benevolence, *auctoritas* and justness … [and] has surpassed the *iudices* of former times in his display of every virtue' (*ILS* 1239: Clodius Celsinus, *praef. urbi* 351); and another fourth-century patron of the same town is thanked by its 'entire plebs [for] distinguished *beneficia* by which he abated long-standing ills of the People'[38] during his governorship.

Amenities repaired 'to pristine state', the 'restored utility' of 'the Eternal City'; a lapsed privilege precisely calculated as renewed 'after 381 years'; boons conferred upon 'most ancient guilds', 'on the model of former times', 'in accordance with the laws of previous *principes*'; 'outstanding patrons' who display in their 'providence' and '*civilitas*', their 'self-control' and 'justice', the emblematic virtues of model Emperors[39] (Augustus the *Pater Patriae* himself and his 'restored republic' seem to hover on the edge of memory as one Prefect shows himself 'more a parent than an official', and another restores to the Senate a mark of its *auctoritas* lost 'since Caesar's times'): the Roman past casts a long shadow in these texts. How is their harping on tradition to be construed? On one view, perhaps, as simple vanity pandered to by abject flattery, of a piece with the questionable claims to long senatorial pedigree that families of the fourth-century Roman elite were prone to make; or the mark, at best, of a compensatory overvaluing of traditional precedent that assuaged the anxieties of an elite in a city of diminished political significance. For the dedications present us, of course, with the patronal services of grandees in rosy terms congenial to the grandees themselves. To modern scholars, the paternalist effusions may easily seem a cloak for vested interest, and some have judged the Roman aristocracy of Symmachus' day very severely as a self-serving class (but what class is not?) whose avarice gave the lie to its patriotic ebullitions and cultural pretensions (e.g. Cameron 1999: 109; Purcell 1999: 159).

In a sense, to be sure, 'philanthropy' in this setting could not be other than self-serving and self-regarding: it affirmed and endorsed the power of an elite class, and the giver's status within it. In raw financial terms, too, the motives of individual benefactors may often have been less than open-hearted. Two of our earlier noticed cases – Volusianus Lampadius' efforts to evade tradesmen's bills arising from his building-repairs, and the elder Symmachus's refusal to sell his surplus wine at a cut rate for distribution to the commons – are both transparently tacky in this regard; and the implication in the latter case that Symmachus was a significant producer of cheap wine for this market may suggest a lesson of wider import. The individuals who occasionally intervened to ensure the supply and affordability to the community of essential commodities were themselves usually owners of large estates, producing and controlling large stocks of such essentials, and profiting from their sale: on a cool estimate, many 'benefactors' might be classified as wealthy speculators who, at times when food prices went notably high, were sometimes prepared to reduce the scale of their speculative activities – but not to abandon them wholly (Marcone 1998: 331). In the case at hand, then, what Avienus Symmachus viewed as popular presumption will have seemed something else to a populace exposed to a shortage of an essential item of consumption if he failed to sell his wine; moreover, his threat to divert the wine for lime-slaking rather than sell at the price demanded suggests that he was hoping to turn a profit by exploiting an alternative captive market, the market in building materials (and insult would be added to injury if, as some suspect, the lime-mortar he had in mind was of a type specially prized for lining aristocrats' fish-ponds).[40] Faced with evidence of this sort, moderns are apt to respond curtly to the notion that an idealising attachment to Rome's civic and cultural tradition nurtured any great sense of *noblesse oblige* in the late Roman aristocracy, and it is easy to feel impatient with a set of immensely rich men whose influence could prompt municipalities to hail them as patrons on the strength of mere hopes, and whose claims to popular gratitude more often rested on access through office to public funds and imperial grants than on the expenditure of private wealth. But even the most astringent of verdicts would not entail that the traditionalist echoes in our patronal dedications lacked any genuinely inspiring resonance for the honorands, or for some, at least, of those who honoured them: avarice can be blind to itself, and avaricious men are not necessarily thorough-going cynics; they can harbour a wishful sentimentalism in their notions of their own worth and others' estimates of it. Implicitly, the echoes affirmed that the public estimation of a grandee's reputation at Rome continued to be bound up with a venerable image of patronal provision and care. Commemorative dedications by client guilds, like the attendance of a dependant at the *salutatio* or the commendatory letter in the personal sphere, were central to patronage's etiquette; like them, they persisted, one suspects, because the established etiquette still counted in the minds of the parties concerned. Widely encountered in Rome's public space on walls and statue bases, the texts of the dedications proclaimed both the fact of a patron's power to influence and protect, and other men's estimate of his virtue. In a similar way, bronze plaques commemorating a patron's taking-on of a town or guild continued to be prominently displayed in aristocratic houses: in the house of the Valerii Proculi on the Caelian, for instance, a clutch of such *tabulae patronatus* hung in the atrium recording a prominent family member's various fourth-century patronal co-options, the dates and hereditary reach of each, and the ratifying visits made to the patron at Rome by deputations from provincial client communities; and in these texts too, it mattered that pride in the arrangements was recorded for the client as well as the patron.[41]

The allusions in our commemorative texts to the civic virtues and traditions of Rome's past, then, seem to have counted as something more than empty flattery cynically elicited in the minds of their elite recipients, however moderns care to judge their class. To exercise influence over individuals and groups as a patron, and to be acknowledged as having played the part effectively, remained central to the self-definition of the fourth-century elite in Rome, and the self-definition was bound up with a broader historical selfconsciousness. It is tempting to make the connexion here with the strong interest taken within some elite circles at this time in Augustan writers, particularly Livy and Virgil. Symmachus himself planned to edit the entire *History* of Livy, and members of the Symmachi and Nicomachi worked actively over two generations on the texts of Livy's first ten Books and on the *Aeneid* (Marcus 1974: 11–12; but note the qualifying comments of Cameron 1999: 118–21). Attachments of this sort rested on more than literary connoisseurship – implicit, surely, is a special pull exerted by Livy's antiquarian patriotism and sentimental 'republicanism' – and they could impinge at times on elite public conduct: when Symmachus as Urban Prefect in 384 wrote to the Emperor urging him to revoke the removal the Altar of Victory from the Senate House, he was speaking, after all, of a monument well known to have been dedicated by Augustus himself, and at which rituals had been performed from Augustus' reign onward. And in the present connexion it is apt, too, to adduce the case of a near-contemporary of Symmachus, Rutilius Namatianus. Rutilius, who pursued a successful career at Honorius' court and served as Prefect of the City in 414, is best remembered for a poem shot through with Virgilian and Horatian echoes in which he recounts a journey made in 417 from the capital to his native Gaul. As we have it, Book 1 of the poem opens with an long passage, much of it apostrophising Rome directly, in praise of the city's greatness as disclosed by her history, her architecture and the excellence of her present senate: grant a safe journey, the writer begs of her, 'if I was pleasing to you when I administered the laws of Romulus, if I honoured and consulted your venerable senators' (Rutilius Nam., *De reditu suo* I.156–8). One such senator (one whose family we have already encountered) was a friend to whom the traveller says a fond goodbye as he sets out from Ostia: 'Rufius, the living glory of his father Albinus, who with Virgil as his witness traces his name back to the ancient line of Volusus and to Rutulian kings ... and whose zealous imitation [of ancestral virtue] has held out to him the prospect of the supreme fasces' (Rutilius Nam., *De reditu suo* 168–76); that is to say, Rufius Antonius Agrypius Volusianus, a man about to take up office as Prefect of the City (417–8), and himself the son and grandson of Prefects (the grandfather was our Volusianus Lampadius, benefactor of Vatican beggars and the Prefect pursued by unpaid tradesmen in 365). By the close of the book, Rutilius has reached Pisa, the scene of an emotionally charged passage which slides in its opening couplets from foundation legends of archaic Greek settlement and Aeneas's arrival in Latium to recent personal experience, and which deserves to be quoted at length:

> Long before fortune grafted the Trojan house on to the stock of the kings of Lavinium, the Elians founded a Tuscan colony at Pisa ... where now my eyes met a statue of my venerable father erected by the Pisans in their civic forum. I was driven to tears by their praise of my dead parent, bitter-sweet tears that flowed down my cheeks. For my father once [AD389] was governor of Tuscia, exercising a jurisdiction confirmed by six *fasces*. I remember how, after a career full of honours, he used to say that he had enjoyed his post in Tuscia the most. Not even his later tenure of the Prefecture [of Constantinople?] was dearer to him than this post (indeed – dare one say it? – he went so far as to put his love of it above the Prefecture); and he was not mistaken, so very dear was he in the eyes of the Tuscans. Their mutual affection sings out eternal thanks [in verses inscribed on the base of his statue], and old men who remember him tell their young how he mingled firmness and kindness. They rejoice that the son has not fallen short of the father in his honours ... All Tuscia reverences the reputation of my father Lachanius as one of its own sons, and as if it were divine.
>
> (Rutilius Nam., *De reditu suo* 571–96)

This passage touches on many of the topics we have been discussing. In the figure of Rutilius the public aspirations of a holder of the most eminent office in late Antique Rome are neatly conjoined with a historically self-conscious and self-defining attachment to Rome's past, and in his poem these feelings merge with ideals of filial piety and patronal virtue: the father beloved of all Tuscia who is honoured by Pisa with a statue can surely be added to those we have found attested earlier in inscriptions, as a governor targeted by a community under his jurisdiction as a helpful patron for their town.

The late Roman elite memorialised by Rutilius alongside their city's history and architectural wonders was also the readership for which he chiefly wrote, and his appeal to the nation's past as the measure of present conduct may well have voiced a sentiment which many such aristocrats shared. But even if we allow their good faith, elite self-assessment in this connexion was hardly likely to be rigorous. Supposing that the allusions to the past in our dedications to prefects and patrons were indeed seriously taken by honorands, may that not merely denote an almost farcically self-deluded elite looking to the past mainly because it sweetened the tart contemporary reality of a Rome having become a political backwater in which the elite's own public standing and extravagant life-style depended on the willingness of the imperial government to continue with subventions on the vast former scale? Dramatic events of the early fifth century plainly give the question a sharper edge: only seven years before Rutilius' journey of AD417 Gothic armies had overrun his father's beloved Tuscia and had sacked Rome itself, and it is tempting to suspect that for the likes of Rutilius there may have been little to look forward to except the past. Perhaps the lesson to be drawn in the case of the late fourth-century texts we have reviewed is really much the same?

A measure of truth may be granted to this notion – but not too much. Even in the fifth century, it can be argued, there remained an optimistic strand to Rutilius' vision of a Rome returning to normal after the trauma of the Gothic sack of 410 (Matthews 1975: 327–8, 353–9; cf Cameron 1999: 117–8). 'That which undoes other kingdoms,' the poet declares, 'renews you: the capacity to grow stronger out of misfortune is the principle of your regeneration' (Rutilius Nam., *De reditu suo* I.139–40) – and in his small way a friend of Rutilius, Decius Acinatius Albinus, can illustrate the sentiment: as the poet's successor as Urban Prefect of 414, Albinus would write to the Emperor informing him that the number of persons entitled to the corn-dole at Rome had recently markedly increased – which may suggest large scale return of former refugees; and an inscription tells how in the same year he undertook the repair of a popular place of resort, the Decian Baths on the Aventine.[42] As for our fourth-century texts, we should not assume too quickly that their allusions to the Roman past had resonance for aristocrats alone, deluded or not. The provision by a guild of an inscribed commemorative monument to a notable entailed significant expenditure by the guild: what justified the expense in the guildsmens' minds? Partly, one assumes, the continuing goodwill of an influential contemporary and the practical advantages that might accrue from it; but an element of self-commemoration is also implicit in the act, the linking of the guild to a prominent civic figure whose high reputation could enhance the guild's own lustre. On this score, it is hard to say how much, if anything, was added to the value and appeal of our dedications to elite benefactors in the eyes of guildsmen, or of the plebs at large, by their evocations of the Roman past. Leading members of large guilds could be persons of some reputation and means on their own account, and for them at least something probably was added: the bland dictates of flattery certainly did not require them to advertise their membership of 'most ancient' guilds, or to commission texts which made them commentators on Roman history and judges of its reflection in their eminent contemporaries. As for the rest, a sort of 'cockney', or populist, civic pride might be surmised: pride in the past can cross classes, and if a popular assumption still indeed held that the proper beneficiary of gifts and services provided or mediated by the elite was the citizen body, not the poor as such, it may be that some broader plebeian memory of historically sanctioned privileges was also still at play. But here fundamental and very difficult questions impinge, not only about the extent and level of mass literacy and about the attention with which public texts whose function was as much performative as informative were actually read, but also a basic demographic question: was there by this time a trans-generational continuity in the plebeian population of Rome substantial enough to nurture an inherited sense of collective identity that might appeal to the past; or was 'the late Roman plebs' a much less stable entity than that implies, with a good part of the population constantly shifting in a pattern of migration towards and away from the city (Purcell 1999: 137–50)? One recent study, for instance, judges that our evidence does suffice to show the plebs acting as a partner of the elite in promoting 'the profoundly historical self-consciousness' of fourth-century Rome, but it makes a crucial proviso that would deny the point much general force: as an institutional collectivity, it speculates, the *plebs Romana* was itself perhaps now no more than 'a dwindling, etiolated, symbolic body', just another decorative feature in a 'theme-park' Rome (Purcell 1999: 137). On this view, a declining civic population at Rome in late Antiquity was threatening to dissolve a structure of economic exchange, dependence, consumption and subvention which had lasted centuries, and without which the urban life-style taken for granted by its aristocracy was unsustainable; and the apparent altruism of the elite's efforts to maintain the city's ancient glory and utility in the public interest masked a desperate attempt to preserve the system which underpinned its wealth and prestige – a system, of course, in which personal patronage and the structures of dependence it engendered had long been significant constituents.

When the population's sense of the city's past in late Antique Rome is in question, another large issue impinges, one that we have deliberately touched on only in passing as yet, and to which we can revert briefly in closing: Christianisation. By the late fourth century, one supposes, the bulk of the Roman populace was Christianised: the power of the Roman Church, manifest in its charitable provisions and its building works by the time of Pope Damasus (AD366–384), offered the population a new source of authority and *beneficia* to contemplate, and, if it wished, an alternative local tradition, a Rome of Peter and Paul, catacombs and martyrs, Constantine's Lateran and the Vatican. So, by the time S Maria Maggiore was completed in the mid-fifth century, the city's inhabitants could be famously addressed by their Pope as *plebs Dei*, the People of God (Krautheimer 1980: 46). By then the bulk of Rome's aristocracy, too, could safely be counted among God's people, and in the long run the Christianising process plainly implies a disruption of traditional patterns of patronal display and exhange. Charity – donation to an economically defined 'poor', irrespective of civic entitlement – is a significant ideological shift, and in this connexion the fate of the Caelian house of the Valerii Proculi, cited earlier for the *tabulae patronatus* that adorned its walls, gives us a telling emblem of the passage from 'patronage' to 'charity' in one elite family. In the early fifth century, after some years of dereliction following the Gothic sack, the house was given over for use as a Christian hospice by Valerius Pinianus and his wife Melania the Younger in the course of a general liquidation of the family's vast estates undertaken by the pious couple for the purpose of poor relief (Matthews 1975: 356, citing *Vita Melaniae*, 14). So too, the funding of ecclesiastical buildings offered a new channel of expenditure to rich benefactors whose efforts had formerly been directed mainly to the provision or upkeep of secular amenities and services (though a channel which plainly could still serve secular needs of self-advertisement). The change was already showing through in the fourth century, and several strands of it are converging in the activities of Ambrose of Milan, his continuing engagement in the web of personal patronage notwithstanding (and all the more pointedly, in his case, for the fact that the church had supplied an alternative career for an aristocrat whose estates could otherwise have funded acts of civic euergetism in the old style). As bishop of Milan, Ambrose directed his resources not to the upkeep of secular amenities, but to the building of the *Basilica Ambrosiana*, a new church to house the bones of SS Gervasius and Protasius ('these [martyrs] are the sort of influential men whose support I am securing', he noted); and he was happy to melt down silver plate donated to the church by rich converts in order to ransom prisoners of war, with a brusque reminder to the donors that 'the property of the church consists of the support of the destitute …'.[43] At Rome, too, by Ambrose's day, rich private donors were contributing to new churches, and founding paupers' hospices.[44] But it remains a rather different question, in the case of Rome itself, whether the Christianising process had already by the late fourth century radically eroded the contours of patronal benefaction: a question resting partly on the nature and dictates of Christianity in elite eyes, on whether Christian ideals of charity made most fourth-century elite converts much less willing in practice to engage in patronal display in the old style.

At Rome, at least, it would seem that this was not the case: the tradition of private secular munificence survived among its elite a century and more after the evidence for it elsewhere in Italy virtually disappears (Ward-Perkins 1984: 44–5), and we have seen that, in their public capacity as prefects, Rome's fourth-century grandees continued to play a long-familiar role as patrons and benefactors of an entitled civic body. The part was played the more readily at Rome, no doubt, for the fact that the established imperial subventions to fund the food supply and keep up the urban fabric still flowed; but fundamentally, these patterns of behaviour, public or private, continued to be enacted and commemorated because they remained close to the heart of elite self-definition in a historically self-conscious city. The *pax deorum*, the notion that Rome's success had been underwritten from the beginning by its ancestral gods, had clearly figured in that self-consciousness, and in the eyes of a senator such as Symmachus pagan cult remained indissolubly part and parcel of what Rome was. Nonetheless, religious allegiances do not look to have been central to the practice of patronage and munificence among the elite of fourth-century Rome. On occasion they could colour an individual prefect's actions, certainly: the restorations of a temple of Apollo by Memmius Orfitus, twice prefect in the 350s (and Symmachus' father-in-law), and of the portico of the *di consentes* by the celebrated pagan intellectual Praetextatus, prefect in 367/8, seem clear cases in point on the pagan side (*ILS* 3222 [Orfitus], 4003 [Praetextatus]). But the great bulk of the epigraphic evidence shows benefaction at Rome at this time as still principally a secularly focussed enterprise (pagan civic cult, indeed, is so rarely the object of private patronage in this connexion that some have wondered whether it was really such a compelling concern in the eyes of Symmachus and his sort[45]). Similarly, while his enriching of beggars from the Vatican in the presence of a scandalised plebs suggests that Volusianus Lampadius could recognise the difference between old style civic philanthropy and Christian charity, the action itself was intended to shock, and aberrant: the inscriptions we have reviewed applaud services and generosity to civically entitled groups, not charitable provision for the destitute; and the elite benefactors commemorated in them belong as often to Christian as to pagan senatorial families. Like their activities as personal patrons, the public display of these men elides the line between Christian and pagan. If the texts we have reviewed sit easily with modern claims that the elite senators of fourth-century Rome are best construed as fundamentally a governing class, only secondarily as pagans and Christians,[46] they also suggest that at Rome the fourth-century elite's notion of what good government was, and of the role of patronage and euergetism within it, was still strongly coloured by a self-defining attachment to Rome's past. Gradually, the old ethos of civic patronage and euergetism would dwindle there, as it had done elsewhere, but it is hardly clear that the espousal of an alternative, Christian, ideal of charity was the prime cause of its undoing: we should view the shift, rather, as part of a gradual and broader pattern of urban and demographic decline that accelerated in the fifth century with the drying-up of the city's old governmental subsidies and the drift away from the city of much of the dependent population which had furnished the body of the entitled (Purcell 1999, citing Brown 1982: 123–45). For most of the fourth century, the elite at Rome persevered in the show of civic benefaction: they did so partly because it was a class role endorsed and enjoined by the past, and if the Christian charitable ideal posed a challenge to the tradition, most elite converts at Rome were still first and foremost aristocrats. But perhaps the voice of the Roman Church itself did not in any case speak so very harshly on this matter in the fourth century. It would certainly be rash to assume that the crowd which so violently pressed Damasus' claim to the papacy in 366 represented a new class of dependent support drawn from outside the circle of the 'entitled' plebs (Amm. Marc. 27.3.12–13); and in the 380s, when two dissident rigorist priests denounced Damasus, the cost and luxury of his ecclesiastical building works were cited as prime proofs of his lack of Christian humility (Pietri 1978: 313–37). A pope who built on a scale that could seem to rival or outdo the public works of a prefect: that too, in its way, is a testimony to the power and claims of the past in the Roman elite's conception of patronage at this time.

Notes

This chapter was written and submitted before the appearance of and without knowledge of J.R. Curran (2000) *Pagan City and Christian Capital: Rome in the Fourth Century*, Oxford: Oxford University Press.

1 For the shift to charity as a key transition in late antiquity, Veyne 1990: 19, 24–34; Brown 1992: 78–103; Patlagean 1977 is fundamental.

2 On difficulties of generalisation in this connexion see e.g. MacMullen 1988: 15–48 (regional contrasts); Brown 1989: 109ff, 151–2 (Syria); Lepelley 1992: 70–2 (Africa).

3 Rouland 1979: 493ff ('depoliticisation' of the *clientela* system in the Principate); cf Johnson and Dandeker 1988: 238–9.

4 A qualified formulation: notions of *generalised* third-century cessation of munificence and municipal collapse are of course problematic (MacMullen 1988: 5–7, 220, and ch.1 *passim*, questioning an earlier consensus).

5 His *liberalitas*/charity: Eusebius *V.C* 1.43 and (critically) Zosimus 2.38; on buildings and endowments, Krautheimer 1980: 20–31; Barnes 1981: 49–51, 222–3, 248–9; Lane Fox 1986: 667–9.

6 Matthews 1989: 270–4; MacMullen 1988: 109–10, on sharpened competition among fourth-century court officials and imperial ladies as brokers of patronage (noting as telling the virtual disappearance in the period of direct response by emperors to individual petitions in the form of rescripts); for petitioners' recognition of the realities, Brown 1992: 30–1.

7 Liebeschuetz 1972: 194–208; de Ste Croix 1981: 224–6; Carrié 1976: 159–79; Brown 1992: 91–5 (bishops). Church wealth and expenditure at Rome: Pietri 1976: 645ff and 1978: 313–37; at Constantinople: Dagron 1984: 496ff.

8 Brown 1971: 80–101 [1989: 103–52]; Mitchell 1993: vol. ii, 124, 134–50; Lane Fox 1986: 774 n25 (qualifying).

9 For late antiquity, Libanius, *Orr.* 47, 48 and 49 are key texts of complaint, *C. Th.* 1.29.8 and 11.24.1–6 good examples of governmental response to 'abusive' forms: discussion in Petit 1955: 174, 293–4, 375–8; Liebeschuetz 1972: 201–4, Carrié 1976: 159–176.

10 Brunt 1988: 393–5; Saller 1982: 10–11, and 1988: 52–4. On the persisting habit in late antique correspondence, Brown 1992: 46–7.

11 The book divisions of Pliny's letters were plainly the model in the final editing of Symmachus' correspondence after his death, and the likelihood that Symmachus himself had read them is very strong: see Cameron 1965: 289–98.

12 Affirmation of an idealised *amicitia* as a dominant impulse in Symmachus' letters: Conte 1983: 634; Browning 1983: 760; on literary allusion and archaism in Symmachus. NB still Kroll 1891: 1–41; for criticism of Symmachus as preoccupied with the past to the exclusion of 'a realistic attempt to grapple with the present', Cameron 1977: 30; cf Paschoud 1967: 71–109.

13 Matthews 1974: 58–99, at 61, with 79 (acutely observing that this rough measure will still exclude a significant portion of Symmachus' patronal activity: the letters do not

touch on his actions while in public office in favour of his own clients and others commended to him).

14 Symm. *Epist.* 1.64, with Matthews 1975: 24–5 for the context (bishop Clemens representing his city at the Imperial Court) and the Mauretanian property interests of the Symmachi.

15 Matthews 1975: 191–2; McLynn 1994: 263–75 (doubting the family connexion). Whether the letters to Ambrose mark personal *friendship* is of course another question: see Matthews 1986: 173–4.

16 Principally Matthews 1975: esp 1–31, with earlier articles there cited (see esp. 1971: 122–8); see also 1989: 414–23, and the studies of Symmachus' correspondence cited above (1974, 1986).

17 Often in Pliny *Epist.* book X: eg at 10; 11; 12; 85; 86a; 86b; 87; 94; 106. Cf MacMullen 1988: 108, aptly citing the Sejanus of Tac. *Ann.* 4.41.1: 'It is natural to wonder whether the crowds sought him out as a praetorian prefect or as a patron. Surely the answer is, as both at once …'.

18 MacMullen 1988: 148; cf Matthews 1974: 78: 'Public office was [now] a function of the private status of senators; it was not the other way round'.

19 MacMullen 1988: 103–4 on Symm, *Epist.* 7.94 (I quote his translation).

20 Ambrose, *Epist.* 20 & 87, with Matthews 1975: 190–1; Symm. *Epist.* 3.33 shows Ambrose commending a protégé to Symmachus.

21 Clemente 1972: 142–229 surveys guild-patronage, noting (226) as a fourth-century development the tendency to appoint as *patroni* officials administratively linked to the guilds – a feature of the 'privatisation in government' noticed above.

22 Ward-Perkins 1984: 23ff (NB MacMullen 1988: 16 (qualifying), and Lepelley 1992: 71, a notice of work in progress). Building, of course, is not the *only* possible expression of local elite patronage: and against the dearth in the archaeological record, we can note late-fourth-century literary testimony (e.g. Symmachus, *Epist.* 1.3, on the elite of Beneventum who 'exhaust their private wealth on the adornment of the town').

23 I quote Meiggs 1973: 211–2. For the former pride of notable Ostian families in local public spending and guild patronage, Meiggs 1973: 420, 494–507, 598: the epigraphic record runs back from Severan to Augustan times, perhaps to the late Republic (see Zevi 1973 on *ILS* 6147).

24 Jones 1973: 554–7; Brown 1981: 34 (wealth 'drained' upwards); cf de Ste Croix 1981: 503 (the elite as 'vampire bats'). Symmachus' letters allow his own case to be reconstructed in some detail: for the range and scale of his family properties, Vera 1986: 231–70.

25 Cullhed 1984: 47–67 (Maxentius' programme); for Constantine's activities, Krautheimer 1980: 20–31; and see now E.D. Hunt in the present volume at pp. 105–24 above.

26 Amm. Marc. 16.10.1–17; cf 17.4.12–23 for the erection of the obelisk, on the background to which, Fowden 1987.

27 *ILS* 771–2 (bridge); 776, 5592 (fora); 781 (arch); 5694 (baths); 797 (walls).

28 Jones 1973: 689–90; with Chastagnol 1960: 43–63 for imperial funds and officials serving the annona and building works.

29 *ILS* 1368 (Lavinium): *patroni plebis et collegiorum.*

30 *C. Th.* 1.29.1 and 4 (AD368: Valentinian and Valens to Petronius Probus).

31 See Matthews 1989: 416–20; and Kneppe 1979; most recently Purcell 1999: 135–6. Horsfall 1996, though not focused on the late period, has broad implications, and many fascinating details (e.g. 10–12, fourth-century survival of a popular tradition of memorising songs from the stage, worried over by Jerome and Augustine).

32 Amm Marc 27.3.4 (for the honour received in connexion with the bridge, see Matthews 1975: 22, noting the grant as assigned to Symmachus as an individual, *after* his tenure as prefect).

33 *C. Th.* 13.5.19 (AD400), 'forum Aproniani', and fifth century e.g. in Matthews 1975: 356–7.

34 AD398, an obsure episode: Symm, *Epist.* 6.66; 8.64–5; 9.81.
35 *ILS* 1222, perhaps relating to procedure at elections of senatorial magistrates; in which case *Caeariana tempora* may allude to a Caesarean law of 44BC noted in Suetonius *Iul.* 41.2.
36 *ILS* 6072. I here cite the edict (a familiar item to students of topography and the *annona*) only for its traditionalist and paternalist verbal tone: for discussion of the criteria of eligibility presupposed, and of the status as *tabernarii* of the plebeians named, see Carrié 1976: 1009.
37 For this interesting suggestion and textual restoration, see Purcell 1999: 144–5, reading the text as: *nomina aere in[cisa taber]nariorum qui sibi pecun[iam locum] spectaculis et panem populi contra / disciplinam romanam derel[icta urbe Roma] vindicare consueverant.* Livy's account of the proposed migration and of the Gallic capture of Rome (*AUC* 5.29–30, 34–55) was much admired by late Roman readers.
38 *ILS* 6506: Tanonius Marcellinus, *v.c., cons. Camp, patrono dignissimo..*
39 Wallace-Hadrill 1981: 298–323; 1982: 32–48. On the *providentia* of Claudius, famously a source of mirth after his death (Tac. *Ann.* 13.3), nb in the present connexion the SC *de aedificiis non diruendis*, AD 47, *ILS* 6043: cum *providentia* optumi principis tectis quoque urbis nostrae et totius Italiae *aeternitati* prospexerit..
40 Purcell 1999: 153; on fishponds nb Matthews 1974: 71.
41 On *tabulae patronatus*, see Nicols 1980: 535–60; for the example of the Valerii Proculi, see *ILS* 6111 (four such commemorations of Q. Aradius Valerius Proculus, AD321–2) with *ILS* 1240–3 (from the same site, a house on the Caelian) on the guild-patronage of L. Aradius Valerius (*pr. urb.* a. 340).
42 Olympiodorus, fr. 25 (Albinus' *relatio*); *ILS* 5715 (Aventine Baths repaired).
43 Ambrose's basilica, AD386: Brown 2000: 82; on his melting church plate, Brown 1992: 95–6, observing 'church wealth' becoming 'public wealth' in the hands of a bishop, and quoting Ambrose *Ep.* 18.17.
44 Krautheimer 1980: 33–42; for Fabiola's sick-house (*c.*AD3 90), Jerome *Epist.* 77.6.
45 To which the probable answer is that in Symmachus' view, it is basic to the *pax deorum* that public cult at Rome must be publicly funded: Matthews 1975: 208.
46 Brown 1961, and often elsewhere; cf Cameron 1999.

References

Barnes, T.D. (1981) *Constantine and Eusebius*, Cambridge, MA: Harvard University Press.

Brown, P. (1961) 'Aspects of the Christianization of the Roman aristocracy', *JRS* 51: 1–11.

Brown, P. (1971) 'Rise and function of the Holy Man', *JRS* 61: 80–101 [= *Society and the Holy in late Antiquity*, 103–52].

Brown, P. (1981) *World of Late Antiquity, AD150–750*, London: Thames and Hudson.

Brown, P. (1982) 'Dalla plebs romana alla plebs dei: aspetti della christianizazzione di Roma'. In P. Brown, L. Cracco Ruggini and M. Mazza (eds), *Governanti e intellettuali: populo di Roma e populo di Dio*: 123–45, Turin: Giappichelli.

Brown, P. (1989) *Society and the Holy in Late Antiquity*, Berkeley: University of California Press.

Brown, P. (1992) *Power and Persuasion in Late Antiquity: Towards a Christian Empire*, Madison: University of Wisconsin Press.

Brown, P. (2000) *Augustine of Hippo: A Biography*, London: Faber.

Browning, R. (1983) 'Learning the Past'. In E.J. Kenney (ed.), *The Cambridge History of Classical Literature II: Latin Literature*: 762–70, Cambridge: Cambridge University Press.

Brunt, P.A. (1988) *Fall of the Roman Republic*, Oxford: Clarendon Press.

Cameron, A. (1965) 'The fate of Pliny's letters in the late Empire', *CQ* 15: 289–98.

Cameron, A. (1977) 'Paganism and literature in late fourth century Rome', *Fondation Hardt: Entretiens* 23: 30–70.

Cameron, A. (1999) 'Last pagans of Rome'. In W.V. Harris and A. Giardina (eds), *The Transformations of Urbs Roma in Late Antiquity* (JRA supplementary series, 33), Portsmouth, RI: Journal of Roman Archaeology.

Carrié, J.-M. (1976) 'Patronage et propriété militaire', *BCH* 100: 159–79.

Chastagnol, A. (1960) *La préfecture urbaine à Rome sous le Bas-Empire.* Paris: Nouvelles Éditions Latines.

Clemente, G. (1972) 'Il patronato nei collegia dell' imp. romano', *Studi classici e orientali* 21: 142–229.

Conte, G.B. (1994) *Latin Literature: A History*, Baltimore and London: Johns Hopkins University Press.

Croke, B. and Harries, J. (1982) *Religious Conflict in Fourth-century Rome: A Documentary Study*, Sydney: Sydney University Press.

Cullhed, M. (1984) *Conservator Urbis Suae*, Stockholm: Aström.

Dagron,G. (1984) *Naissance d'une capitale: Constantinople et ses institutions de 330 à 451*, 2nd edn, Paris: Presses Universitaires de France.

de Ste Croix, G. (1954) 'Suffragium: from vote to patronage', *Brit. Journ. Soc.* 5: 32–44.

de Ste Croix, G. (1981) *The Class Struggle in the Ancient Greek World: From the Archaic Age to the Arab Conquests*, Ithaca, NY: Cornell University Press.

Fowden, G. (1987) 'Nicagoras of Athens and the Lateran obelisk', *JHS* 107: 51–57.

Garnsey, P. and Saller, R. (1987) *The Roman Empire: Economy, Society and Culture*, London: Duckworth.

Harmand, J. (1957) *Le patronat sur les collectivités publiques, des origines au bas-empire: un aspect social et politique du monde romain*, Paris: Presses Universitaires de France.

Horsfall, N. (1996) *La cultura della Plebs romana*, Barcelona: Departament de Filologia Clàssica, Universitat de Barcelona.

Johnson, T. and Dandeker, C. (1988) 'Patronage: relation and system'. In A. Wallace-Hadrill (ed.), *Patronage in Ancient Society:* 219–45, London: Routledge.

Jones, A.H.M. (1973) *The Later Roman Empire, 284–602*, Oxford: Blackwell.

Kent, F.W. and Simons, P. (eds) (1987) *Patronage, Art and Society in Renaissance Italy*, Oxford: Clarendon Press.

Kneppe, A. (1979) *Untersuchungen zur städtischen Plebs des 4. Jahrhunderts*, Bonn: Habelt.

Krautheimer, R. (1980) *Rome: Profile of a City, 312–1308*, Princeton: Princeton University Press.

Kroll, W. (1891) *de Symmachi studiis graecis et latinis*, unpublished dissertation, University of Bratislava.

Lane Fox, R. (1986) *Pagans and Christians*, Harmondsworth: Penguin.

Lepelley, C. (1992) 'The survival and fall of the classical city in late Roman Africa'. In J. Rich (ed.), *The City in Late Antiquity*: 50–76, London: Routledge.

Liebeschuetz, J.H.W.G. (1972) *Antioch: City and Imperial Administration in the Later Roman Empire*, Oxford: Clarendon Press.

MacMullen, R. (1988) *Corruption and the Decline of Rome*, New Haven: Yale University Press.

Marcone, A. (1998) 'Late Roman social relations', *CAH*[2] 13: 338–70.

Marcus, R. (1974) 'Paganism, Christianity and the Latin classics'. In J.W. Binns (ed.), *Latin Literature of the Fourth Century*, London: Routledge and Kegan Paul.

Matthews, J. (1971) 'Symmachus and the Magister Militum Theodosius', *Historia* 20: 122–8.

Matthews, J. (1974) 'The letters of Symmachus'. In J.W. Binns (ed.), *Latin Literature of the Fourth Century*: 58–99, London: Routledge and Kegan Paul.
Matthews, J. (1975) *Western Aristocracies and Imperial Court,* AD*364–425*, Oxford: Clarendon Press.
Matthews, J. (1989) *The Roman Empire of Ammianus*, London: Duckworth.
Matthews, J. (1986) 'Symmachus and his enemies'. In F. Paschoud (ed.), *Colloque genevois sur Symmaque*: 173–4, Paris: Belles Lettres.
McLynn, N. (1994) *Ambrose of Milan*, Berkeley: University of California Press.
Meiggs, R. (1973) *Roman Ostia*, 2nd edn, Oxford: Clarendon Press.
Mitchell, S. (1993) *Anatolia: Land, Men, and Gods in Asia Minor*, 2 vols. Oxford: Clarendon Press.
Nicols, J. (1980) 'Tabulae Patronatus: a study of agreement between patron and client-community', *ANRW* ii(13), 535–61.
Nordh, A. (1949) *Libellus de regionibus Urbis Romae*, Lund: Gleerup.
Paschoud, F. (1967) *Roma Aeterna*, Rome: Institut Suisse.
Paschoud, F. (ed.) (1986) *Colloque genevois sur Symmaque: à l'occasion du mille six centième anniversaire du conflit de l'autel de la Victoire*, Paris: Belles Lettres.
Patlagean, C. (1977) *Pauvreté économique et pauvreté sociale à Byzance: 4–7 siecle*, Paris: Mouton.
Petit, P. (1955) *Libanius et la vie municipale à Antioche au IVe siècle après J.-C*, Paris: P. Geuthner.
Pietri, C. (1976) *Roma christiana: recherches sur l'Église de Rome, son organisation, sa politique, son idéologie de Miltiade à Sixte III (311–440)*, Rome: École Française de Rome.
Pietri, C. (1978) 'Evergetisme et richesses ecclésiastiques dans l'Italie du ive a la fin du ve s: l'example romaine', *Ktema* 3: 313–37.
Purcell, N. (1999) 'The Populace of Rome in late antiquity'. In W. Harris and A. Giardina, (eds), *The Transformations of Urbs Roma in Late Antiquity*: 135–6, Portsmouth, RI: Journal of Roman Archaeology.
Robert, L. (1948) *Epigrammes du Bas-Empire. Hellenica* 4.
Rouland, N. (1979) *Pouvoir politique et dépendance personnelle dans l'Antiquité romaine*, Brussels: Latomus.
Saller, R. (1982) *Personal Patronage under the Early Empire*, Cambridge: Cambridge University Press.
Saller, R. (1988) 'Patronage and friendship'. In A. Wallace-Hadrill (ed.), *Patronage in Ancient Society:* 249–62.
Vera, D. (1986) 'Simmaco e le sue proprietà'. In F. Paschoud (ed.), *Colloque genevois sur Symmaque*: 231–70, Paris: Belles Lettres.
Veyne, P. (1981) 'Clientèle et corruption au service de l'état: la venalité des offices dans le Bas-Empire romain', *Annales* 1981, 339–60.
Veyne, P. (1990) (O. Murray, trans. and ed.) *Bread and Circuses* (abridged translation of *Le pain et le cirque* (1976) Paris: Seuil), London: Penguin.
Wallace-Hadrill, A. (1981) 'The emperor and his virtues', *Historia* 30: 298–323.
Wallace-Hadrill, A. (1982) 'Civilis princeps', *JRS* 72: 32–48.
Wallace-Hadrill, A. (ed.) (1988) *Patronage in Ancient Society*, London: Routledge.
Ward-Perkins, B. (1984) *From Classical Antiquity to the Middle Ages: Urban Public Building in Northern and Central Italy,* AD*300–850*, Oxford: Clarendon Press.
Zevi, F. (1973) 'P Lucilio Gamala *senior* e I "quattro tempietti" di Ostia', *MEFRA* 85: 555–81.

INDEX